AUTHOR .... M 56245

TITLE ....
D0811000

M.S.C.

WANDSWORTH PUBLIC LIBRARIES

19

Includes 8 map extracts at the back of book

METROP...
METROPOLIT...

THIS BOOK SHO...

L. 36

101 128 786 CE

Man and Landscape

by the same author

ADVANCED PRACTICAL GEOGRAPHY

MAN AND LANDSCAPE

A PRACTICAL HANDBOOK OF CASE STUDIES
AND TECHNIQUES IN HUMAN GEOGRAPHY

ARTHUR GUEST

Head of Geography Division
Derby College of Art and Technology

Heinemann Educational Books
London

Heinemann Educational Books Ltd

LONDON   EDINBURGH   MELBOURNE   AUCKLAND   TORONTO
HONG KONG   SINGAPORE   KUALA LUMPUR
IBADAN   NAIROBI   JOHANNESBURG
LUSAKA   NEW DELHI

ISBN O 435 35354 3

© Arthur Guest 1974
First published 1974

910.03 GUES

~~940.55 GUÉ~~

M56245

~~X 11015~~

101 128 786

Published by Heinemann Educational Books Ltd
48 Charles Street, London W1X 8AH

Printed in Great Britain by
Fletcher & Son Ltd, Norwich

Preface

WANGANUI PUBLIC LIBRARIES M.S.C.

Studies offered to senior sixth-form and to first-year college and university students should possess intrinsic academic merit, simplicity of explanation and be built on a sound quantitative base. I trust that these educational aims are sufficiently true to permit examination targets to be hit and pleasing scores attained.

This work is primarily intended to stimulate interest in human geography but not to the exclusion of the physical environment, for, as we are reminded by Sir Halford Mackinder, 'Geography is like a tree which early divides into two great branches, whose twigs may none the less be inextricably interwoven.'[1] If geography is to be grasped as a whole, then a selection of twigs from our physical and human branches should be cut with very sharp tools, the sharpest of which, suggests David Harvey, are those provided by mathematics and statistics.[2] The use of appropriate statistical techniques permits data to be objectively analysed and tested.

An understanding of our environment can also come by building theories and models, but since a geographer's first model is the map we shall use one in each of our areas of study, as in *Advanced Practical Geography*, for which this book is unashamedly a companion.

The case studies are located in Europe since we are more likely to visit our west European neighbours than to travel to our other more distant cousins.

I hope that this practical guide for students of modern geography will enable them to see a Europe, as the visionary Winston Churchill saw it, 'Where men and women of every country will think as much of being European as of belonging to their native land and wherever they go in this wide domain will truly feel "Here I am at home".'

ARTHUR GUEST

[1] Mackinder, H. J., *The Scope and Method of Geography* (1887).
[2] Harvey, D., *Explanation in Geography* (1969).

Acknowledgements

This text owes its statistical and literary clarity to my wife who has also thoroughly criticized concepts and tested exercises in her joint-capacity as lecturer and school examinations assistant examiner. Her teaching ability shines throughout the pages of this handbook. I am much indebted to my colleague Dr Michael Barke and to Mr Robin Holmes of St Lawrence College, Ramsgate, for reading through the proofs and for their advice. Dr David Collins of Liverpool University has also read the manuscript. Dr Hans-Joachim Späth, of the School of Earth Sciences at the University of Duisburg, has helped with critical comments on population studies and physical geography of the Middle Rhine Valley.

Mr Robert Whitehead, mountaineer and geomorphologist, has checked my data in Koblenz. His wife, Ann, a linguist of no mean ability, has solved many translation problems and I am also grateful to her for the field report on farming conditions in the Saas communes.

The Chief State Administrator of the Statistical Office of the Municipality of Koblenz has provided population data and the harbour authorities at Koblenz were also delighted to help. The Bureau Fédéral de Statistique at Bern has sent pre-publication data on the population composition of the Saas communes and has answered my many queries. Monsieur J. P. Marty, Director of the Parc des Volcans D'Auvergne, has been a mine of information on the growth and development of that park. The officers in Paris of the Conférence Permanente des Parcs have also been most helpful.

The telling photographs of the urban scene in Canterbury (Photographs II and III) are the property of Mr J. S. Curl, and the copyright of the Koblenz pictures is held by Herbert Gauls of Koblenz (Photographs V and VI). The Massif Central prints (Photographs IX and X) were provided by Aerofilms, London, who also own the copyright of pictures used for Photographs I, XVI and XVII.

The vertical air photograph of the Saas glacier is the property of the Aufnahme der Eidgenössische Landestopographie, Wabern-Bern.

The sixteenth-century map of Canterbury (Photograph IV) was specially photographed in the British Museum for the *Geographical Magazine*, whose editor generously allowed me to use their print. The Librarian of *Punch* permitted me to search for the 1920 Summer Number, in which appeared the delightful advertisement for Welwyn Garden City (Photograph XI).

The Passenger Sales Manager, British Railways, Eastern Region at York allowed me to use the topological map, Figure 25.

Many officials of the Development Corporations of New Towns and of the Commission for New Towns gave freely of their advice, and kindly supplied statistical data and relevant copyright photographs (Photographs XII, XIII, XIV and XV).

Mr Hamish Ramsay, Chief Planning Officer at Dundee, and also the Advertisement Manager of D. C. Thomson & Co. Ltd, gave up time to the solving of my Tayside problems and gave permission for appropriate statistical data to be issued.

The copyright for other maps, diagrams and statistics is acknowledged in the appropriate places but I am grateful to the Ordnance Survey for permission to base sketches and diagrams upon their printed maps. I extend this gratitude to the appropriate overseas survey officers and also acknowledge their copyright.

I am indebted to Professor Peter Hall of the University of Reading for stimulating my interest in German settlement and to Dr A. F. A. Mutton for her infectious enthusiasm for Switzerland that both my wife and myself have caught.

I have been very fortunate with my excellent typists, Evelyne Booth, Jill Twyford and Joan Bonser. I am pleased with the painstaking cartographic help from my technicians and especially thank Paul Cooper, Mark Pegg and Donald Wise. Mr T. O'Neale, Librarian, has obtained new sources of data most efficiently and, of course, I must warmly thank my students for being such devastating critics. My colleagues Mr A. Tomson, Dr G. O'Hare and Mr J. Gold have provided useful points for discussion.

The staff at Heinemann have been such models of patience and tact that any defects in this work must surely be due to my own shortcomings.

The photographs used on the cover of this book are reproduced by kind permission of Milton Keynes Development Corporation.

Contents

Maps and Figures

Photographs

Map Extracts

To E.M.G.

'. . . the harbour of explanation can only be reached by
crossing the sea of theory.' *W. M. Davis, 1900*

1. Evolution of Settlement in SE England

Geography is the science of locations. Regional geography classifies locations and theoretical geography predicts them.

W. Bunge

ON THE western margins of Europe lie the off-shore islands of Britain to which came invading continental peoples who changed its economic and social geography. Our voyage in search of an explanation of such changes is fascinating if we first reduce the scale of our exploration and then sail out of sight of facts before returning home much the wiser for our adventure.

Scale is a spatial concept as well as an information line on a map. A large-scale plan of our home area depicts such detail as the floor space of our house and shows that also of a neighbour. A small-scale map may merely mark our street or village, and the fact that we may have neighbours is obscured by the generalized pattern. In the same way, an intensive exploration into the complex settlement patterns of part of Britain nearest to the Continent reveals to us spatial relationships and provides explanations much more clearly than if we were to undertake an extensive survey. We know our friends better than we know a crowd, but at the same time we are individuals who form a total population located on a particular part of the earth's surface. One explanatory guide is the historical geographer.

ROMAN INVASION

At the time of the Roman invasion of 55 B.C. Kent was heavily forested and partly settled by the Belgae (an Iron Age C people), who had originated in northern France and who had established themselves in hamlets, or in tribal capitals on fertile lowlands. They used a simple plough to cultivate their wheat lands which had been made by cutting and burning down the forest. It was into this landscape that the invading Romans came from the small Channel ports which they had established at Dover, Lympne and Richborough (near to present-day Sandwich). In any invasion communications are vital, and new straight roads soon linked these fortified ports to Celtic centres. The best known of these, when Romanized, was called Durovernum Cantiacorum or, to give it its modern name, Canterbury. Being at the crossing point of the river Stour, it soon established itself as a head of navigation as well as a route centre. By A.D. 200 its defence had been ensured by its enclosure within a wall. Although the walls now remaining are medieval, they appear to follow the line of the earlier wall, since they incorporate fragments of Roman masonry at their base.

EXERCISE 1:
(a) *Using Figure 2, measure in hectares and acres the approximate area of walled Roman Canterbury. (One hectare is 10 000 square metres; one acre is 4840 square yards.)*
(b) *With the aid of the air photograph (Photograph I) and the Ordnance map extract, suggest to what extent physical factors may have influenced the shape of the walled area.*

During the third and fourth centuries Roman towns in Europe had developed curved lengths of wall for easier defence of the urban area, which could be as small as 8–12 hectares (20–30 acres), as at Amiens and Dijon in France, or as large as 100 hectares as at Cologne (Köln) in Germany. Roman Canterbury's urban area is thus seen to have been modest in size, and it is possible that it also included non-residential land, although perhaps some two thousand people were living within or adjacent to Durovernum Cantiacorum at that time.

In the countryside the Roman occupation resulted in the creation of a dual society. On the one hand, there was the Roman villa or estate, built on cultivated light soils and consisting of a courtyard around which were set buildings housing both cattle and Romans, together with their associated Celtic families. Occasionally a villa developed into a rural manufacturing centre where the cleaning and finishing of woollen cloth took place. On the other hand, there still existed the Celtic peasant farmers living in hamlets linked to a central non-Roman settlement. This complex unit has been called a Federal Manor, and it existed prior to and during the Roman occupation of Britain.[1] Unfortunately, no evidence of the rural settlement of this age is discernible on the Canterbury map extract, although villas have been excavated at Ickham and Wingham.

EXERCISE 2:
'New concepts of settlement, trade, law and order were created by the Romans.' Attempt to explain this statement by reference to a map of one specific area of south-east England. Include a geographical sketch map to show the positions of any Roman villas and Roman roads in your study area.

Mineral extraction was a major feature in the economy of Roman Britain and in this respect the Weald of Kent made its contribution through the quarrying of iron ore.

But the most permanent effect of the Roman occupation was clearly urban rather than rural or industrial, for town walls with their gateways and roads converging on bridge locations are survival features even today.

ANGLO-SAXON INVASION

With the withdrawal of the Roman legions the Britons brought in German mercenaries to help in their fight against the Picts and the Irish. Thus, during the fifth century, when small waves of Anglo-Saxon warriors and settlers came to Britain, it was already peopled by Celts,

---

[1] Glanville Jones, 'Settlement Patterns in Anglo-Saxon England', *Antiquity*, XXXV (1961), p. 224.

Photograph I *Canterbury—the cradle of English Christianity—a city of 33 150 people in 1971.*

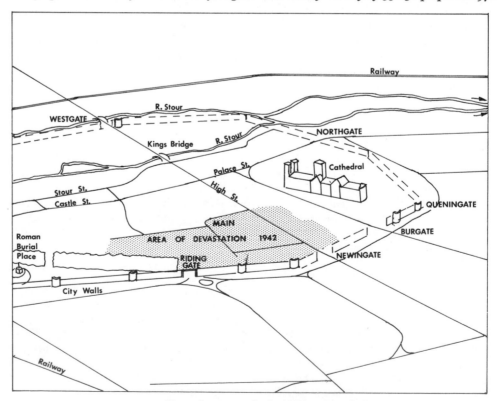

FIG. 1. Canterbury: analysis of Photograph I.

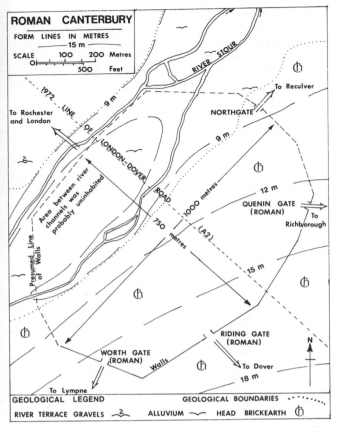

FIG. 2. Roman Canterbury, Durovernum Cantiacorum. The present urban street pattern is not that of the Roman system except where it is aligned according to a presumed NE–SW/NW–SE grid.

Romans and Germanic mercenaries. It was also a Britain dominated by subsistence arable farming, which persisted into the eleventh century, when 90 per cent of the inhabitants were still rural dwellers. But during these centuries pastoral farming was also important, with the extensive uncleared woodland of the lowlands being used for pig or swine farming, since acorns and beech-mast (nuts) provided food. After an initial period of stagnation or decay, associated with the departure of the Romans, towns grew rapidly. Canterbury, for example, outgrew its walls by the ninth century. Romanized towns and the central settlements of the Federal Manors became market centres. The evidence for Anglo-Saxon settlement can be discerned either from archaeological evidence or from a study of place names on Ordnance Survey maps.

PLACE-NAME INVESTIGATION

Most names of places are made up of several elements or parts, as, for instance, the name of the settlement of Kingston. Elements other than the first of compound names usually related to the physical character of a place. In this example -ton means hamlet. Some names, however, possess three or more elements, and therefore a student should try to ascertain which element describes the geographical character of a place. A sequence of settlement can be discovered when, for example, name endings are classified according to the age during which they came into common usage. Prior to the coming of the major invasions of the Anglo-Saxons certain major physical features associated with rivers or hills had Celtic names, and many of these still survive. The names of such rivers as the Aire, Ure and Earn are even pre-Celtic.

Pre-Anglo-Saxon Place-name Endings

CELTIC (BEFORE FIFTH CENTURY A.D.)		ROMAN (LATIN)	
Place-name ending	Meaning	Place-name ending	Meaning
Avon; Esk; Eye; Dee }	river	-caster -cester -chester }	fort, camp, (later a town)
-hamps	a dry stream in summer	-port	gate, harbour
-aber	river mouth	-street	paved way
-bre; -drum -don }	hill	-fos(s)	ditch
-caer	fortress		
-coed	wood		
-pen	hill; head		
-porth	harbour		
-tre	hamlet		

Anglo-Saxon Place-name Endings
(mid-fifth to eleventh century A.D.)

PRIMARY SETTLEMENT INVASION PHASE		SECONDARY SETTLEMENT EXPANSION PHASE		
Sequence 1	2	3	4	5
Homestead or Farmstead names		Daughter settlements	Wood clearance	Drainage settlements
-ing -ingas	(a) -ham -ton -tun (b) -ingham -ington	-cot; -cote (outlying hut or cottage) -croft (small enclosure) -field (open field) -stead (place) -stoke (daughter settlement) -stow (holy place) -wike; -wick; -wich; wic (outlying, inhabited place, usually a dairy or cattle farm)	-den; -dene (swine pasture) -hurst; -hirst (coppice on a hill) -fall (place where trees have been felled) -holt (wood) -leaze; -lee; -lea; -ley; -leah; -leigh (clearing in a forest or wood) -riding; -rod (cleared land) -weald; -wold (high woodland or wasteland) -wood (wood) -worthy (enclosed land)	-delph; -dic (dyke or stream) -eg; -ey; -ea; -eig (island) -fen (fen) -lake -mere } (lake) -moss (swamp)

Scandinavian (ninth to eleventh century A.D.); Norse, Danish and Jutish Place-name Endings

NAME ENDING	MEANING	NAME ENDING	MEANING
-beck	stream	-kirk	church
-booth	{ summer pasture { centre	-laithe	barn
-by	village	-lund	grove
-fell; -how	hill or mound	-slack	stream in a valley
-gate	road	-tarn	lake
-garth	enclosure	-thorp	daughter settlement
-gill	ravine or valley		
-holm;	an island in a fen	-toft	homestead
-wray	remote place	-thwaite	forest clearing or meadow
-ings	marsh; meadow	-wath	ford

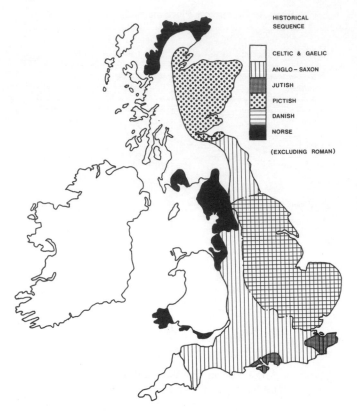

FIG. 3. Major areas of pre-Norman colonization based on place-name evidence.

As seen from Figure 3 the area under study in this chapter was one invaded by both Anglo-Saxons and Jutes. These latter peoples left their original native homes in Denmark and settled in the Romanized lower Rhinelands where they intermarried with the Franks. Groups of these Germanic–Jutes invaded Sussex and Kent and adopted Canterbury as their royal capital. The positions of these Germanic–Jutish villages are now recognized by the place-name ending of -inge. They were sited along or near Roman roads which suggests that these invaders were principally traders or that they utilized the Roman roads in their colonization.

EXERCISE 3:

Make a tracing of the map extract area and on it show the development of Anglo-Saxon settlement. With the help of the table of Anglo-Saxon place-name endings distinguish clearly between primary and secondary settlements using contrasting symbols.

EXERCISE 4:

'A study of place-names is to be preferred to that of settlement forms.' Discuss.

The Value of Place-name Studies

1. The mapping of settlements according to their relative age shows how a region may possibly have developed in terms of its human occupance.
2. Any sequence of events that has been assumed leads to an enquiry into what physical or economic conditions existed at the time of settlement growth.
3. An understanding of the general meaning of place-name endings provides a simple description of the environment at the time of settlement.

4. The occurrence of a number of places with names derived from the same language suggests that a region could have been originally settled by a group of people from a common source area.
5. The growth of settlements affects land use. The destruction of woodland or the reclamation of moor or fen could be deduced from a study of place-name endings.

While these are an aid to understanding the historical geography of an area it must be stated that place-name interpretation is not as simple as it might appear. Nevertheless, with the aid of such reference books as *The Concise Oxford Dictionary of English Place Names* and the various volumes issued by the Place Names Society, the evidence offered by this type of study can be used to provide an outline of the changing historical geography of a region which is a guide to the understanding of the geography of location.

Problems Associated with Place-name Studies

1. Since word elements survive for long periods of time, an already existing name could be adopted by invading settlers. Thus the invasion itself might be concealed since there would be no apparent change of language.
2. Migrating people may speak different languages within their own community and even move into a region where one or more different languages are already spoken. Place-names, therefore, could exist simultaneously in two differing forms. Although one of these would ultimately survive, it might not be the earliest form and would therefore provide misleading evidence as to the origin of that settlement.
3. Even modern settlements are given Celtic, Anglo-Saxon or Norse names and thus suffixes of recent towns should be ignored when seeking to study areas of invasion.
4. The use of historical documents will certainly add to the list of place-names in any given region but care should be taken to list a settlement once only since, for example, some English 'Scandinavian' settlements are in fact renamed Anglo-Saxon villages.

For historical geography the Domesday Book is probably the best-known document and its information has been made accessible to students through a series of volumes edited by Professor H. C. Darby.

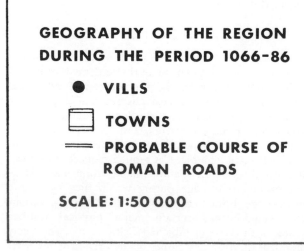

GEOGRAPHY OF THE REGION
DURING THE PERIOD 1066-86

● VILLS

▭ TOWNS

═ PROBABLE COURSE OF
ROMAN ROADS

SCALE: 1:50 000

FIG. 4. Canterbury region during the period 1066–86.

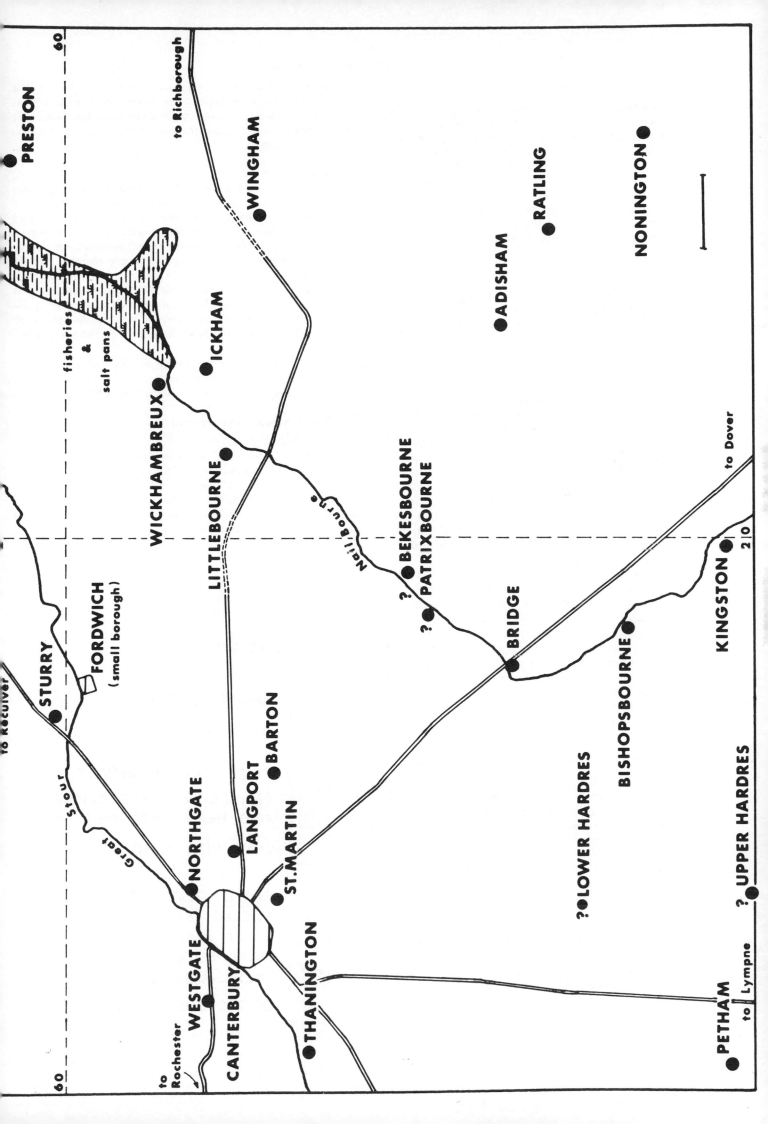

NORMAN INVASION

The Normans landed at Pevensey Bay, Sussex, in September 1066 and Canterbury and London quickly surrendered to William, Duke of Normandy. So began yet another period of foreign influence in the geography of these Islands. As in Anglo-Saxon times the extensive woods provided pasturage for pigs or, as the Domesday record states, there was 'pannage for swine' attached to manors in settled areas. Eventually such denes or swine pastures became areas of settlement because of the availability of both pasture and timber. The pasturage would later be cultivated and the dene house a village.

EXERCISE 5:
(a) *Examine the topographical map and list the three different place-names using the element 'dene' or 'den'. For each state the four-figure grid reference of the locating square.*
(b) *Using Figure 4, briefly describe and account for geographical distribution of settlement in this part of Norman Kent.*

From your answer to Exercise 5 it will be seen that Kent offered contrasts in settlement between the thickly settled regions and those lands, such as woodland and marsh, which were virtually unsettled. At Wickhambreux the Domesday survey records 80 swine, 300 sheep and 31 other animals kept in the park and woodland belonging to that settlement. Thus the countryside of Norman Kent had a wooded aspect; cultivation was of a limited extent and settlement was in dispersed hamlets some of which were in clearings. Each village sought the right to build a water-mill for grinding corn and along the streams were 'fisheries' yielding eels and fresh-water fish.

Other economic resources included salt, obtained by the evaporation of sea water, and reeds and rushes from the Nail Bourne (Little Stour) estuary which then probably extended as far inland as Wickhambreux. Large royal 'forests' or deer parks were also created.

The Normans thus added new place-names to the English language such as *park, forest, grange, close, bourne* (a stream) and, of course, *castle.* At Canterbury the building in 1090 of the Norman castle inside the walls adjacent to Worthgate must have involved the destruction of houses for it was within the crowded 'urban' area.

MAPPING DOMESDAY GEOGRAPHY

Apart from language problems it is difficult to identify Domesday settlement on modern maps. Domesday vills (hamlets or manors) could have disappeared or have been absorbed into neighbouring vills. A farm name may be the only map evidence of the former existence of a Norman settlement. The regrouping of hamlets may have been associated with a new field layout and the only evidence could be documentary or archaeological. Another difficulty is that the Domesday Book seldom makes it possible to draw a clear distinction between neighbouring villages with regard to their *exact* location if they have the same place-name element. This is certainly true for Patrixbourne and Bekesbourne, for Burna (a stream) is the eleventh-century name for each. Similar difficulties arise for Upper and Lower Hardres.[1] (On Figure 4 all four settlements are

---

[1] Eila Campbell, *The Domesday Geography of South East England*, ed. H. C. Darby and E. M. J. Campbell (1962), Chapter X, 'Kent', pp. 483–562.

plotted but a question-mark is placed against each.) It is also important not to draw the conclusion that a particular site has had continuous occupation since the Domesday survey merely because the historical name is printed on modern maps.

EXERCISE 6:
(a) *Using a 1:25 000 map of a lowland rural area construct a map to show the boundaries and names of the modern parishes. Boundary lines between adjacent parishes which share the same name element should be distinctly indicated. Place a dot for the position of each parish church and, by using local histories or by visiting the churches, add the date of their foundation to your map. If your reference library has a volume on the Domesday Geography or a copy of* The Victoria County History *of the county, distinctively underline the names of those located settlements which are referred to in these books as Domesday settlements.*
(b) *Describe the type of information that you would need to help you write an account of the 'moving frontier of settlement' (ie. process of colonization) in lowland England.*

The Physical Environment
EXERCISE 7:
  Study the geological outline map (Figure 5) and compare it with the topographical map of the same area. Write two brief paragraphs, one on 'The Stour Valley', the other on 'The Dissected Chalk Hills', describing in each the distribution of the various rocks in the relevant areas. (The geological term 'rock' includes alluvium and periglacial deposits as well as the solid rock of the country.)

LEGEND

SCALE 1:50 000

DRIFT GEOLOGY

ALLUVIUM

RIVER TERRACE GRAVELS

PERIGLACIAL HEAD BRICKEARTH AND HEAD DEPOSITS

CLAY WITH FLINTS

SOLID GEOLOGY

EOCENE SANDY CLAYS SAND AND PEBBLE BEDS

MAIN EOCENE – CRETACEOUS BOUNDARY

CRETACEOUS CHALK

FIG. 5. Simplified drift geology of the Canterbury region.

The Eocene age rocks here are either the blue-grey London Clay or the sandy clay with sand and pebbles of the Thanet, Oldhaven and Woolwich Beds. The back slope of the North Downs is composed of chalk of the earlier Cretaceous period. But the recent and periglacial (Ice Age) drift deposits must have been of equal significance to the early settlers. While water and potential farm land would be hard won on the chalk hills, the dissecting valleys of these uplands and the Stour Valley itself were floored by river alluvium or river terrace gravels and the valley slopes were covered by a veneer of well-drained, fertile 'Head' deposits due to slumping under freeze–thaw action.

It is suggested that the settlement pattern of eleventh-century England was strongly influenced by the location of light, well-drained soils since they were suited to the light plough and could easily be cleared of woodland. This hypothesis could be tested by working the exercise set below.

EXERCISE 8:
(a) *From the map extract, make a tracing of the outline of the main built-up areas of the village settlements and place over the geological outline map (Figure 5). Use a copy of the table below to list the settlements according to their site on the appropriate geological strata. (Where there is overlap on to two or more rock types choose the village core around the church as the site.)*

	HEAD BRICKEARTH AND HEAD DEPOSITS	RIVER TERRACE GRAVELS	EOCENE ROCKS	CHALK	CLAY WITH FLINTS
1					
2					
3					
4					

(b) *From your evidence state whether or not the above hypothesis is correct.*
(c) *What other factors do you consider important for the founding of settlements?*

COLONIZATION SIMULATION

The development of new rural settlements due to migration can be simulated. A model in the form of a game can be devised in which the rules and method of play are based on events and situations that could be experienced in real life. The decisions we make in our daily lives may not always be correct, wise or even logical and occasionally what we do depends on mere chance or luck. Early colonizers, hiving off or 'swarming' from their parents' homes, no doubt took risks, made both foolish and wise decisions and sometimes gambled on their luck holding out and providing an answer as to where they might establish their new homes. This simulation game must therefore have an element of chance or probability built into it and the method of play would resemble that seen at a Monte Carlo casino. The table of random numbers may be less exciting than the roulette wheel but it serves the same purpose.

Aim

To create new daughter settlements around mother settlements which have outgrown their home resources in a typically varied English landscape.

Method of Play

Stage 1: Choose your area

1. First establish and arrange in order of importance the various geographical factors which could have affected the site and situation of settlements in the area selected for study. The list below suggests some factors which could have played a part in decision making by the unknown people who founded settlements.

SITE FACTORS
{
Sheltered by hills
Area free from steep hill-slopes
A defensible site when danger threatened
Water supply available
Timber near by for fuel and building
Nearness or distance from parent settlement
Roads easy to construct in area chosen
Absence of clay soils—land easy to work
— — — — — — — — — — — — — — — —
— — — — — — — — — — — — — — — —
}

If evidence other than that provided by topographical, geological or soil maps is available then a more extensive list including economic, social, religious and health factors could be compiled.

2. Arrange your site factors in order of merit or significance. For example, if the availability of water is of prime importance then it will head your list and if you have chosen ten factors then number 10 is the numerical value allocated to water supply. The next item of slightly lesser importance will be given a value of 9 and so forth down to 1. Where only 8 factors are being considered then the numbers 8 to 1 would replace 10 to 1.

Stage 2: Prepare a board for play

1. On *tracing-paper* draw an inked copy of a matrix such as that illustrated in Figure 6. This consists of kilometre squares covering an area lying within approximately 3 kilometres (2 miles) radius of the mother settlement. The matrix is placed centrally over this settlement on the topographical map and oblique lines are drawn across the four central squares. No play is permitted in this area which is within the sphere of influence of the existing central settlement.

2. Each of your site factors (listed under Stage 1) is now studied in relation to each square of the extract map and a 'weighting value' allocated. For example, if an assessment of the region is to be made on a basis of rock types, place your matrix 'board' over a geological map *of the same scale* as the topographical map being used and consider the rock type represented in each kilometre as a factor in helping to determine the suitability of that area as a place for a new settlement. (Work systematically from left to right along each row of squares, starting in the top left corner.) In the original list of siting factors the number 6 may have been allocated to rock type and therefore assign to each square a number between 0 and 6 according to the degree of favourability that you yourself consider appropriate to the square. Where the rock type is considered to be highly favourable its value will be 6. However, if you consider the rock type to be virtually useless give a value of 0. The full range of numbers for each factor will be used over the whole area of the matrix. Where one square covers varied rock types select the major outcrop for consideration. Insert the number in pencil in the respective square on the matrix.

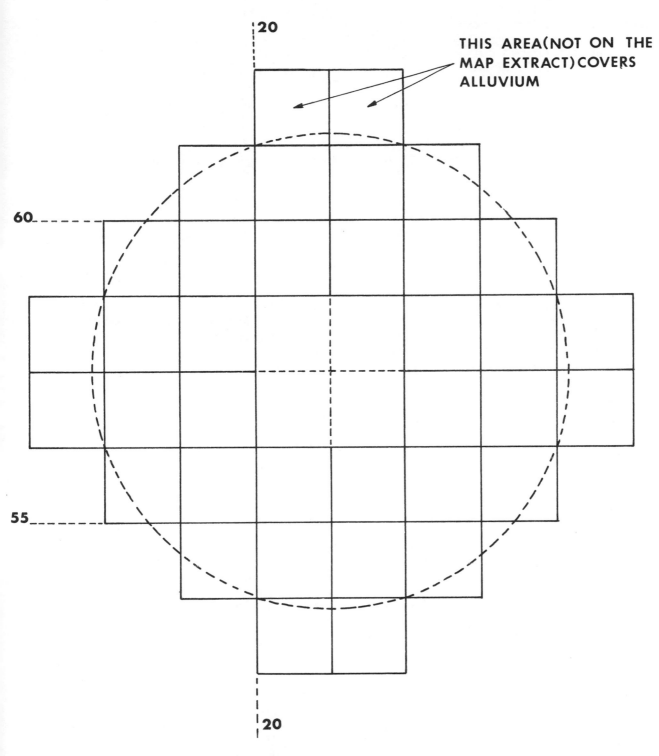

FIG. 6. Matrix for the Monte Carlo simulation game.

Clay lands are usually wet and cold but with drainage will suit cereal crops especially when the plough had been improved to work these heavy lands. Sandy and gravelly soils give rise to warm soils which being naturally well drained are light to work and favour vegetable production. *Alluvium* could be avoided if such areas were marshy or liable to flood. *Head Brickearth* on lowlands give rise to light and fertile soils which drain easily. *Head deposits* on summit areas are also lighter than *clay-with-flints*. The dry *chalk* lands could, however, have been clothed with scrub and forest or have been used for pasturage.

3. The same procedure is adopted for each siting factor and the appropriate weighting value noted in pencil in each square.
4. Total up all the weighting values in each square and write this final number clearly in the respective square.

8/1/4/6
3/2/2/8
= 34

5. With all the squares bearing values it is now necessary to build the chance element into the game since, for example, it may be sheer luck that a group of migrants turned left instead of right at a division of a path. To include this chance factor either use the same matrix or trace a second copy and convert the square (or cell) totals into a probability matrix as shown below.

Conversion of cell matrix into probability matrix
Having computed the weighting factor in each grid square under consideration, we can now interpret this in terms of chance. Thus, using the cell shown, the first square shows a weighting value of 2 but the square next to it has a value of 5. This simply means that each of these numbers can be considered as the number of chances that the individual squares possess as possible future sites for settlement. Thus a square of value 2 has two chances and will be allotted two consecutive numbers starting with unity. The square of value 5 has five consecutive numbers allotted to it to give it greater opportunity of being selected. A quick estimate of the total values in all the cells added together will indicate how many numbers should be used. Thus if the sum total lies between 1 and 100 it is only necessary to use two digits, but if the total lies between 1 and 1000, then three digits are necessary. In our example therefore a cell value of 2 requires two probability matrix digits. Hence allocate to the first square numbers 001 and 002. (With a smaller sum total of values this could equally well be 01 and 02, or with a larger sum total it might well be 0001 and 0002.) The second square requires five digits, and these must consecutively follow on those of the first square. Thus numbers 003, 004, 005, 006 and 007 are assigned to this square—written as 003–007 on the probability matrix. The third square in our example has the value 3 and takes the next three numbers 008, 009, 010—written 008–010. Allocate probability matrix numbers to all squares (cells).

	Cell totals		
2	5	3	1
6	5	4	7

Probability matrix and random number matrix			
001 002	003 007	008 010	011
012 017	018 022	023 026	027 033

A method of using the random numbers table (Figure 7)
Select any starting-point on the table, that is any row and any column. You may, for example, decide to start in the third double column and on the tenth row in that column, that is with the number 17. In our probability matrix three numbers have been utilized and thus the third number in the probability matrix is obtained from the first figure in the next double column (i.e. column 4) on the right. Thus our starting-point with 3 digits is 177. We may now work either across the table horizontally reading for example 177, then in the next pairs of columns, in the same row, 036, followed by 662, 247 and so forth or vertically in columns, in which case the succession of numbers would be 177, 590, 009, 958 and so forth. (In the random numbers table 11 is read as 100 and 000 as 1000.)

Suppose the maximum number recorded on your final cell total is 417, then any number occurring in the random table greater than 417 must be rejected and the next one used, since these larger numbers are not represented on the probability matrix. This is 'the discarding method' as some numbers are rejected.

Stage 3: The game and its rules
1. Decide how many daughter settlements you wish to establish, for example say 5, by means of a predetermined number of 'landings', e.g. 15, 25 or 50, etc.
2. Commence play by selecting any three adjacent digits on the random number table. Mark a cross in the square of the matrix which contains the number. This represents the first 'landing'.
3. Select the next three adjacent digits, and find the square containing this number and mark another cross to represent your second 'landing'. Continue this process until the predetermined number of crosses has been plotted on the board. The five squares with the greatest number of crosses would then be the positions of the new settlements.
4. As stated earlier no play is permitted in the four central squares since new settlements would not be created within three-quarters of a mile of the central mother settlement.
5. The first round ends when five new settlements have been located.

Stage 4: Mapping the theoretical settlements
Ink in a larger circle for the old central settlement and five smaller circles for daughter settlements placing them in the most advantageous position with reference to the original siting factors. A diagrammatic map showing the diffusion of settlement resulting from a 'swarming' or 'hiving-off' process has thus been created based partly on chance and partly on decision-making by its founders.

It will be observed that when the game is run once only and neighbouring students results compared, quite dissimilar patterns will emerge when different starting positions on the random numbers table have been selected.

Thus in the above game it is possible to play either as an individual or as a group to reach an average solution following a number of rounds related to a given situation in a selected area. The Monte Carlo technique therefore yields the best results to a theoretical solution of problems where answers are averaged. A daughter settlement could in turn be regarded as the new mother settlement and the process of 'swarming' would begin again. Thus the third- and fourth-generation settlements could be stimulated, and a theoretical pattern of settlement, with a reasonable degree of acceptability, created. On a limited map area it is probably desirable to average the results to obtain the solution, and leave the hierarchy of settlement to be considered only on a larger area of land.

EXERCISE 9:
(a) *For an area centred on Littlebourne make a diagrammatic map to show the location of six new settlements due to migration. Use the Monte Carlo method, the Canterbury map extract, a sheet of tracing-paper, the matrix (Figure 6) and the geological base map (Figure 5). Do not be influenced by existing settlements.*
(b) *Compare your ideal distribution with the real one on the map extract. Is there any degree of similarity? (It is not necessary that this should be so.) Comment on the likely decisions that could have been made by the unknown founders of the existing settlements in the Littlebourne area.*

```
20 17   42 28   23 17   59 66   38 61   02 10   86 10   51 55   92 52   44 25
74 49   04 49   03 04   10 33   53 70   11 54   48 63   94 60   94 49   57 38
94 70   49 31   38 67   23 42   29 65   40 88   78 71   37 18   48 64   06 57
22 15   78 15   69 84   32 52   32 54   15 12   54 02   01 37   38 37   12 93
93 29   12 18   27 30   30 55   91 87   50 57   58 51   49 36   12 53   96 40

45 04   77 97   36 14   99 45   52 95   69 85   03 83   51 87   85 56   22 37
44 91   99 49   89 39   94 60   48 49   06 77   64 72   59 26   08 51   25 57
16 23   91 02   19 96   47 59   89 65   27 84   30 92   63 37   26 24   23 66
04 50   65 04   65 65   82 42   70 51   55 04   61 47   88 83   99 34   82 37
32 70   17 72   03 61   66 26   24 71   22 77   88 33   17 78   08 92   73 49

03 64   59 07   42 95   81 39   06 41   20 81   92 34   51 90   39 08   21 42
62 49   00 90   67 86   93 48   31 83   19 07   67 68   49 03   27 47   52 03
61 00   95 86   98 36   14 03   48 88   51 07   33 40   06 86   33 76   68 57
89 03   90 49   28 74   21 04   09 96   60 45   22 03   52 80   01 79   33 81
01 72   33 85   52 40   60 07   06 71   89 27   14 29   55 24   85 79   31 96

27 56   49 79   34 34   32 22   60 53   91 17   33 26   44 70   93 14   99 70
49 05   74 48   10 55   35 25   24 28   20 22   35 66   66 34   26 35   91 23
49 74   37 25   97 26   33 94   42 23   01 28   59 58   92 69   03 66   73 82
20 26   22 43   88 08   19 85   08 12   47 65   65 63   56 07   97 85   56 79
48 87   77 96   43 39   76 93   08 79   22 18   54 55   93 75   97 26   90 77

08 72   87 46   75 73   00 11   27 07   05 20   30 85   22 21   04 67   19 13
95 97   98 62   17 27   31 42   64 71   46 22   32 75   19 32   20 99   94 85
37 99   57 31   70 40   46 55   46 12   24 32   36 74   69 20   72 10   95 93
05 79   58 37   85 33   75 18   88 71   23 44   54 28   00 48   96 23   66 45
55 85   63 42   00 79   91 22   29 01   41 39   51 40   36 65   26 11   78 32

67 28   96 25   68 36   24 72   03 85   49 24   05 69   64 86   08 19   91 21
85 86   94 78   32 59   51 82   86 43   73 84   45 60   89 57   06 87   08 15
40 10   60 09   05 88   78 44   63 13   58 25   37 11   18 47   75 62   52 21
94 55   89 48   90 80   77 80   26 89   87 44   23 74   66 20   20 19   26 52
11 63   77 77   23 20   33 62   62 19   29 03   94 15   56 37   14 09   47 16

64 00   26 04   54 55   38 57   94 62   68 40   26 04   24 25   03 61   01 20
50 94   13 23   78 41   60 58   10 60   88 46   30 21   45 98   70 96   36 89
66 98   37 96   44 13   45 05   34 59   75 85   48 97   27 19   17 85   48 51
66 91   42 83   60 77   90 91   60 90   79 62   57 66   72 28   08 70   96 03
33 58   12 18   02 07   19 40   21 29   39 45   90 42   58 84   85 43   95 67

52 49   40 16   72 40   73 05   50 90   02 04   98 24   05 30   27 25   20 88
74 98   93 99   78 30   79 47   96 92   45 58   40 37   89 76   84 41   74 68
50 26   54 30   01 88   69 57   54 45   69 88   23 21   05 69   93 44   05 32
49 46   61 89   33 79   96 84   28 34   19 35   28 73   39 59   56 34   97 07
19 65   13 44   78 39   73 88   62 03   36 00   25 96   86 76   67 90   21 68

64 17   47 67   87 59   81 40   72 61   14 00   28 28   55 86   23 38   16 15
18 43   97 37   68 97   56 56   57 95   01 88   11 89   48 07   42 60   11 92
65 58   60 87   51 09   96 61   15 53   66 81   66 88   44 75   37 01   28 88
79 90   31 00   91 14   85 65   31 75   43 15   45 93   64 78   34 53   88 02
07 23   00 15   59 05   16 09   94 42   20 40   63 76   65 67   34 11   94 10

90 08   14 24   01 51   95 46   30 32   33 19   00 14   19 28   40 51   92 69
53 82   62 02   21 82   34 13   41 03   12 85   65 30   00 97   56 30   15 48
98 17   26 15   04 50   76 25   20 33   54 84   39 31   23 33   59 64   96 27
08 91   12 44   82 40   30 62   45 50   64 54   65 17   89 25   59 44   99 95
37 21   46 77   84 87   67 39   85 54   97 37   33 41   11 74   90 50   29 62
```

Each digit is an independent sample from a population in which the digits 0 to 9 are equally likely, that is each has a probability of $\frac{1}{10}$.

FIG. 7. Random sampling numbers.

ECONOMIC CHANGES IN MEDIEVAL KENT

The human geography of medieval Canterbury reflects the influence of continental Europe upon this region. While it is true to say that the majority of people in England then lived by subsistence farming, villages, as well as towns, were centres of the wool trade. In Kent the export of cloth was of major economic significance and wool was a leading export to the Low Countries, France and Italy. Canterbury and near-by Sandwich became early 'staple' ports or depôts where wool was deposited against a toll or tax which was levied prior to its export. In the fourteenth century, established settlements such as Canterbury grew as Flemish weavers arrived in great numbers and brought with them their craft of silk-winding and weaving. Another wave of Flemish refugees arrived during the reign of the Protestant Queen, Elizabeth I. The close links with Europe could therefore be expressed in terms of language, religion and heritage or race and there were similar economic interests between the island and continental peoples.

The pattern formed by mapping the location of old and new villages and the growing towns leads directly to a study of the spatial patterns made by parishes associated with this early settlement.

The Parishes of England and their Patterns

The first parishes appear to have been formed from the land area held by lords of the manor, and on these lands churches were built. The priest of each parish was largely maintained by the tithes paid by the tenants who lived in that ecclesiastical parish. During the early nineteenth century civil parishes were created since by that time the parishes had come to have considerably more administrative functions that those concerned purely with church affairs. The civil parishes usually had the same boundaries as the ecclesiastical ones, but some detached portions were absorbed. New civil parishes were needed as industrialization and urbanization increased. Thus the shape and size of parishes not only reflects the political geography of an area but also provides a glimpse of economic changes that have occurred in conjunction with the evolution and growth of rural settlement.

In England the Local Government Re-organisation Act (1972) made *urban* parishes largely obsolete. On the O. S. First Series 1:50 000 maps existing civil parishes are shown, but they are omitted on the Second Series maps, except on the Outline Editions of such maps.

Is There a Limit to the Sizes of Parishes?

The area worked by tenants or cottager-farmers of any individual village would be initially limited by the distance that a plough-team of men and horses could travel to their daily work in the cultivated fields. M. Chisholm, writing of the Lincolnshire parishes, states that the median distance (a term explained below) from all the villages to the furthest point on their parish boundaries is 3200 metres or about two miles.[1] Although he draws no firm conclusion from this evidence and although grazing, rather than arable farming, would be practised on the fringe areas of the parishes, he mentions that the 'economic distance' for medieval daily travel would appear to be one of the factors controlling parish size. Once this distance became too great, then the likelihood of a daughter settlement being born would be a strong possibility. This process of hiving off would create new hamlets on an adjacent 'waste' which would be part converted from woodland or heathland to arable. Parent parish areas in regions of equal opportunity would therefore have a tendency to remain constant in area with linear distances limited to two or three thousand metres from the villages to the parish perimeters.

MEANS, MEDIANS AND MODES

Subjective or descriptive means of comparison allow too great a flexibility in its conclusions, for one person's opinion may differ significantly from that of another, as each is using his own scale of values. To overcome this type of difficulty the geographer has introduced some statistical methods into his investigations. This enables him to quantify his results, which can then be compared to similar situations elsewhere.

Means, modes and medians are all central values which can be determined from a population of statistics and which help to provide more information about such a population and its distribution within the extreme limits of its values, that is the dispersion of that data. The term population is used here in the statistical sense meaning a set of data.

Mean

The summation (addition) of a population in which the variable is x is divided by the number of individual items (n) to give the average or arithmetic *mean* of that data. Using mathematical shorthand, this is expressed as $\bar{x} = \dfrac{\Sigma x}{n}$, where Σ (sigma) means 'sum of' and $\bar{x}$ (x bar or bar x) is used to denote the arithmetic mean or average. When calculating mean values every figure in the set is utilized, but some of these may be very high or very low values when compared with the rest of the data, and thus the mean value will be affected by these non-typical extremes. Thus the mean is an expression of the total of all values being shared out equally, and since the true value of all items is taken into account, it can be used in further mathematical calculations. It is the best known of all central values, but where data are discrete (i.e. only of whole number value) the mean may give an 'impossible' result, e.g. 0·8 persons per square mile.

Median

The median, another form of central value, is the midpoint in a series, the position of which takes account only of the *number of items* in the data and *not* the individual values. To find the median the individual values are arranged in order of magnitude or a column dispersion diagram is constructed. To do this a vertical line is drawn to scale, representing the range of the data. Each item is then plotted in its correct position on the diagram, and thus by the simple operation of counting, the middle point is found so that half the points are above and half are below this middle value (Figure 8). If an even number of values is being used, then the mean of the two middle values is taken as the median, i.e. in a 24-unit series the median

---

[1] M. Chisholm, *Rural Settlement and Land Use* (1968), p. 129

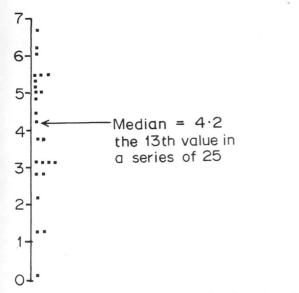

FIG. 8. Dispersion diagrams showing the position of the
median in odd and even series.

would lie at the mean of the 12th and 13th points. As the median takes no account of the true values of the data it is not influenced by extreme values.

Mode

The mode is the third type of central value used to help describe the distribution of a series. This is the value which occurs most frequently in the series, hence it is 'the most fashionable'. The mode may be the least useful of these three middle values since it cannot be used for further calculations.

If the following figures represent the number of faults developed in a colour television set in each of ten successive years:

$$0\ 0\ 1\ 0\ 0\ 3\ 0\ 1\ 0\ 10$$

then the mean $\bar{x} = \dfrac{\Sigma x}{n} = \dfrac{15}{10} = 1\cdot5$ faults

The median is calculated by finding the mid-point of the series rearranged in ascending order

$$0\ 0\ 0\ 0\ 0\ 0\ 1\ 1\ 3\ 10$$

5th   6th

With an even number of items in this series the median lies at the mean value of the 5th and 6th points. The mean of $0 + 0 = 0$. The mode is 0. In this particular data series the median and mode both have the same value but the mean has been 'swung' upwards since the exceptional value of 10 faults occurring in one year has affected its value and thus, in this case, the mean would be the least effective way of describing this population.

The relative positions of the mean, median and mode are an indicator of the distribution of the data and thus the shape of the histogram of the series (see Figure 9).

In a large set of data even the rearrangement of the numbers into an ascending or descending order may convey little or no impression of any pattern that may be present in the series, and thus the data may be grouped into classes and a histogram constructed. The class boundaries must be clearly defined to avoid any overlapping in adjacent groups,

and should ideally contain a 'spread' of the data throughout the class.

For example, the following data could represent the number of passengers arriving each day in April at Canterbury by one of the rural mid-morning buses: 25, 18, 29, 32, 8, 5, 20, 15, 25, 26, 35, 7, 10, 23, 17, 27, 29, 11, 3, 26, 20, 21, 28, 26, 8, 22, 30, 31, 31, 24.
By regrouping these figures into classes the following result would be obtained:

Class	Frequency
0–4	1
5–9	4
10–14	2
15–19	3
20–24	6
25–29	9
30–34	4
35–39	1

Mean = 21·1 persons.
Modal class = 25–29 persons which in this instance is a useful concept even if it cannot be used for further calculations.
Median = 23·5.
The positions of the mean, mode and median relative to each other indicate the type of distribution and thus the shape of the histogram, as illustrated in Figure 10 (overleaf).

STANDARD DEVIATION

A method of expressing the dispersion of a set of data is that of the standard deviation. While the concept of this deviation is difficult to comprehend, it is not complex in its mathematical evaluation. Of all the methods of expressing dispersion this is the one of greatest value in further statistical work. Its principal advantages are that it is a measure directly related to the area under a normal distribution curve (see page 16) and it uses every value in the data set, but at the same time it over-emphasizes the extreme values, since it involves the use of the squares of the deviations.

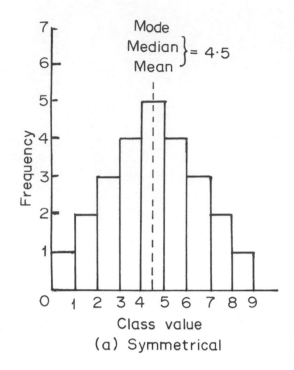

(a) Symmetrical

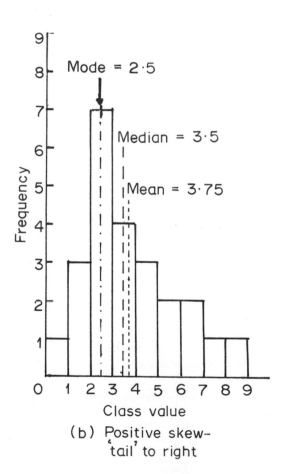

(b) Positive skew–
'tail' to right

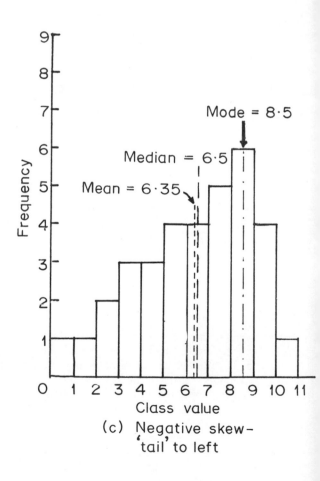

(c) Negative skew–
'tail' to left

It should be noted that the actual value of the mode has been
determined from the data and only class boundary values
are shown on the graph

FIG. 9. The shape of histograms.

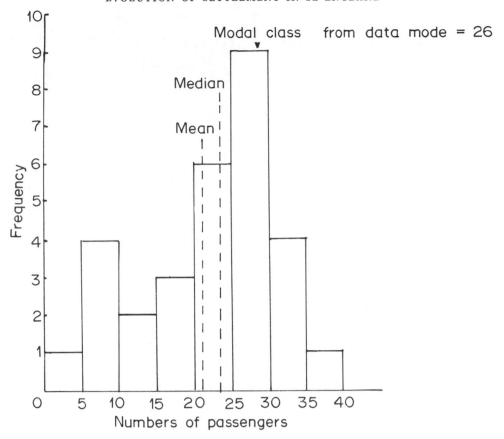

FIG. 10. Histogram for frequency of passengers on
Canterbury buses.

The total sum of the deviation of an array of data can be easily determined and from it the *mean deviation* calculated using the table below.

DATA ARRAY	DEVIATION		DEVIATION SQUARED
Value = x	Including direction $d_1 = (x-\bar{x})$	Excluding direction d_2	$d^2 = (x-\bar{x})^2$
5	−2·5	2·5	6·25
6	−1·5	1·5	2·25
7	−0·5	0·5	0·25
8	+0·5	0·5	0·25
9	+1·5	1·5	2·25
10	+2·5	2·5	6·25
$\Sigma x = 45$ $\bar{x} = \frac{45}{6} = 7\cdot5$	$\Sigma d_1 = 0$	$\Sigma d_2\ 9\cdot0$ $\bar{d_2} = 1\cdot5$	$\Sigma d^2 = 17\cdot50$

A useful check on the accuracy of your arithmetic is to find the sum of all the deviations which should always equal 0.

The mean deviation, $\bar{d} = \dfrac{\Sigma|x - \bar{x}|}{n}$

$$= 1\cdot5$$

By using $|x - \bar{x}|$ (i.e. the modulus of $(x - \bar{x})$), it implies that no account of direction (i.e. sign) is considered, but this is mathematically unsound, and hence the use of squares to eliminate the negative signs. From the above example the mean of the sum of the deviations squared, i.e. the variance, is calculated, and this is expressed by the formula:

variance, $\sigma^2 = \dfrac{\Sigma d^2}{n}$

$$= \frac{\Sigma(x - \bar{x})^2}{n}$$

standard deviation, σ, is the square root of the variance

i.e. $\sigma = \sqrt{\dfrac{\Sigma(x - \bar{x})^2}{n}}$

variance, $\sigma^2 = \dfrac{17\cdot50}{6}$

$$= 2\cdot917$$

and the standard deviation,

$$\sigma = \sqrt{2\cdot917}$$
$$= 1\cdot7$$

A shorter method and one involving less calculation is that using the formula

$$\sigma = \sqrt{\frac{\Sigma x^2}{n} - \bar{x}^2}$$

Thus it is seen that the standard deviation is an indication of the dispersal of the data.

No matter what the dispersal of the data of a normal distribution curve, a given percentage of occurrences always falls within given limits. Thus:

68·3% of the occurrences lie between $+1\sigma$ and -1σ
95·45% of the occurrences lie between $+2\sigma$ and -2σ
99·7% of the occurrences lie between $+3\sigma$ and -3σ
99·99% of the occurrences lie between $+4\sigma$ and -4σ

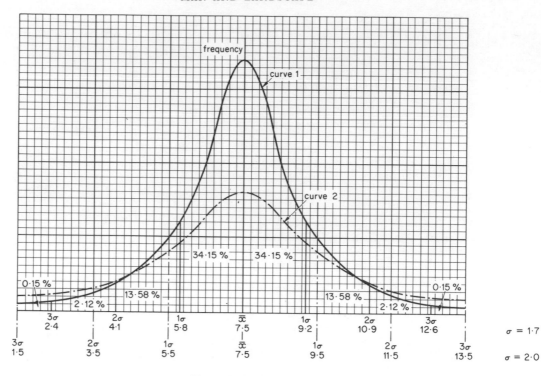

FIG. 11. Normal distribution curves.

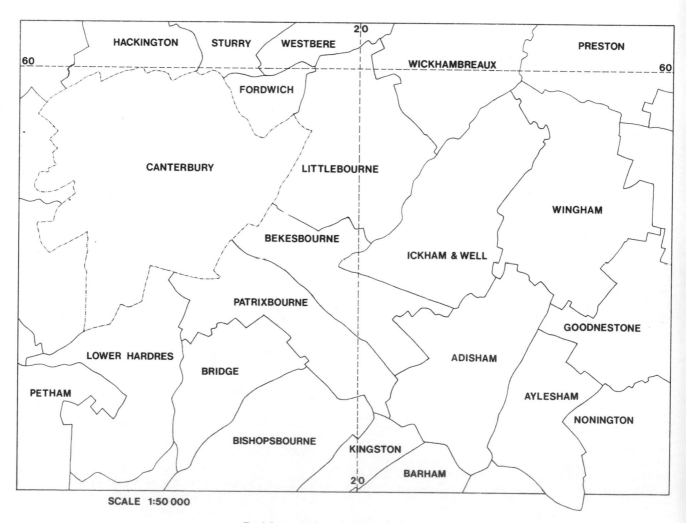

FIG. 12. Parishes south-east of Canterbury.

It is important that the concept of the standard deviation be understood, for it forms the basis of all advanced statistical work.

At the beginning we said that the standard deviation is a measure of the dispersion of a set of data and that it is related to the area under a normal distribution curve. This is a curve which is derived from a symmetrical histogram, for the smaller the class values then the more nearly will the shape of this curve equate to that of a bell. But this shape is only obtained when the array of data is symmetrically arranged about the mean of the data. The perfect normal distribution curve shows typical features, apart from the bell shape.

These are: 1. a peak about the mean;
2. symmetrical about the mean;
3. the two tails never reach the x-axis but always tend to approach it.

In Figure 11 two normal curves have been drawn. In both cases the mean is the same with a value of 7·5 but the standard deviation of the data from which curve 1 is drawn (table on page 15) has a value of 1·7 and the standard deviation of a second set of data from which curve 2 has been constructed has a value of 2·0. It immediately becomes apparent that because of the greater numerical value of the standard deviation in curve 2, the shape of this curve, while still retaining its bell shape, is 'flatter' than that of curve 1.

EXERCISE 10:
(a) Choose ten parishes whose boundaries are shown complete on Figure 12. Trace off these boundaries and from the topographical map mark the positions of all the parish churches which can now be assumed to be the village centre. From here find and measure in metres the maximum straight line distance to the farthest point of each parish. Tabulate the results and calculate the mean, median and mode of these measured values for the ten selected parishes.
(b) Which of your three values do you consider to be the most meaningful for the area under study?
(c) Compare your median value with that found for the Lincolnshire parishes (see page 12) and briefly give geographical reasons for any degree of similarity or divergence between the two values.

THE CONCEPT OF SHAPE

A simple method has been devised for measuring shape to avoid such descriptions as 'almost rectangular' or 'approximately triangular' since such terms are differently interpreted by different people. By adopting an index of measurement and using elementary mathematics, a comparison can be made between any two shapes: one unknown such as that formed by the boundary of a parish and the other known such as a rectangle, hexagon, circle or equilateral triangle, or in fact any geometrical figure.[1]

Method

1. Trace the outline of the unknown shape on to a sheet of graph paper or draw it on sectional tracing-paper.
2. On a small piece of ordinary tracing-paper draw any regular geometrical figure that appears to be nearest in

[1] D. Lee and T. Sallee, 'A Method of Measuring Shape', *Geographical Review* (1970).

shape and size to the unknown figure. This is now termed the 'known standard'.

3. Place the known standard over the unknown figure and enlarge or reduce it or change its orientation so that it covers the maximum area of the unknown shape. Now draw this 'best-fit' standard on top of the unknown figure.
4. On this diagram clearly mark the longest perimeter of the combined shapes and by counting the number of graph grid squares find the area enclosed by this perimeter (area A on Figure 13). It is unnecessary to convert the number of graph squares into real areas as the estimation shape is based on an index number (r).
5. Measure the area of coincidence of both figures as shown by the shaded areas in Figure 13. This is area B entered in the table below.
6. Divide area B into area A and subtract the result from the value 1 to give an index number.
7. Establish the index numbers for other regular shapes that appear to be a close fit to the unknown shape and tabulate the results.
8. The lowest value of r in the table below thus gives the best-fit-standard for the shape under investigation for if A and B were coincident the ratio of $\dfrac{A}{B}$ would be unity and r would equal zero.

Comparison of the Unknown Shape in Figure 13 with Known Shapes

| PARISH SHAPE | NUMBER OF SQUARE UNITS | | INDEX NUMBER (r) $1 - \dfrac{A}{B} = r$ |
	TOTAL AREA A	COINCIDENT AREA B	
(a) Square	736	496	0·148
(b) Rectangle	651	490	0·132
(c) Circle	1026	571	0·177
(d) Hexagon	763	500	0·152
(e) Right-angled triangle	662	518	0·127
(f) Parallelogram	724	536	0·135

In Figure 14 the shape of the parish is closest to that of a right-angled triangle.

This method can be used with a series of neighbouring parishes to test the hypothesis that one shape is dominant in a particular area. It also provides an objective means of discovering similarities that exist, or individual parishes which diverge from the general regional shape. And thus explanations can be investigated. It can be argued that if in real life daughters take after mothers then daughter parishes could resemble the shape of their mother parishes! This supposition could be tested.

EXERCISE 11:
Use the shape index method to describe the shape of selected adjacent parishes south-east of Canterbury (see Figure 12).

If you examine the shape of all the parishes shown in Figure 12 it will be seen that the best-fit regular figures representing each parish can be joined together to form a geometrical pattern which can then be referred to as the parish lattice.

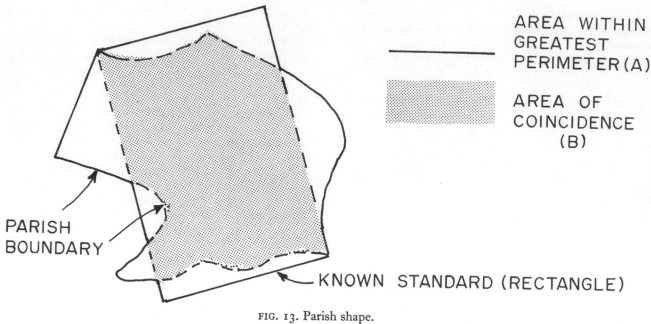

FIG. 13. Parish shape.

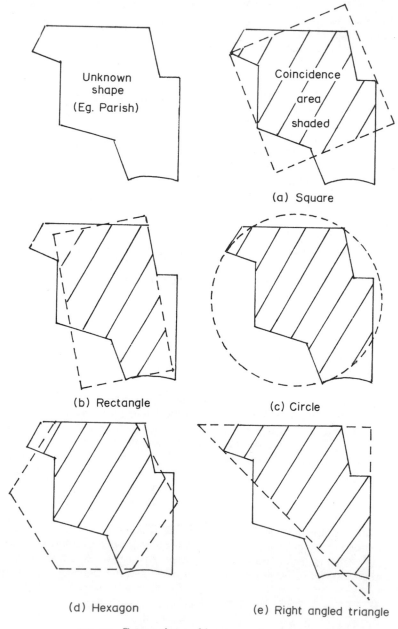

(a) Square

(b) Rectangle

(c) Circle

(d) Hexagon

(e) Right angled triangle

FIG. 14. Comparison of known and unknown shapes.

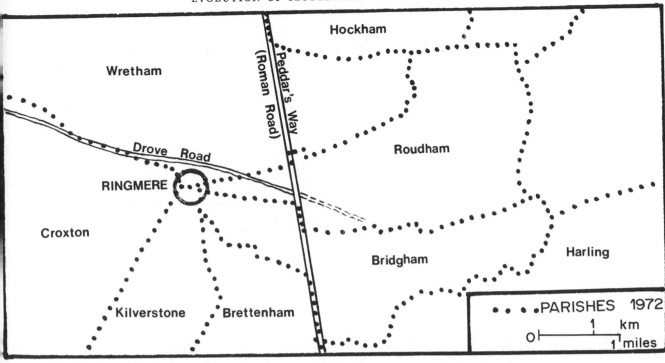

FIG. 15. Breckland heath parishes.

PARISH LATTICES

EXERCISE 12:

(a) *Geometrically subdivide an imaginary land area, which is represented by a square of 100 mm side, into a series of uniform circular parishes. Each village is centrally placed and the distance between each is 25 mm. On your diagrammatic map construct uniform equilateral triangles. Repeat the exercise but substitute regular hexagons for the triangles.*

(b) *Examine the parish lattices and comment on the advantages and disadvantages that each figure would possess if used to divide a uniform area into parishes.*

(c) *State which regular shape is the best from the point of view of both 'minimum energy requirement' and of trouble-free land division.*

Geographers, seeking a uniform parish lattice to use as a model, commonly use a hexagon. Theory and actuality do not always coincide and it is unlikely that the student will see many hexagonal parishes on a map. The value of using both the test of best-fit for parish shapes and of superimposing a hexagonal lattice over the parishes of a region is seen in the extent to which parishes achieve a hexagonal shape. If they do differ widely from the model shape then the geographical reasons for this fact should be unravelled.

SIGNIFICANCE OF SHAPE

In the past when villagers needed water either for themselves or for livestock, access to rivers or lakes would be of prime importance and their territory would reach out to the water supply. In the sandy, dry heathlands of the East Anglian Brecklands temporary natural lakes are found. Near Thetford the parishes of Wretham, Croxton, Kilverstone, Bridgham and Roudham all meet at the Ringmere Lake as depicted in Figure 15. Although Brettenham parish fails to reach the mere the villagers were wise enough to negotiate the right to pass across the Kilverstone heathland in order to obtain water.[1] These water-seeking tongues of land give an elongated shape to their parishes even to the extent of their reaching across a Roman road, the Peddar's Way. This fact is even more remarkable when it is realized that twenty Breckland parishes allow this road to form part of their boundaries and thus to dominate their shape. A still earlier influence upon parish boundaries was the Drove Road. This prehistoric trackway still forms a small part of the boundary between Wretham and Croxton parishes.

Elsewhere downslope elongation of parishes reflects the need for soil type variety within it. Access to valley alluvium and fertile silty soils would be of inestimable value to upland farmers. However, the reverse is also significant since heath and forest were important for pasturage. In the area between Cambridge and Newmarket, as shown on Figure 16, the elongation of such parishes as Brinkley and Westley Waterless reflect this need for pasturage and timber, these areas being called the 'waste' by the Anglo-Saxons. Thus waste-edge settlement is as significant as scarp-foot or fen-edge settlement and the right to use the 'waste' was as significant as the right to use water supplies.

Where parish boundaries follow dykes then the antiquity of both is suggested since these great defensive earthworks of lowland Britain belong to the Dark Ages. The Devil's Dyke in Cambridgeshire, for example, is a parish boundary for seven miles and even today is a linear rampart some 4·5 metres (15 feet) high which begins in the fenland and ends on the clay hills—the 'waste' of Anglo-Saxon times.

However, one aspect of medieval rural settlement frequently overlooked is that short period of time when the size of some settlements was reduced. During the fourteenth and fifteenth centuries cornfields were changed into pasture and open fields converted into parkland with a resultant change in the rural economy. Some small hamlets became depopulated and eventually deserted. With the houses in ruins, the parish would cease to exist and the neighbouring parish would absorb this area and so extend

---

[1] W. G. Clarke, *In Breckland Wilds* (1937), p. 84.

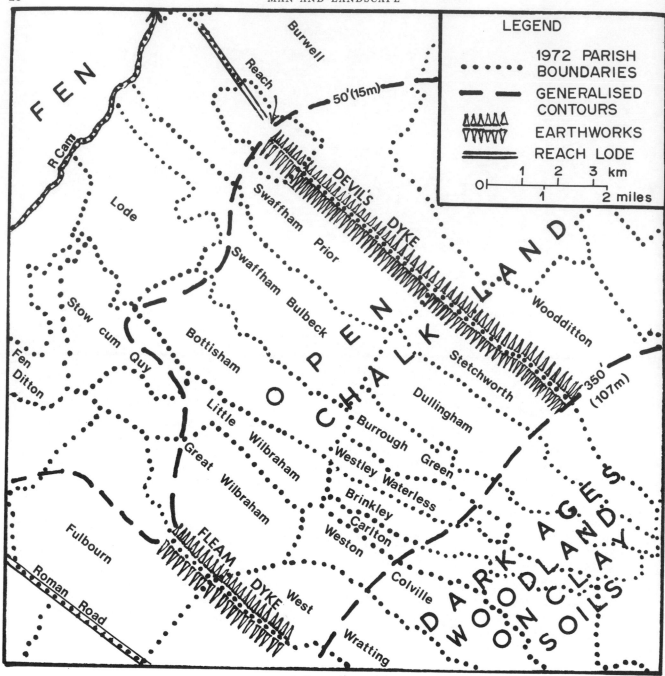

FIG. 16. Fen-edge parishes.

its boundaries. A bulge in the parish boundary may be but a hint that such an event might be entered in the parish records or be revealed by an archaeological excavation. Lost medieval villages could also be the result of epidemics such as the Black Death (1348–49) which almost annihilated entire village populations.[1]

EXERCISE 13:

(*a*) *On the Canterbury topographical map name the parishes which appear to have had the line of their boundaries modified or influenced by communications.*

(*b*) *Examine the shape of the parishes of Bekesbourne and Patrixbourne and suggest physical reasons why it is advantageous for both to possess their present shape.*

---

[1] E. M. Yates, 'Dark Age and Medieval Settlements on the Edge of Wastes and Forests', *Field Studies* (1965), vol. 2, no. 2, pp. 133–53.

Distortion of parish shapes from that of a regular hexagon may be due to one or more of the following factors:

1. the need for a water-supply—lakes, rivers or springs;
2. avoidance of or access to roads or navigable rivers;
3. the presence of a sea coast;
4. the need for defence in the form of earthworks;
5. changes in the economic structure of the village territory;
6. 'lost villages' due to poverty or disease and hence absorption of the territory of the lost parish;
7. improvements in farming practices and techniques;
8. the seeking out of either fertile soils for cultivation or the heath and woodland glades for pasturage.

If an English village is defined as 'a community organized for work' then it is to be expected that important changes will have occurred since its foundation. Only if all the village populations have equal opportunity and equal capability and desire for work in a uniform environment will parish areas evolve into regular geometrical shapes.

Photograph II *Redeveloped Canterbury: view looking towards the Cathedral and 'Roman Pavement', August 1970.*

Photograph III *A glimpse of 'old Canterbury': a lane leading to the Cathedral from High Street, August 1970.*

Which view do you prefer—open vista or medieval glimpse? Old gabled buildings with strong vertical lines contrast with the horizontal lines of the new box-type structures which surround the Cathedral. In both photographs the service function of Canterbury and the intrusion of vehicles can be studied.

MODERN CANTERBURY

In 1971 Canterbury with its 33 000 inhabitants was principally a market and distributive centre for SE Kent. Its
other interests, then as now, lay in the new university and
in meeting the requirements of some 300 000 annual
visitors. Its few light industries are linked to its chief
function as a service centre.

EXERCISE 14:

'*The approach to Canterbury from any of the gently rising
lands around it reveals the breathtaking cathedral, still
dominant as its builders intended and still nobly presiding over
the close-knit fabric of the medieval city. The eye is bewitched
and the traveller looks forward to the experience of penetrating
the matrix of buildings lying before him . . . with anxiety the
traveller moves forward into Canterbury.*' (*J. S. Curl*)
   *As James Stevens Curl came towards the city walls he
experienced 'a sense of unease'. Study Photograph I. (a) Suggest two reasons why this writer may have been disappointed by
what he saw. (b) Give your impression of this urban landscape.*

A major problem for Canterbury is that of the heavy
traffic which enters it, since as yet (1973) the motorway
linking London to Dover has not been completed and the
city attracts thousands of tourists as well as those regularly
using its shopping and service facilities.

EXERCISE 15:
(*a*) *Here is a list of possible solutions to the urban planning
    problem of dealing with traffic in cities. Select any four
    of these which you consider to be the most useful and discuss
    their merits, giving reasons why you think these to be more
    satisfactory than those excluded.*
    (*i*) *Devise special traffic lanes for buses.*
    (*ii*) *Separate through traffic from the rest.*
    (*iii*) *Build peripheral car parks and close the city centre
         to traffic.*

(*iv*) *Create complex one-way route systems to discourage
     city traffic.*
 (*v*) *Provide more parking places and ban all street
     parking and waiting.*
(*vi*) *Redevelop the city to provide wider roads.*
(*vii*) *Provide a free bus service and prohibit the use of
     private cars within the city centre.*
(*viii*) *Charge tolls for cars to enter the central area.*
(*ix*) *Raise city centre car park fees to high levels.*

(*b*) *Examine the air photograph (Photograph I) and the other
    two photographs (II and III) and state which solutions
    appear to have been selected by the authorities to try to
    solve the traffic problem of Canterbury. Have they been
    successful?*

A substantial part of the medieval city was destroyed during
the Second World War (see analytical sketch, Figure 1). If
you compare this with the same area on the air photograph
(I) and contrast the redevelopment area with that of the old,
then a clear distinction between modern box-style structures
and medieval-gabled buildings is obvious. Planning the
rebuilding of historic cities to satisfy both the inhabitants
and the tourists is clearly a difficult exercise. Is it preferable
to open up the area near the cathedral to give distant views
or to provide glimpses of it from narrow alleys? What
about the cost of land? If the profit motive is a powerful
factor in the redevelopment of urban centres then tall,
straight-line structures, closely packed together may result.
Yet new, light and airy buildings are attractive both to
shoppers and shopworkers, but such new properties ought
to have a style and spatial distribution which harmonizes
with the old. To what extent has this been achieved in
Canterbury or in any similar historic town?
   This survey of the establishment and growth of rural and
urban settlements in part of Kent has led to the selection of
certain themes and to the stressing of one aspect at the
expense of another. The study of local geology, history,
technology and social and economic conditions through
time all contribute to the understanding of the environment.
Because of the complexity of geographic studies it is
sometimes necessary to express data in mathematical terms
and to accept guidance from theories.
   This fascinating voyage may have taken us 'out of the
sight of the land of existing fact' but we should have
returned to harbour with a mind enriched through a clearer
understanding of the past and of our present place on the
globe.

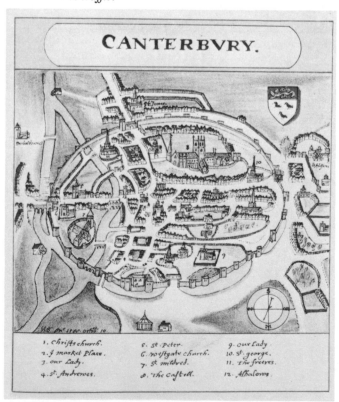

Photograph IV *A sixteenth-century map of Canterbury.*

2. Settlement and Communications in the Middle Rhine Valley of West Germany

Here, man and nature have achieved a rare harmony, a union whose mellow perfection is emphasised by contrast.

K. A. Sinnhuber

WHERE THE meandering river valleys of the Rhine and Mosel (Moselle) converge is the confluence city of Koblenz (Coblence). The rivers cut deeply into the mountains and settlement location reflects the presence or lack of cultivated land and building land. The deeply entrenched rivers have helped to create steep hill-slopes one of which experiences long hours of sunlight while the opposite one is deprived of warmth. As the rivers swing in large bends, the relative orientation to the sun of the valley sides is constantly changing thus producing a similarly changing pattern in the receipt of sunshine on the slopes. The varied land use and the presence or absence of early settlement partly reflects the influence of this consideration.

SETTLEMENT ORIENTATION

The direction of one settlement in relation to another, or the direction in which the majority of the buildings face is stated by either giving the compass direction or by means of bearings. The *bearing* of a distant object is the angle between north and a line from the position of the observer (A) to that distant point (B). This angle is to be regarded as the amount of angular rotation made by turning *clockwise* from the direction of the true north, grid north or magnetic north to the direction of the observed object. Thus N120°E implies

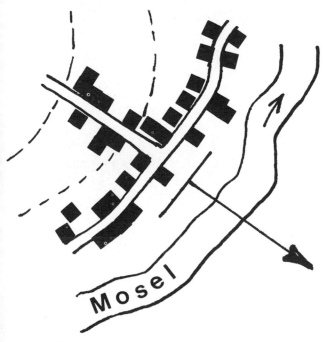

FIG. 17. Settlement orientation line at right-angles to main street.

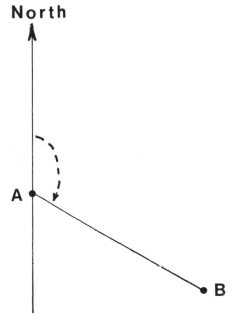

FIG. 18. Bearing diagram: the bearing of B is N120°E.

an easterly movement through 120°. True north is the direction of the meridian (line of longitude) leading to the North Pole of the earth and if a bearing is made from true north then this bearing is called an *azimuth*. On maps bearings can be most easily made from grid north if a circular plastic protractor is used.

Duration of sunlight especially in spring could make or mar a settlement's economy. The sunny side (*adrêt*; *Sonnenseite*) of steep river valleys which reaches down to alluvial terraces on meander slip-off slopes is planted with vines adjacent to the riverside settlements. The shady slope (*ubac*; *Schattenseite*) is wooded and where river cliffs abound settlement is absent. The truth of these observations can be verified by studying the scene depicted on Photograph VI together with the relevant map area.

EXERCISE 1:

(*a*) *Complete a copy of the following table:*

SETTLEMENT	GENERAL ORIENTATION	ON SUNNY OR SHADY SLOPES	AVERAGE ALTITUDE	SITE GEOLOGY
Güls				
Lay				
Ober-Lahnstein				
Rübenach				
Winningen				

(*b*) *With the aid of sketch maps make a geographical comparison between Winningen and Lay.*

Photograph V *The confluence of the Rhine and Mosel at Koblenz viewed from Ehrenbreitstein.*

Photograph VI *The village of Lay on the Mosel. Orientate the map extract and identify the viewpoint from which this photograph was taken.*

THE VINEYARDS—THEIR ASSOCIATED CLIMATE AND SETTLEMENT

EXERCISE 2:

(a) For the Koblenz map extract area plot the positions of all vineyards using the map symbol of parallel rows of short vertical dashes.

(b) Measure the total area of the map and of the vineyards and state the percentage of land given over to the cultivation of vines.

(c) Comment on the orientation and geographical location of the vineyards.

The extract gives but a mere hint as to the importance of the Mosel (Moselle) as an area of viticulture, but vines have been cultivated here since Roman times.

The Highlands, known also as the Slate Plateau (Schiefergebirge), provide cleaved rocks which are used for building the attractive dividing and retaining walls of the artificial terraces of the vineyards and appear as gigantic brown and green stairways flanking the river gorges.

During the Middle Ages a rapid expansion in vine cultivation coincided with settlement expansion for the crop was of economic importance to villagers. Considerable cash benefits could be obtained from a few hectares of land and the near-by expanding towns, with their non-agricultural population, created a demand for such specialized products as wines.

The vineyards have also influenced the compact shape of settlements, for houses are built close together to conserve land. Cattle rearing was of lesser importance and so isolated farms were not required.

The Mosel Valley has been described as an 'elongated climatic oasis' since the temperature is usually 1 to 1·5°C higher than the surrounding country and it experiences exceptionally early springs. Apple orchards are covered with blossom in late April. The geographical conditions for viticulture in this region can thus be summarized:

1. Slaty rock is available for terrace wall construction along the valley sides.

2. The stony slate-earth soil stores heat derived from the sun (insolation) and thus raises night temperatures on the slopes.

3. The well-drained, steep, sunny slopes experience a high degree of insolation since the angle of the sun on the mountain slopes approaches that of 90° at midday during the Northern Hemisphere summer.

4. Down-slope air drainage prevents the formation of frost which would otherwise damage the vines. The open construction of the dry stone walls allows cold air to flow down to the valley floor where it forms a cold 'air-lake'.

5. Woodlands on the plateau summit above the vineyards deflect the down-slope movement of cold air and therefore also help in the prevention of frost damage to the vines. Nevertheless during severe winters frost protection in the Mosel vineyards is achieved by using rotating water sprinklers which give a heavy fall of spray. Latent heat is thus liberated at the ice–water boundary on the wet leaf surface and this keeps the temperature at or above 0°C when otherwise it might be −2°C or below, with the plant consequently being severely damaged or killed.

EXERCISE 3:

For the settlement and environs of Winningen (9476) discuss the extent to which:

(a) The above statements 1 to 5 apply

(b) The settlement shape appears to reflect the dominance of viticulture.

EXERCISE 4:

Draw an annotated cross profile or a transect diagram from the spot height 284 (938 781) in the Rübenacher Wald to the triangulation point 203 (940 744) west of the Kondermuhle to illustrate the contrasts found on the opposite slopes of the Mosel Valley.

EARLY SETTLEMENT

By travelling into the Rhine Valley and reaching Koblenz the geographer has arrived in an area that has been described by Elkins and Yates as 'the microcosm of Western Germany' for this is the region where the evolution of settlement typically reflects that found in Central and Southern Germany.[1]

USING AND MAPPING PLACE-NAME EVIDENCE

The earliest invaders of this region probably came from the Baltic lands and the oldest surviving place-names have an ending such as -ithi, or in its shortened form -the or -de. This map extract unfortunately does not cover these localities but the next oldest endings, -ing and -heim, together with their abbreviated forms of -em and -um, are scattered throughout the lowlands and are a result of the movement of the Franks from the mouth of the river Elbe to the territory now known as France. These peoples conquered the early Celtic tribes in the Rhinelands and by the end of the first century A.D. had spread over most of what is now Germany even pushing the Slavonic peoples eastward (see Figure 19). But the Franks, when they arrived, found settled areas of mixed culture, including Roman.

FIG. 19. Germanic people and their neighbours at the end of the first century A.D.

[1] T. H. Elkins and E. M. Yates, 'The Neuwied Basin' *Geography*, 45 (1960), p. 50.

Whether one is studying rivers, paintings or settlements it is easier to study small-scale rather than large-scale features. Fortunately for our investigations, the movement of European peoples was on a small scale. Individual great migrations only affected a few thousand persons and were the exception rather than the rule.

To study growth and migration it is possible to group place-name elements into three main chronological orders and to call them primary, secondary and tertiary, although some writers use the terms early primary, late primary and secondary. In the following account the ease of using numerals in practical exercises makes it preferable to use the former rather than the latter classification. After all classification is to help us over difficulties.

The English-speaking student should have few problems in understanding the early history of German settlement since certain name elements are virtually the same in both languages and the form -heim in German can be equated with -ham in English, for as we have seen Anglo-Saxon and Celtic influences were also felt in Great Britain.

Primary—Fourth and Fifth Centuries A.D.

GERMAN	ENGLISH
-ithi (-de; -the)	
-ing	
-ingen	
-heim (-em; um)	home
-mar; -ar; -aha	
-stedt	

Secondary—Fifth to Eighth Centuries A.D.

GERMAN ELEMENT	ENGLISH MEANING
-burg	defended home
-dorf	village
-haus; -hausen	dwelling(s) (village)
-hof; -hofen	farm(s)
-hurst	hill
-ach; -ich	personal place
-becken	basin
-weil; -weiler	villa (seventh to tenth centuries)
-kirch; -kirchen; -kappell	church(es); chapel (fifth to thirteenth centuries)
-zell; -zel; -cell	religious settlement

Settlements bearing these elements, such as Lützel (originally Lützelkoblenz) show the influence of the invading Franks upon the region. Lützen would originally provide the bridgehead for the invasion of the Mosel Valley.

Tertiary—Ninth to Thirteenth Centuries A.D.

Clearing land by burning down the forest was so common that newly established places within this territory acquired name endings such as '-seng' indicating singeing or scorching and '-brand' suggesting burning. Other settlements were created either in clearings, where timber had been hewn, or near streams which gave direct access into the mountains. The newly built homes on these types of sites were fenced or walled in as a protective measure.

GERMAN ELEMENT	ENGLISH MEANING
-bach (possibly a survival from an earlier period)	a stream or brook
-berg	hill or mountain
-brand	burning, fire
-brunn	spring settlement
-deich	dam, dyke or ditch
-fels	rock
-hau	hewing of wood around a village
-hagen; -heide	fence or hedge round a heath
-lah	a small wood
-metz	hewing of wood
-ried	marshy place
-reut; -reute; -reuth -rode; -roth; -rod	rooting up of woodland
-sand	sandy settlement
-scheide	wall or barrier
-schlag	attack (the waste)
-schwand; -schwanden	burning
-stein	rock or stone
-stock	stick (fenced area)
-tal	valley
-wald	wood

EXERCISE 5:
(a) *Construct a map to show the relative ages of settlement for the area of Koblenz using place-name endings.*
  (i) *The base map should include the outline of the courses of the Mosel, Lahn and Rhein (Rhine) together with the main roads (numbered 9, 42 and 49), distinctly marked.*
  (ii) *Place the numerals 1, 2 or 3 on your map over the approximate centres of your settlements, to represent primary, secondary and tertiary, respectively.*
  (iii) *Draw continuous lines to separate the area of primary settlement from the rest of the region. Shade this zone by means of widely spaced parallel lines drawn across it.*
(b) *Using your map discuss the nature and extent of the suggested primary colonization of this region.*

EXERCISE 6:
Using place-name evidence arrange the following small towns in chronological order beginning with the earliest (number 1) and enter in a copy of the table below.

Oberlahnstein
Rübenach
Winningen

Examine the location of each of these settlements with the aid of the geological map (Figure 20) and the topographical map. Complete your copy of the table:

SETTLEMENT		GEOLOGY OF SITE	GEOGRAPHICAL SITUATION
Age	Name		
1			
2			
3			

FIG. 20. *Facing page.* Simplified geology of Koblenz region.

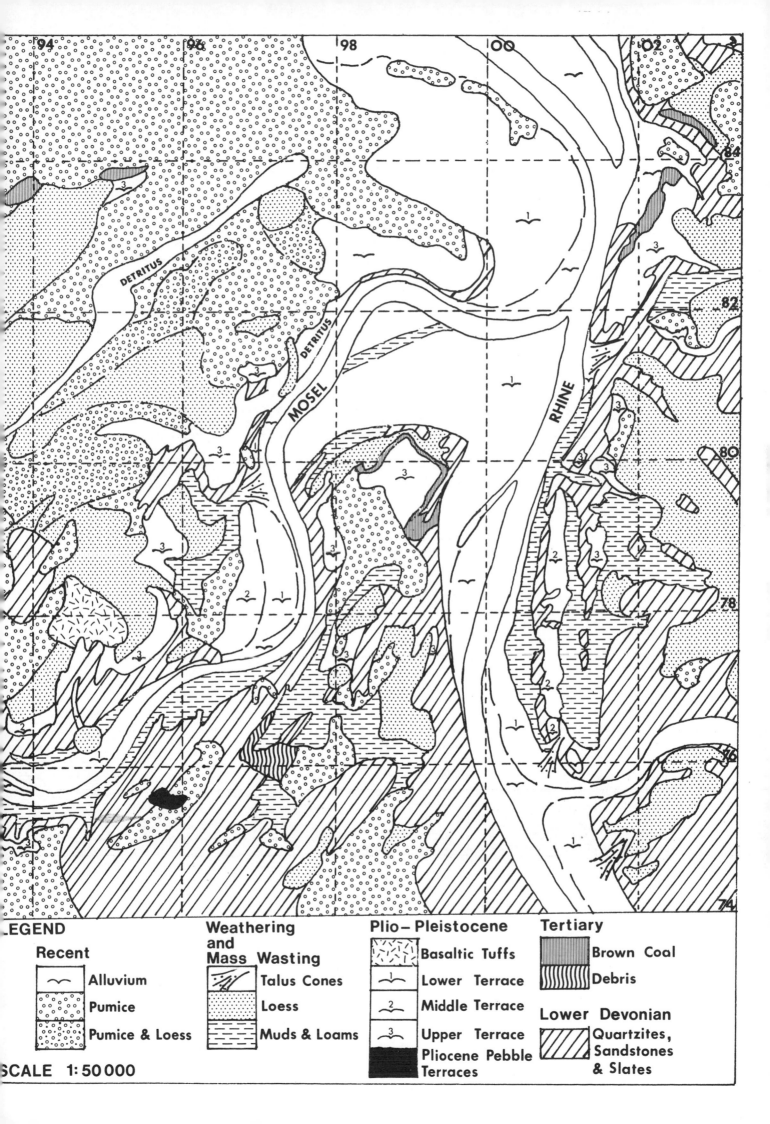

LEGEND

Recent

Alluvium

Pumice

Pumice & Loess

Weathering and Mass Wasting

Talus Cones

Loess

Muds & Loams

Plio–Pleistocene

Basaltic Tuffs

Lower Terrace

Middle Terrace

Upper Terrace

Pliocene Pebble Terraces

Tertiary

Brown Coal

Debris

Lower Devonian

Quartzites, Sandstones & Slates

SCALE 1:50 000

DETRITUS

MOSEL

RHINE

In general terms the growth and development of German villages shows a movement from productive soils to marginal areas with the result that by the end of the eleventh century only the poorest areas were still available for new settlement.

FACTORS INFLUENCING SETTLEMENT

Obviously place-name evidence is only one type of evidence concerning the origin and growth of settlements. The type of village structure and associated field patterns, the form of farmhouses and the method of using land are also of great significance in understanding regional contrasts seen in the landscape of western Europe. Unfortunately these other aspects of settlement foundation and growth are not easily studied from maps or even from actual visits to the area concerned since the main source of information has to be sought in historical documents.

It is possible to start with a broad generalization that early settlement was irregular in form and that more recent settlement had a planned layout of streets and buildings. Although this is a simple and attractive explanation of village form it is not always true, for the growth of farming was a result of a complex relationship between land and the social and economic conditions prevailing at given times in the past. For example, the development of types of ploughs or the structure of rural society involving landlord and tenant meant that in certain regions of western Europe the enclosure of land, by walls or hedges, was due as much to social as to technical developments, all of which must have influenced village growth.

On the other hand there were large areas of medieval France and Germany where large villages were associated with an open-field system, with cultivation on a crop rotation basis. A rising population led to a division of land into smaller units. The establishment of territorial lords and church (monastic) authorities meant that they could state the conditions of settlement to anyone wishing to settle on their land. The manorial system was a new force, the strength of which would be reflected in the freedom the peasants had either to extend the open-field system or to develop, adjacent to the medieval open field, new clearings in which they built isolated farms. Hence the shape, size and spacing of settlements were influenced by social and population changes.

In the Koblenz area the open-field system permitted settlement to develop into large villages (Haufendörfer) with the courtyard farms concentrated into villages while between these villages were the single farms (Einzelhöfe). Today the villages also house commuters to Koblenz and have some industry 'spilled-over' from the city. This has tended to break up the old closed village form.

The map (Figure 21) shows that during the Ice Age this region was adjacent to the ice front and thus experienced a periglacial climate. With retreating ice, bare land dried out and the top surface became wind-blown. This unstratified wind-blown material, usually of a light yellow colour and known as loess, weathered down to a rich soil and was quickly recognized as fertile land by early settlers. The forest in such areas would be cleared and arable land created around the new hamlets. Loessic lands were early providers of arable, pasture and forest and the relationships of these would vary according to economic demands. Also such fertile territories were commonly free from physical restrictions since they were plains, low plateaux or river terraces. Small villages quickly grew to towns under such conditions.

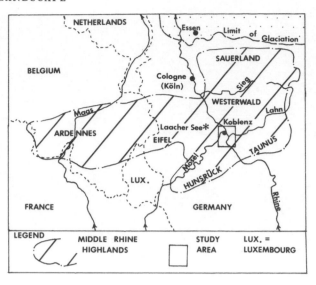

FIG. 21. Location of Koblenz area.

EXERCISE 7:

By reference to named examples in the Koblenz region relate the areal size of settlements to:
(a) the physical availability of building land;
(b) the geological nature of the site.

The advantages of loessic soils for settlement can be demonstrated by comparing landscapes developed on loess and clay materials.

LOESS (LÖSS) LANDS	CLAY LANDS
Complex nucleated villages	*Small dispersed settlements*
1. Ease of felling timber and of ploughing the relatively dry soils	1. Early settlers could only work this land during drier periods
2. Moisture is retained at depth thus maintaining crops during dry periods	2. Because of difficult working conditions financial returns from the crops were uncertain
3. The soil is rich in humus and minerals	3. Land excellent for growing cereals but these were usually only for subsistence
4. Communications are easy on the open dry land	4. Communications are difficult on marshy or wet clay lands

Contrasts between loess and clay lands are not always clearly recognizable in the Koblenz region since volcanic explosions such as that which resulted in the Laacher See in the near-by Eifel not only produced lava flows but ejected ashes and dust into the air. The shattered, but finely fragmented material is known as tuff and the light foamy lava as pumice which is referred to as bimsstein (bims) in Germany. This bims formed a blanket over large tracts of this area and subdued the relief. At a later period loess covered part of the bims landscape and also provided a layer of fine fertile black soil over the gravels of river terraces which became superb sites for settlement.

EXERCISE 8:
(a) Describe with the aid of Figure 20 the distribution of:
   (i) periglacial loess and (ii) volcanic pumice (bims) in the Koblenz region.
(b) Draw a sketch map of the area which lies north-east and east of Mülheim to show the positions of all quarries, which are in fact bimsstein workings.

The majority of this pumice was laid or re-deposited in water and this is referred to as 'trass' which, with cement added to it, is manufactured into building bricks. The economic importance of the pumice stone industry to the region is relatively declining due to the rapidly expanding iron and steel, paper, chemicals and food-processing industries. Nevertheless some 4000 persons are actively employed in the stone industry of the Koblenz–Neuwied Basin.

FUNCTIONS OF URBAN SETTLEMENTS

Settlements have acquired their urban status through their special socio-economic functions. They have grown to be the chief market centres of an area because such functions as retail shops, wholesale warehouses, banks, garages and offices have developed to meet the requirements not merely of the town's own population but of that of the surrounding area. The range for selling a product or for providing a service for a firm is the distance over which people will travel to purchase goods or obtain a service. To a shopkeeper this is the fluctuating market area and a study of supply and demand within it is undoubtedly complex. W. Christaller, in attempting an explanation of market areas in terms of the provision of services, construed a theory based upon the smallest units of settlement which developed in areas of uniformity.[1] He suggested that the most efficient system of clearly defining market areas was one based upon a hex-agonal lattice. This geometrical form is one which most nearly approaches that of the circle, but a circular lattice suffers from the disadvantage of allowing unsupplied or overlapping areas to occur as indicated by the shaded areas in the diagram below.

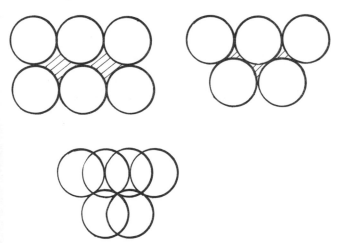

FIG. 22. Packing of circles.

If 'the chief profession of a town is to be central to its rural surroundings' then the centre of the hexagon is the location of the 'central place'. Christaller clearly indicated that there is mutual dependence between the central place and the supply region.

Equal spacing of settlements in self-sufficient agricultural areas results in competition developing between them in the provision of services. Village shops, for example, usually stock a limited range of goods and thus villages are low-order central places and have but a small market area,

[1] W. Christaller, *Die Zentralen Orte in Süddeutschland* (1933). (The Central Places in South Germany. English translation by C. W. Baskin, 1966.)

whereas towns provide a wider range of services for a larger area and are therefore higher-order central places. If higher-order and lower-order centres are considered to be equally spaced then the hexagonal market area of higher-order is larger than that of lower-order central places and the latter areas are contained within the former. This orderly nesting of market areas indicates that, in this model, a hierarchy of central places is conceived, ranging from small hamlets to large towns, and that high-order places perform not only their own varied functions but also those of lower-order places. Within this hierarchy villages survive as economic units because they have developed their own trading area and can therefore compete with the pull of the towns in limited fields.

EXERCISE 9:

(a) *To create a model to simulate the development of a hierarchy of central places, draw a horizontal straight line and construct a series of touching circles of uniform size, each with its centre on the straight line. Use the points of contact between adjacent circles as centres for an overlapping series of similar uniform circles. Using the points of intersection on the circumferences as centres construct lines of circles above and below the first. This procedure may be continued for any number of places.*

In the first circle which is centred on the line, join all points of intersection on the circumference to form a hexagon. Repeat this construction in every fourth overlapping circle along the straight line. The intermediate hexagons are now drawn between the first series of figures using the intermediate lengths of the initial straight line as one side of the second row of the lattice. Continue this construction for any number of hexagons as required.

(b) *Place dots at the six vertices of each hexagon to represent hamlets and larger dots at the centres to indicate village central places which have arisen by successful economic growth.*

Each hamlet is located at the meeting-point of three uniform market areas and hence with equal numbers of people having equal ease of movement and uniform purchasing power one-third of the hamlet's trade will be with each central place village. Thus the total hamlet trade of any hexagonal area around a village can be numerically represented by the value 2. The village also can enjoy the total of its own population's trade and this can be represented by a value of unity thus giving a total of numerical value 3 to the village. Christaller used the term 'K value' to refer to the total 'number' of settlements served by each central place. Hence, in this instance, K = 3. He also assumed that in any one region the K values would be fixed, by which he meant that they apply equally to the relationships between hamlets and villages and between villages and small towns, and so forth.

(c) *Continue the construction by creating a market area to represent that of the next higher-order central place. Join up by coloured lines six village 'centres' to form a larger hexagon. The former central place village can now be regarded as a town and the market area contains the equivalent of 9 units of trade. If space on your paper permits, the central place development can continue, as shown in Figure 23, by the creation of an even larger hexagon in the market area of which there will be 27 trade units.*

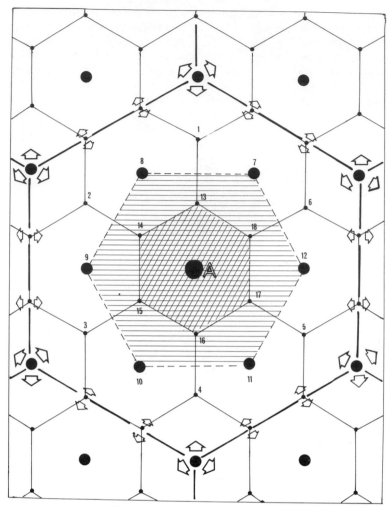

FIG. 23. Trade in a third-order hexagonal area.

When third-order settlements are established the number of units of trade of the central place is 27, as shown in Figure 23 and is calculated as follows:

The 6 centres at the vertices of the hexagon each share their trade between 3 centres and therefore the central place A has $\frac{6}{3} = 2$ units of trade. The other 12 peripheral settlements each share their trade between 2 centres and therefore A's share is $\frac{12}{2} = 6$. Within the hexagon lie 18 other centres whose entire trade is directed towards A and therefore a further 18 units are added. Likewise the entire trade of A is conducted in that centre.

Hence the total trade of A is found by summing all the above parts, i.e.

$$2 + 6 + 18 + 1 = 27$$

As the hierarchy of the settlements is established so the trade of each central place grows in the relationship 1, 3, 9, 27, 81 . . .

i.e.   1, 3, 3², 3³, 3⁴ . . . $(K = 3)$

This central place model suggests that it is possible that the function of such places controls their size and the size of their supplying area. Also this theory offers a partial explanation of why settlements scattered throughout a region differ in size as they do in southern Germany, for example.

Christaller's Urban Hierarchy
in Southern Germany ($K = 3$ hierarchy)

URBAN CLASS	GERMAN NAME AND ABBREVIATION USED		AVERAGE RADIUS OF SUPPLYING AREA IN KM	TYPICAL POPULATION SIZE
Market town	Markort	M	4·0	1 000
Central township	Amtsort	A	6·9	2 000
County town	Kreistadt	K	12·0	4 000
District city	Bezirksstadt	B	20·7	10 000
State capital	Gaustadt	G	36·0	30 000
Provincial capital	Provinzhaupstadt	P	62·1	100 000
Regional capital	Landeshaupstadt	L	108·0	500 000

EXERCISE 10:

Assess the significance of Christaller's market principle by considering the distribution of actual settlements in a lowland agricultural area.

(a) Select a map of a lowland area such as eastern England, the American prairies or the Netherlands, and on tracing-paper plot the distribution of hamlets, villages and towns. Superimpose a uniform pattern of nested hexagons and assess the near-fit of the lattice.

(b) Comment upon the result of this experiment.

EXERCISE 11:

Discuss Christaller's own comment upon the hierarchy as shown in the table above: 'This mathematic scheme is imperfect in some respects; it is even incorrect in its strictness.'

Workers since Christaller have suggested that the fixed K system was unrealistic since a town with a very specialized function might only possess a small tributary area and have few central place functions. Important transport routes may distort the central place scheme and create rectangular or irregular spatial patterns since settlements develop adjacent to the main lines of communication.

The theoretical pattern of hexagons can also be affected by the growth of specialized agriculture, by the intensity of cultivation, by topographic restrictions or by government economic assistance. Although social rather than economic services may be the prime support of some central places, the central place theory is still one useful basis for making a comparative analysis of settlements. The concept is not worthless because variations occur or because modifications have taken place or because it was first applied to southern Germany, where a regular distribution of settlements has developed through time in what was a uniform agricultural region.

The Value of Central Place Theory

1. It enables a comparative analysis of regional centres to be made.
2. It shows the interdependence of town and region.
3. A hierarchy of functions and of settlements is devised.
4. The idea of competition between centres is stressed.
5. The intensity and spacing of centres suggests further investigation as to how these service centres have evolved and are changing their character at the present time.
6. On the basis of a theoretical structure it is possible to make a number of predictions about the pattern of future settlement location.

Criticism of the Theory

1. This theory of Christaller is concerned only with one central place activity, that of the servicing functions for surrounding regions. Other aspects such as places of residence or industrial growth are glossed over irrespective of any local factors such as:
    availability of mineral resources;
    favourable climate;
    strategic position;
    growth of a port;
    railway development;
    urban 'overspill' requirements.
2. The theory of Christaller, which may have played a significant part in the development of that settlement, was devised for an agricultural area. It obviously works well in poor, thinly settled farm districts which are nearly self-contained, but works less well in manufacturing areas.
3. There could be planned delay in establishing full services in centres such as 'New Towns' until they have increased their populations. The theory also may not work well in areas where expanding industries are retarded or encouraged by government decree.

Of course Christaller suggested that there were concepts other than that of the marketing principle which are of value to the understanding of the problem of supply and demand, such as the part played by traffic and politics. Unfortunately an introductory survey such as this text must regretfully leave aside his further considerations and also those of his successors.

(Another simple way of examining variation in settlement sizes is to use the Rank Size Rule. This is explained later—see pages 97 and 98.)

SERVICES AND INDUSTRIAL EMPLOYMENT

EXERCISE 12:

From a study of the statistics given below:
(a) *State the chief function of Koblenz.*
(b) *From the point of view of the numbers of actively employed persons give, in order of importance, the four dominant economic activities of Koblenz, and for each calculate the percentage of persons employed in each category.*

Number of Places of Employment and Employees in Koblenz on 27 May 1971

ECONOMIC DIVISION	NUMBER OF PLACES OF EMPLOYMENT	PERSONS ACTIVELY EMPLOYED	
Agriculture and forestry	23	317	
Power production, water supply and mining	11	931	
Manufacturing:			
Chemical industry	8		331
Plastics and rubber	14		548
Quarrying, fine ceramics and glass	32		291
Metal production, foundry and steel making	35		1 573
Machinery, steel products and vehicle construction	105		3 119
Electrical engineering, precision instruments, optical, toys, sports and musical instruments	74		1 756
Wood, paper and printing	105		1 966
Leather, textiles and clothing	138		412
Food and luxury foodstuffs	185		2 147
Total manufacturing (industry and crafts)	696	12 143	
Building industry	310	5 623	
Commerce including retail trade	1 583	13 694	
Communication and transmission of news	256	6 358	
Banking and insurance	198	3 559	
Service industries and professional services	1 403	8 621	
Non-profit making organizations	203	2 441	
Local authority and social services	186	18 586	
FULL TOTAL	4 869	72 273	

Source: Statistical Office of the Municipality of Koblenz.

EXERCISE 13:

Using the data for Koblenz in the above table draw a divided circle to illustrate the proportion of actively employed workers in each of the ten listed economic divisions.

The establishment of markets and the development of commerce would be encouraged by the advantageous siting of settlements. Koblenz, at the confluence of the navigable Mosel and Rhine, is also built upon a river terrace where the roads parallel to the Rhine intersect those leading into the Mosel and Lahn valleys. The railway came to this nodal settlement in 1858 and within six years the routes along both banks of the Rhine were linked by a bridge.

EXERCISE 14:

Draw an annotated sketch map to show the importance of Koblenz as a communication centre.

In the past the town, which had Roman origins, was orientated towards the Mosel. On the tourist map (Figure 35 on page 40) the semicircular area between Kornpfortstrasse and the Balduinbrücke was the earliest trading centre. A wooden bridge over the Mosel then carried the main road along the left bank of the Rhine to Cologne. When the Franks ruled the area from A.D. 402 the town was fortified and a palace built on the Mosel bank. In the Middle Ages, however, the town grew towards the Rhine and the economic centre gravitated in this direction. During the eighteenth century the chief trade was in coal, wood, wine and cloth and a network of roads developed in response to the growth of trade.

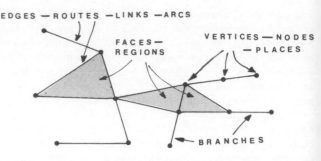

FIG. 24. Terms used in network analysis.

TRANSPORT NETWORK ANALYSIS

A network is a pattern of routeways interconnecting a series of points. A road or rail network may be drawn from a map showing such routeways interlinking the terminal points and intermediate localities and if drawn to scale the lines would represent real distance values. However, the pattern could be simplified to retain the relationship between the places while ignoring accurate map distance and orientation. Such a pattern becomes a topological map in which all termini, junctions and intersections are known as nodes or vertices and all routeways are constructed as direct straight lines between the nodes. These form the links or edges. Distances are now topological distances measured by totalling the number of links between any pair of nodes. Figure 24 below shows the meaning of the many terms used in network analysis.

Passengers using the London underground trains are familiar with topological maps, for the sequence of stations along each of the routes is shown as a transport network.

British Rail also use topological maps and one showing the local stations linked to Leeds is a striking example. (See Figure 25.)

If a graph is an array of points then any array of points may or may not be linked by edges to form a variety of patterns. If any pair of nodes is joined by only one link then a 'tree graph' network is created. On the other hand when an alternative route is possible between any pair of nodes the network becomes a circuit graph. When all intersections at the nodes meet at ground level or in any similar plane a planar graph is produced. But the crossings may be at different levels, that is in more than one plane, such as at the intersection of two motorways. In this instance the graph is classified as non-planar. (See Figure 26.)

The study of networks is, however, probably best begun with an understanding of the concepts of topological central place and of connectivity.

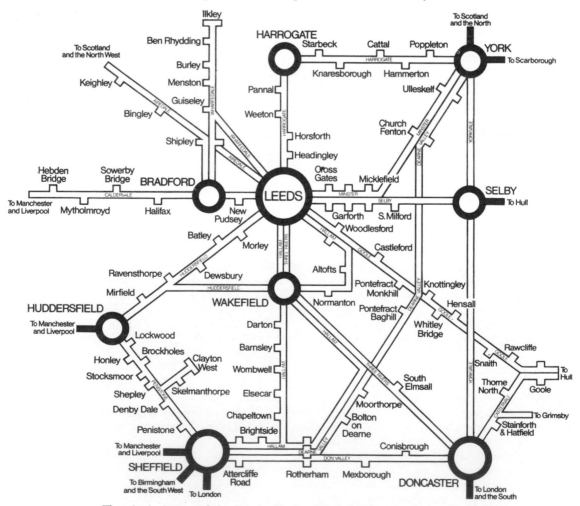

FIG. 25. Topological map of the Leeds district (Yorkshire) passenger train services.

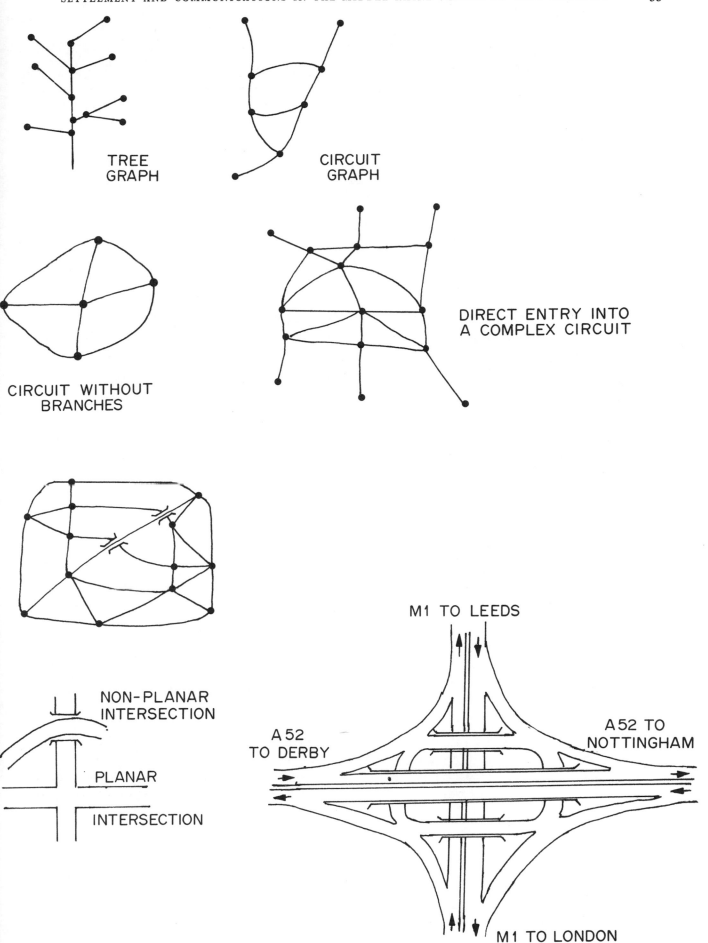

FIG. 26. Planar and non-planar networks.

Topological Central Place

Road transport networks on topological maps possess the following characteristics:

1. Two separate settlements (nodes) are joined by a route (link).
2. Only one single direct route (link) can join any two different nodes.
3. A collection of routes is called a path.
4. The length of a path is the number of individual links along it.
5. It is possible to move along a path in two directions and hence the concept of remoteness of a place is determined by the direction of the movement and the number of routes.
6. Every node on a path has an associated number which indicates the shortest topological distance from that place to the most remote place in the network.

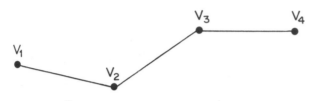

FIG. 27. A network path.

Thus in the above example when travelling from V_1 to V_4 the topological distance associated with V_4 is 3, i.e. 3 links. Conversely if travelling in the opposite direction, from V_4 then V_1 has the same number, namely 3.

7. The node with the lowest associated number is the topological central place.

In the above example V_4 is the central place. This is found by counting the number of individual direct links from V_1 to each node along the path and writing the numbers within round brackets. The process is repeated by travelling in the opposite direction from V_8 to V_1 and placing these numbers within square brackets. At each eliminate the lower of the two numbers and from the remaining numbers select the lowest to find the central place(s) of the network. (See Figure 28.)

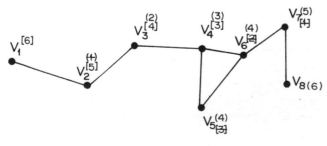

FIG. 28. Topological central place.

EXERCISE 15:
(a) *From the topological map below (Figure 29) give each place its associated number and find the topological central place.*
(b) *Using Figure 32 construct a topological map from Bassenheim to Vallendar with links to Winningen and find the topological central place.*
(c) *Based upon your findings as to the identity of the central place comment upon the limitations of such an analysis.*

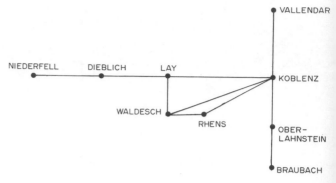

FIG. 29. Network exercise.

In the real world central places are nodes of economic significance in a region for they are commonly market towns and service centres.

EXERCISE 16:
(a) *From the network map of Dundee (Figure 68 on page 94) draw a topological map to represent paths between Edinburgh and Dundee.*
(b) *Mark individual nodes on your network and calculate topological distances from Edinburgh and Dundee.*
(c) *Name the topological central place of your network. After studying an atlas map of the region give suggested reasons why this place could or could not become a centre of a transport system as well as a topological centre.*

In the above exercises the networks under examination were studied in isolation and thus they were assumed not to form part of a larger system. In western Europe or in highly developed areas of the world such networks are in fact an integrated part of a larger and more complex network.

When any two nodes have been connected by one straight line representing a direct route then this is the concept of minimum connectivity. Theoretically all nodes can be linked to each other thus establishing maximum connectivity. In reality the existing situation in a highly developed area usually lies between these two extremes but may tend towards a network of maximum connectivity. On the other hand, in those regions of the world of only limited economic development, the network may be of the simplest kind showing minimum connectivity.

THE DEGREE OF CONNECTIVITY OF A NETWORK

This technique compares the existing number of routes (edges or links) with the maximum number that is possible for any given network (see Figure 30).

1. Make a topological map of the existing network by marking the positions of intersections, junctions, origins and destinations (i.e. all nodes) and by drawing straight-line links between them.
2. Construct a connectivity matrix as shown below. To construct the matrix draw a pattern of cells according to the number of nodes and observe whether they are connected *directly* to other nodes. Obviously it is not possible for a node to be connected to itself and therefore a value 0 is given to all origins as shown in the diagonal in the matrix below.

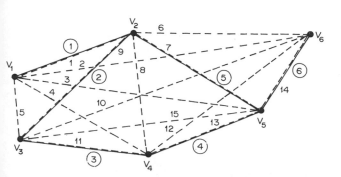

FIG. 30. Connectivity: the numbers in circles are the links of the network. The pecked lines show maximum connectivity for this network.

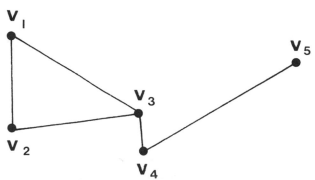

FIG. 31. A simple network 'X'.

Direct Connectivity Matrix for 'X'

$\overset{m}{\underset{\downarrow}{\rightarrow}}$	V_1	V_2	V_3	V_4	V_5	Total
V_1	0	1	1	0	0	2
V_2	1	0	1	0	0	2
V_3	1	1	0	1	0	3
V_4	0	0	1	0	1	2
V_5	0	0	0	1	0	1
Total	2	2	3	2	1	

$m = 5$ in this matrix

Most connected to destinations

Least connected to destinations

If places are *directly* linked the figure 1 is inserted into the appropriate cell. Place a zero in cells where pairs of nodes are *not* directly linked. In the matrix m stands for the number of nodes. When completed total each row and the node with the largest number indicates that it is from here that the largest number of destinations can be reached direct.

The concept and use of a matrix is familiar to motorists since this is a popular way of presenting mileage or kilometre distances to travellers. An example of such data in matrix form is illustrated below.

Matrix of Shortest Kilometre Road Distances between Selected European Cities

	LONDON	BERN	BRUSSELS	KOBLENZ	PARIS	ROME
LONDON	0	960	320	680	430	1920
BERN (SWITZERLAND)	960	0	670	570	590	1030
BRUSSELS (BELGIUM)	320	670	0	310	290	1580
KOBLENZ (GERMANY)	680	570	310	0	470	1510
PARIS (FRANCE)	430	590	290	470	0	1500
ROME (ITALY)	1920	1030	1580	1510	1500	0

3. In the network 'X' used here for demonstration purposes $V_1.V_2.V_3.V_4$ and V_5 are nodes and therefore represent both origins and destinations in that network. The number of cells within the matrix is therefore $m \times m$ (or m^2). Included within this number 5 (the value m) are the links such as $V_1–V_1$, which cannot exist in reality since no place can be connected to itself. Thus the maximum number of cells is given by $(m^2 - m)$.

4. However, if the network is one of transport then theoretically it is symmetrical. In other words for any one route there are two origins and two destinations. A car can travel from V_1 to V_2 or from V_2 to V_1 but two such independent routes would not be built and the matrix shows a duplication of routes which in reality would not exist. This means that half the number of routes on symmetrical networks are excluded. If there were six nodes then any one node can only be connected to five others and with a two-way traffic flow the maximum number of separate direct routes would be $\frac{1}{2}(m^2 - m)$.

$$= \frac{1}{2}(6^2 - 6)$$
$$= \frac{1}{2}(36 - 6)$$
$$= 15$$

Thus the maximum connectivity of a network is given by $\frac{1}{2}(m^2 - m)$ and to use it creates an index of connectivity which can be employed to compare networks of similar or of contrasting regions.

5. As suggested six nodes (towns) are interconnected by five direct road links. What degree of connectivity exists? The ratio

$$\frac{\text{observed connectivity (i.e. the actual links)}}{\text{maximum connectivity}}$$

gives an index number indicative of the degree of connectivity. In the above example observed connectivity $= 5$, maximum connectivity

$$= \frac{1}{2}(m^2 - m) \text{ where } m = 6$$
$$= 15$$

Index of connectivity $= \dfrac{5}{15} = 0.33$

In a region where every possible interconnecting route-way exists then the observed connectivity = maximum connectivity and the index is thus 1. At the other extreme where perhaps the 6 nodes represent 6 isolated farmsteads in a mountain region of exceptionally difficult terrain then no interconnectivity might exist and in this instance the observed value would equal 0. Thus the index of connectivity would also equal 0. Hence if these two cases represent the extreme situations it follows that all values of the index of connectivity must lie between 1 and 0, thus demonstrating that as the index value approaches 0 the fewer direct links there are in a system but the nearer to 1 and the more highly integrated is the transport system, as in industrialized or urban areas.

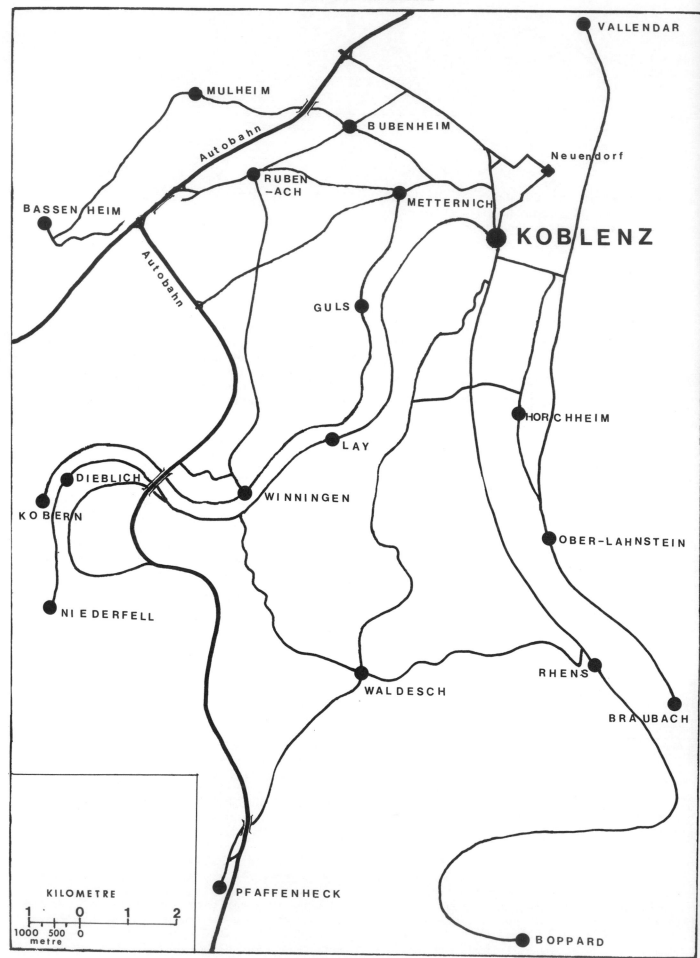

FIG. 32. Major road network in the Koblenz region.

EXERCISE 17:

Using Figure 32 construct a topological map and calculate the degree of connectivity of the road transport network in the Koblenz region west of the Rhine. Describe briefly the network thus examined.

Clearly it is not practical to build a maximum connectivity network but where an existing network shows a low connectivity index then users of it could be involved in high travel costs and loss of time on circuitous routes.

The lack of direct links frequently reflects the influence of relief or the intervention of a major physical feature such as an estuary, a broad river or an area of marshland. A study of the influence of such factors is achieved by initially removing these temporarily from the investigation. To do this it is necessary to compare a topological map with the real-life situation and to calculate the detour index.

DETOUR INDEX

The most economical network from the point of view of the user is one with direct straight routes. This could be a very costly network to build and so either for this reason or on account of the terrain few routes follow a direct line. The extent to which detours are necessary can be computed by measuring the direct distance and the shortest actual land surface distance of the existing routeways between any two places. When one is compared with the other a measure of the detour is obtained. The shortest actual distance can never be less than the direct distance, though it is possible that these two values could be the same as in a reclaimed Fenland landscape. The ratio of these measures must always be greater than or equal to 1. Hence to create a detour index and at the same time eliminate decimal points the ratio is multiplied by 100. Where the entire network of a region is being investigated the results should be recorded in matrix form—one of direct distances, one of actual distances. This makes for clarity.

$$\text{Detour index} = \frac{\text{shortest actual distance}}{\text{direct straight-line distance}} \times 100$$

The closer the value to 100 the more efficient is the network with respect to the cost of using it as a transport system. The calculation of the mean detour index for several networks provides a means of comparison.

EXERCISE 18:

(a) Using Figure 32 and the Koblenz map extract measure the straight-line distances and the actual road distances between:
   (i) Winningen and Koblenz (the bridge at Güls is a railway bridge)
   (ii) Waldesch and Koblenz.
(b) For each 'path' calculate the detour index.
(c) Explain the significance of your findings in part (b) and suggest why route detours are necessary.

EXERCISE 19:

(a) On tracing-paper placed over Figure 32 draw straight lines between each of the seven towns listed in the table below and measure and tabulate the direct distances.

Distance in kilometres	Boppard			Kobern		
	Direct	Actual	Detour index	Direct	Actual	Detour index
Boppard						
Kobern						
Koblenz						
Niederfell						
Pfaffenheck						
Rubenach						
Vallendar						
TOTAL						

(b) Complete a copy of the above table by measuring the actual road distances between each and by calculating the detour index.
(c) Which journey has (i) the largest, (ii) the smallest detour index? For each give reasons suggested by a study of the map extract.
(d) State the mean detour index for the network.

Is directness to be equated with efficiency? It is not always possible to reduce to the minimum both distance and time and thus the direct path is not automatically the 'least effort' solution to the problem of the cheapest way from one place to another. Motorways (autobahns, autoroutes or autostrada) are direct routes but they are not built regardless of expense.

EXERCISE 20:

(a) You wish to travel from Pfaffenhoch to your work in the industrial area of Neuendorf. Your car uses 5 litres of petrol every 40 kilometres (1·10 Imperial gallons to 24·86 miles). You travel at an average speed of 50 kilometres (31·1 miles) per hour on main roads and at 100 kilometres (62·2 miles) per hour on the autobahn. Which route for you is (i) the cheapest, assuming that you are not paid while travelling to work? (ii) the fastest, assuming an average constant speed?
(b) In real life what other factors would influence your choice of route?

Network analysis, at its simplest, leaves many questions unanswered but its value lies in that it stimulates enquiry into geographical relationships and draws attention to changes and influences arising from economic and technical developments.

RIVER TRAFFIC AND INLAND PORTS

Richard Graafen believes the new industrial quarter, north of the Mosel confluence with the Rhine at Koblenz, possesses a spaciousness and ease of communication which is unparalleled in the mid-Rhine area.[1] On this 250 hectare industrial estate between Wallersheim and Kesselheim are food manufacturing concerns, a steel rolling mill, an aluminium works and car accessory firms. Adjacent is the motorway network to the west and the Rhine harbour for Koblenz to the east.

---

[1] Richard Graafen, 'The Middle Rhine Basin with special reference to the Koblenz–Neuendorf Vale'. Die Mittelrheinlande Festschrift zum 36. *Deutsch Geographentag* (1967), pp. 208–16.

Both the Rhine and Mosel rivers are navigable for the latter was canalized during the period 1958–64 to permit barges of up to 1500 tons to travel along it as far as Thionville in France. The use of the Mosel 'canal' has shown a significant increase during the 1960s, reaching some 15 per cent of the river traffic using the inland port of Koblenz by 1970.

NUMBER OF VESSELS PASSING KOBLENZ

	1960	1969	1970
On Middle Rhine	126 377	101 030	89 851
On Mosel	3 683	15 588	16 807

The apparent decline in traffic on the Rhine does not give the true economic picture for although there has been a fall in the number of vessels there has not been in general a decline in the amount of goods carried, due to the increasing size of vessels now in use. Competition from road and rail transport, the increasing use of oil pipelines together with a decline in the transport of Ruhr coal has, however, affected the volume of traffic on certain reaches of the Rhine.

GOODS PASSING ALONG THE RHINE IN 1970 IN MILLION TONNES

Lower Rhine (Emmerich–Dutch/German frontier)		Middle Rhine (Koblenz)		Upper Rhine (Karlsruhe–Neuburg-weier, German/French frontier)	
Upstream	Downstream	Upstream	Downstream	Upstream	Downstream
68·6	43·8	34·0	17·6	10·1	21·1

EXERCISE 21:
(a) *Construct three percentage bar graphs to illustrate the composition of freight traffic (by nationality) along the Rhine in 1970.*

(b) *For the years 1960–70 draw a graph to show the changing pattern of traffic along the Mosel at Koblenz using the table below.*

PERCENTAGE OF FREIGHT TRAFFIC ALONG THE RHINE IN 1970, BY NATIONALITY

	Lower Rhine	Middle Rhine	Upper Rhine
German	32·5	53·7	59·7
Belgian	10·0	5·9	4·9
French	3·4	5·0	5·2
Dutch	50·4	25·8	16·5
Swiss	3·0	9·3	13·5
Others	0·7	0·3	0·2

MOSEL TRAFFIC AT KOBLENZ

TOTAL TRAFFIC IN MILLION TONNES

	Upstream	Downstream	Total
1970	6·93	3·80	10·73
1969	5·90	3·54	9·44
1968	5·05	3·47	8·52
1967	4·26	2·89	7·15
1966	3·49	2·30	5·79
1965	2·67	1·92	4·59
1964	1·16	0·67	1·83
1963	0·60	0·82	1·42
1962	0·83	0·61	1·44
1961	0·62	1·29	1·91
1960	0·42	1·07	1·49

PERCENTAGE OF FREIGHT TRAFFIC ALONG THE MOSEL AT KOBLENZ BY FLAG 1970

German	41·6
Belgium	14·4
French	22·4
Dutch	18·8
Swiss	1·6
Luxembourg	1·1
Others	0·1

The goods landed at the *Mosel harbour* at Koblenz include fuel oil, petrol, building materials and coal. The exports are insignificant.

EXERCISE 22:
(a) *Using Figure 33 and the method of located bar graphs illustrate the change in traffic recorded at the twelve chief inland ports of the Rhine river system between 1960 and 1970.*

TRAFFIC IN THE TWELVE PRINCIPAL HARBOURS ON THE RHINE RIVER SYSTEM (IN MILLION TONNES)

		1960	1969	1970
1	Duisburg	34·2	40·4	41·2
2	Strasbourg	5·8	12·3	12·4
3	Mannheim	6·9	9·1	9·4
4	Ludwigshafen	7·3	9·2	9·3
5	Basel	7·0	8·0	8·9
6	Köln (Cologne)	6·0	9·1	8·5
7	Wesseling	5·8	7·1	7·7
8	Karlsruhe	3·9	7·2	7·7
9	Frankfurt	6·6	7·6	7·5
10	Heilbronn	4·3	5·6	5·9
11	Rheinhausen	3·0	4·8	5·1
12	Walsum	5·1	4·0	3·9

The majority of the traditional Rhine tugs are of 250 to 400 h.p. and out of the total of 1357 some 75 per cent are Dutch. Most barges have a fully loaded capacity of only 700 to 1400 tonnes but the newer 'Push-tugs' are much more powerful and their lighters have a capacity of either 1640 or 2240 tonnes. Obviously these new vessels cause less congestion on the river and one composite unit has enormous capacity. At the beginning of 1970 the largest 'Push-tug' on the Rhine was the *Pierre Brousse*, flying the French flag, which was of 4800 h.p. and able to pull a lighter train of 15 600 tonnes freight capacity.

Number of Power Units Used for Freight Traffic on the Rhine in 1970, According to Flag

FLAG	TRADITIONAL TUGS	NEW 'PUSH-TUGS'
Dutch	1026	32
German	299	32
French	3	27
Belgian	14	1
Swiss	15	1
TOTAL	1357	93

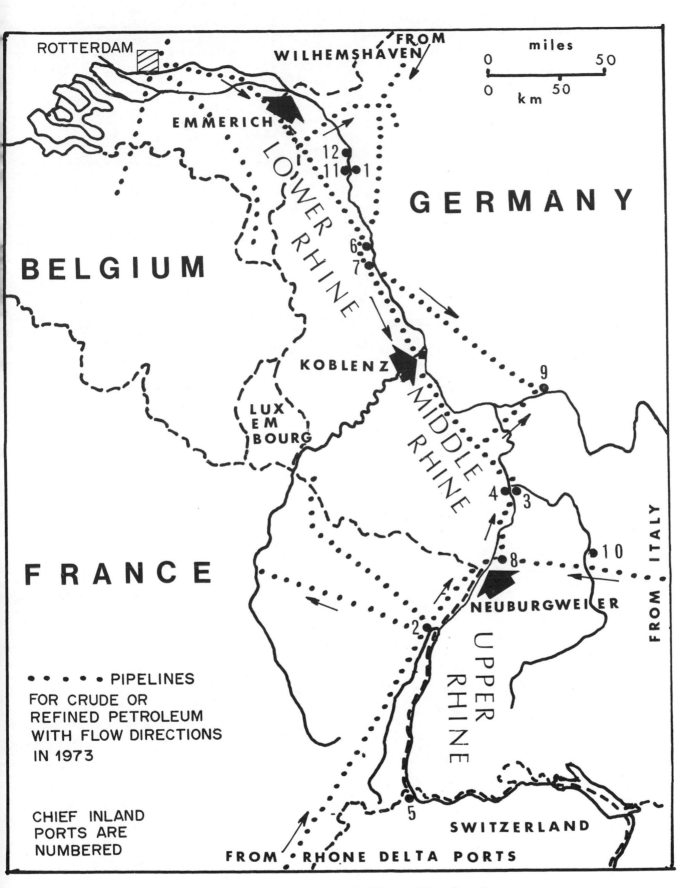

FIG. 33. Chief inland ports on the Rhine and its tributaries.

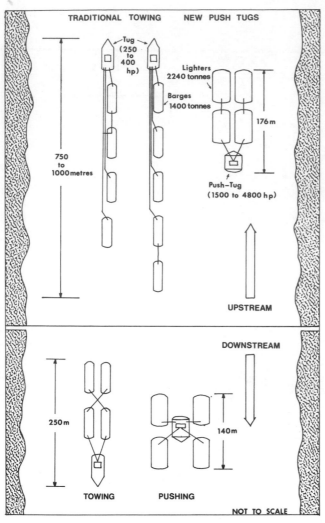

FIG. 34. Barge and lighter trains on the river Rhine.

Number of Non-motorized Freight Vessels on the Rhine 1970

FLAG	TOTAL NUMBER OF TOWED OR PULLED VESSELS	NUMBER OF PUSH TUG LIGHTERS	NUMBER OF BARGES
Dutch	8 796	148	8 648
German	2 450	178	2 272
French	1 117	85	1 032
Belgian	1 526	8	1 518
Swiss	408	22	386
TOTAL	14 297	441	13 856

EXERCISE 23:
  Study the various statistical tables and Figure 33 and then write a geographical essay on 'River Traffic at Koblenz'.

SCALES—OR NO SCALES

Koblenz as a tourist centre provides its visitors with brochures and maps. The geographer will notice that tourist maps may have different orientation and a different scale from 'official' topographical maps such as those published by government survey departments. On occasion tourist maps may fail to give a scale and the map chosen to illustrate this point and shown as Figure 35 has had the scale deliberately omitted.

Map scale is stated by drawing a subdivided line representing measured units or by means of a ratio which relates the distance on the map to that on the ground. This representative fraction is of universal application since the numerator is always one and the denominator a multiple

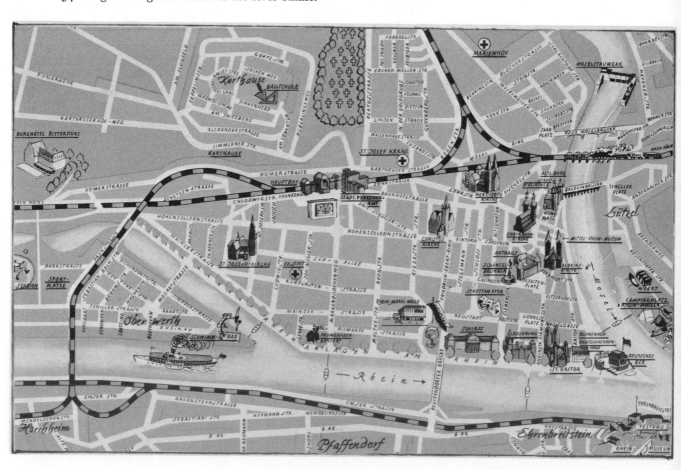

of that unit. For example $\frac{1}{50\,000}$ is the Representative Fraction (R.F.) for a map on which 1 centimetre represents 50 000 centimetres ($\frac{1}{2}$ kilometre) on the ground, or 1 inch represents 50 000 inches on the ground.

This concept is useful when unscaled, accurately drawn field or tourist maps are used in conjunction with official maps. If the actual distance is known then a simple calculation can provide the Representative Fraction. If the map distance from A to B is say 500 mm and this represents 6 kilometres then:

$$500 \text{ mm} = 50 \text{ cm} \equiv 6 \text{ kilometre}$$

$$\equiv 6000 \text{ metre}$$

$$\equiv 600\,000 \text{ cm}$$

$$1 \text{ cm} = \frac{600\,00\cancel{0}}{5\cancel{0}} \text{ cm}$$

$$\equiv 12\,000 \text{ cm}$$

$$\therefore \text{ R.F. is } \frac{1}{12\,000}$$

EXERCISE 24:

(a) *Select the letter which corresponds to the most nearly correct answer:*

The tourist map of Koblenz (Figure 35) is drawn by an observer looking in the general direction North (A); West (B); East (C); WSW (D); WNW (E).

(b) *Using the official topographical map of Koblenz state the bearing of the western end of the railway bridge across the Rhine from the tip of the Deutsches Eck at Koblenz (the confluence of the Rhine and the Mosel). Use grid north.*

(c) *Given that the distance along the left bank of the Rhine at Koblenz from the railway bridge crossing it to the confluence point is 3·4 kilometre, calculate the approximate scale of the tourist map. Give your answer as a representative fraction.*

Koblenz is both a tourist centre and a city whose influence reaches far into the surrounding country. The thirty or so insurance organizations and the numerous wholesalers give the city an importance which extends throughout the Federal Republic. Satellite towns are dormitory settlements for workers in newly developing industries and in the expanding service trades. The autobahn-main road network, the excellent rail communications and the expanding river traffic all favour the growth of industry and the growth of the city. The Koblenz region is richly endowed for its role as an expanding central place in the heart of the Rhenish Uplands.

FIG. 35. A tourist map of Koblenz.

3. Mountain Settlements and their Populations—the Saas Valley, Switzerland

This is a corner of the earth which multitudes cherish and admire. Here is a people who follow their own way of life, a people whose spirit remains eternally strange to us. W. Schmid

THE NARROW alpine valley of the Saaser Vispa river is one of a number of parallel valleys running in a south to north direction from the Italian frontier to the broad trench of the Rhône. It is reasonable to assume that prior to the twentieth century valleys such as the Saas were cut off from the main commerce of Europe, and that among these mountains villages were merely the homes of peasant farmers and their small herds of cattle and sheep. Yet in summer, traders passed along the Saas valley mule tracks *en route* for Italy, crossing the Alpine divide by way of the Monte Moro pass which retained some of its former medieval importance until the Simplon Pass superseded it in the seventeenth century.

In 1938 a metalled road was constructed to connect the valley-floor villages with Stalden and the main Rhône valley, although Saas Fee itself had to wait until 1952 to be joined to this road network.

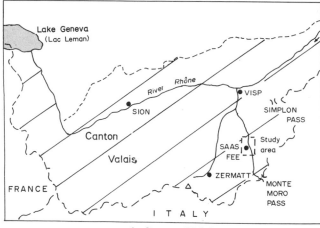

FIG. 36. Canton Valais.

A GLACIAL ENVIRONMENT

The immensity and grandeur of the alpine landscape creates a lasting impression upon a visitor. The majestic size of the peaks can, however, cut off the sun's heat and light until later in the morning and result in the dark night coming earlier to the valley floor than to the upper slopes. Thus the orientation of the deeply eroded valleys is of profound importance, for in those trending north–south the receipt of insolation in the lower parts is affected by the configuration of the east and west crestlines. Even in an east–west valley in summer, when the sun is high in the sky, its north facing walls are deprived of much of the sun's warmth.

EXERCISE 1:

Study the topographical map and the insolation maps, Figure 37, made by field study observations, for the settlements of Saas Grund and Trift.

(a) *Why is one settlement better sited than the other to serve a farming community?*

(b) *Suggest reasons why Saas Grund has progressed and Trift declined in importance.*

Obviously neither raw materials nor markets were responsible for the location of those villages which are sited where the valley floor opens out sufficiently to give increased amounts of sunlight, but yet avoid those areas subject to avalanches of snow and rock debris—some of which now overlies morainic debris—such as is seen on the eastern side of the Saas valley.

The geology of the region has also exerted a strong influence on the siting of settlements, for the sedimentary rocks of Triassic and Jurassic age have been changed by alpine metamorphism into schists, gneisses and quartzites. The strong folding, by earth movements, of resistant rocks, together with denudation processes has created such peaks as the Mittaghorn. (Grid square 638 103.)

The geographer is thus in a complex area of both metamorphosed crystalline and sedimentary rocks. The forces of erosion and mass wasting have shattered valley walls whose lower slopes are covered by morainic debris and scree. With the overdeepening of valleys tributary streams enter main valleys over steep drops. On the valley floors are old moraines which provide evidence that ice once covered the entire region. Although the Fee glacier has advanced 20·3 metres between 1966 and 1968 and the Allalin glacier has moved forward some 110 metres during the same period, the ice front has by no means reached the positions of the major moraines that can be so clearly seen on the air photograph (Photograph VII). Since 1963 a series of cool summers has reduced melting (ablation) and in the Saas valley a local advance of the glaciers has been recorded, although this is not the universal situation throughout the Alps.

EXERCISE 2:

(a) *Based on a study of the vertical air photograph (Photograph VII) and the analytical sketch map (Figure 38) state the evidence for identifying former positions of the glaciers and illustrate your answer with a sketch map.*

(b) *Measure the approximate area covered by the Fee glacier (Feegletcher) and for the map extract area calculate the percentage of land now covered by glaciers.*

The Fee glacier, from its extensive catchment area, descends steeply towards the village of Saas Fee. Where it slides down over the uneven rock floor and where it is compressed by the narrowing restrictive valley, ice falls and intensive crevassing can be seen on the photograph. The material on and within the glacier is considerable. 'For the moving of large masses of rock, the most powerful engines, without

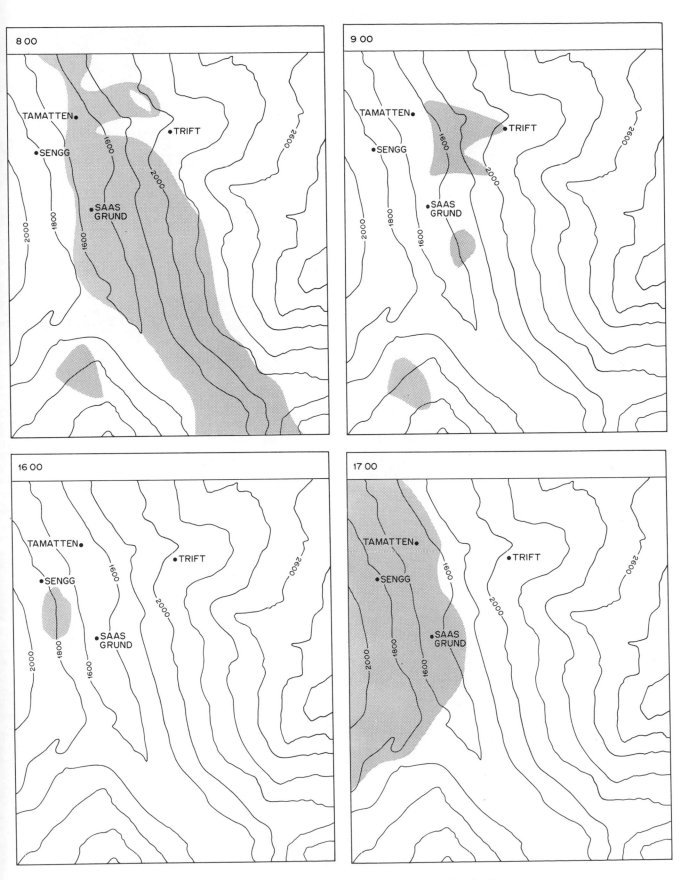

FIG. 37. Morning and evening shadows recorded in the Saas
Valley in early April (contours in metres).

Photograph VII *Saas Fee and the Saas Fee Glacier, April 1972.*

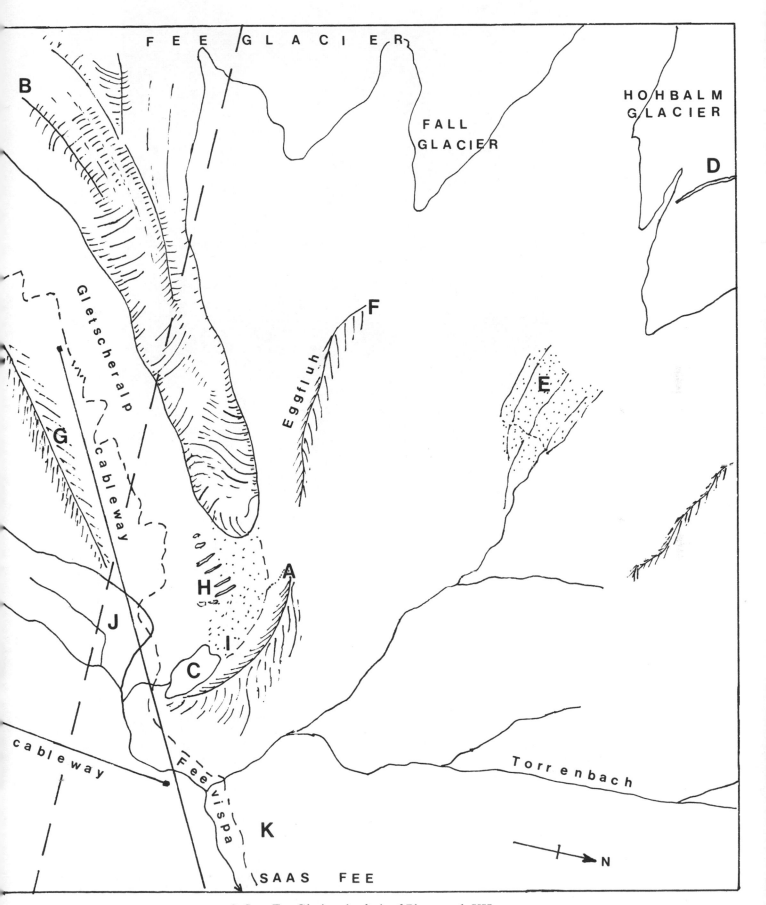

FIG. 38. Saas Fee Glacier. Analysis of Photograph VII.

Photograph VIII *Saas Fee. A traffic-free village in the Swiss Alps.*

doubt, which nature employs are the glaciers,' observed J. Playfair as long ago as 1802, and the impressive end moraines of the Fee glacier substantiate this.[1] With the approach of summer, as Photograph VII shows, there is more debris than snow on its surface. The grey shades on the ice represent dirt bands, but these will be covered by the deep winter snows. 'I counted in a rent, or crevasse, of a glacier which we passed many years of snow,' wrote G. Greenwood after climbing in the Alps. 'The top of each of these annual beds was clearly marked in black.'[2] The rock fragments in the ice are thus exposed by ablation or melting of the glacier surface during summer and may be washed away or retained as layers of debris to be later preserved under fresh snow. At all extremities of the glacier the debris that has fallen on to it, and has been carried on or within it, accumulates as mounds or moraines. Fragments and blocks of rock falling through crevasses find their way to the floor and if fine enough can be carried along by sub-glacial streams. Englacial streams also redistribute the 'dirt'. Glaciers as powerful engines appear to exert some wear and tear on the track but their meltwater streams are considerably more erosive.

[1] J. Playfair, *Illustrations of the Huttonian Theory of the Earth* (1802), p. 388.

[2] G. Greenwood, *Rain and Rivers* (1876), p. 153.

GLACIAL DEPOSITION

1. *End Moraines* (Frontal Moraines)
   (*i*) *Terminal Moraines.* Ridges or mounds of debris which accumulate at the end of the glacier from the fall-out of material carried in and on that glacier when it is more or less stationary.
   (*ii*) *Ablation Moraines.* As a result of downmelting of a thinning glacial tongue, a broad, hummocky sheet of material is spread out in the terminal area.
2. *Lateral Moraines*
   Debris bands along the sides of glaciers are due partly to the accumulation of fallen rock fragments which have been loosened by freeze–thaw and plucking action from the valley walls, and partly to the fall-out of material carried on or in the ice.
3. *Medial Moraines*
   The union of two or more lateral debris bands from former independent glaciers, which have now joined, creates a surface 'dirt' zone located along the middle of a glacier.
4. *Recessional Moraines*
   These are a number of more or less parallel crescentic ridges of debris left at the end of a glacier which has had a history of alternate retreats and still-stands.
5. *Ground Moraines*
   Thin sheets of material deposited from within the glacier and added to by debris falling through crevasses are located under glaciers.

6. *Fluvio-glacial Deposits*
   Sandy and gravelly material washed out from glaciers by sub-glacial streams mixed with meltwater deposits are located as sheets in front of end moraines.

7. *Outwash Plain*
   A plain of fluvio-glacial material.

Use the above definitions to help your study of the physical features of the Saas glacial tongue which is shown in the vertical air photograph.

EXERCISE 3:
   Examine the air photograph (Photograph VII) and the analytical map (Figure 38).
(a) *Identify the landscape features listed below:*

Glacier	*Pro-glacial lake*
Lateral moraine	*Area of outwash gravel*
Terminal moraine	*Area of forest*
Medial moraine	*Ridge*
Recessional moraine	*Eroded rock bars*
Crevasse	*Snow patch*
Ice fall	*Cultivated area*

   Write, in alphabetical order from A to K, a list of those features which can be identified by the analytical sketch map letter.
(b) *Orientate the analytical map in relation to the topographical map to identify the Easting marked by a dashed (pecked) line. State its number.*
(c) *Was the photograph taken before or after noon? Briefly state the evidence you used to make your decision.*

A factor of economic significance is the amount, duration and location of snow, especially since the tourist industry is heavily dependent upon skiing. At Saas Fee, for example, during the 'winter' of 1966–67 snow lay for 187 days with a maximum depth of 136 cm. The succeeding year saw a cover which lasted for 142 days at a maximum depth of 80 cm. Clearly, winter sports are not the only thing influenced by snow. Cattle spend the winter in stalls. Snow accumulation is also water supply storage and snow patches remain long in sheltered areas but vary in size and depth according to the amount of woodland, degree of slope of the ground and the orientation of the slope. These factors combine to assist in the development of landslips when meltwater is available as a lubricant for loose rock, slabs of ice and soil particles. Settlements on southward-facing mountain shoulders, spurs or ledges are favoured by the rapid melting of snow. The direction of the prevailing winds and the frequency of exposure to gales all play a part in influencing choice of sites for habitation.

EXERCISE 4:
(a) *List all the geographical factors which may have played a part in the siting of alpine settlements.*
(b) *Examine the map extract to make a comparison of the sites of the major settlements in the Saas Valley.*

POPULATION STUDIES

A study of mere population numbers is dull. An analysis of the age structure, sex composition, nationality, language and religion of a community is fascinating. Is it interesting to know that in almost all European countries there are more young women than young men? Have you ever considered the implication of the fact that there are more European people speaking Germanic languages than any other—the Austrians, Dutch, English, Germans, Scandinavians and, of course, the German-speaking Swiss, just to mention some of these peoples? Is it of any economic consequence that the growth of population in Europe is the lowest in the world? Migration—does the term relate to our friends who emigrated to Australia or to our neighbour who left for the city? Can we speak of stability when all we seem to do is to gad about in private cars? 'There was a time', pleaded Mackinder in 1919, 'when a man addressed his "friends and neighbours". We still have our friends, but too often they are scattered over the land and belong to our own caste in society. Or if they happen to be near us, is it not because our caste has gathered apart into its own quarter of the town? With too many of us, in our urban and suburban civilisation that grand old word Neighbour has fallen into desuetude.'[1]

It is therefore appropriate that we study certain aspects of the population geography of Switzerland for, as all the world knows, it is here that Protestant and Catholic, foreign refugee and Swiss national, and Germanic and Romance-language speakers are neighbours. Such a study may answer some of our questions or help to provide a partial explanation of the 'paradox of stability and harmony in diversity' which characterizes the human geography of Switzerland.[2]

EXERCISE 5:
   Study a physical geography atlas map of Switzerland, the language zones map (Figure 39) and the cantonal map (Figure 40).
(a) *Do the linguistic (language zone) boundaries follow the boundaries of the cantons?*
(b) *Are the main boundaries between French, German and Italian speaking zones marked by natural features?*
(c) *The linguistic map shows boundaries that separate areas in which at least 50 per cent of the population claim one specified language as their mother-tongue. Make a list of the cantons in which two major language zones are located.*
(d) *How does the linguistic map (Figure 39) oversimplify the true situation?*

Kurt Mayer's study of Switzerland stresses the fact that in spite of a higher birth rate in the French- and Italian-speaking areas a state of relative stability exists in the linguistic composition of the Swiss cantons as indicated in the table below. This he ascribes to internal migration, since more German-speaking migrants move to French-speaking areas than the reverse. Many German-Swiss also speak French, but when the French-speaking people move to dominantly German-speaking areas they have two languages to contend with, one being the classical German and the other the Swiss-German (Schwyzerdütsch) dialect which is used in daily conversation.

---

[1] H. Mackinder. *Democratic Ideals and Reality* (1919), pp. 148–9.

[2] K. B. Mayer. *The Population of Switzerland* (1952), p. viii.

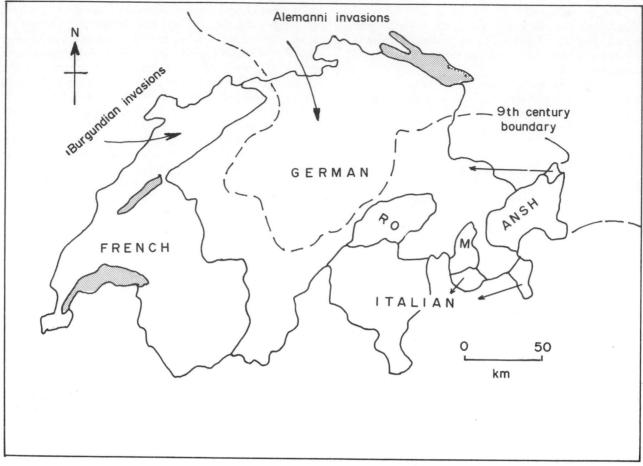

FIG. 39. Switzerland: principal areas of speech, 1973.

Percentage Distribution of the Swiss Population by Language

YEAR	GERMAN	FRENCH	ITALIAN	ROMANSH* AND OTHERS
1850	70·2	22·6	5·4	1·8
1880	71·3	21·4	5·7	1·6
1900	69·8	22·0	6·7	1·5
1930	71·9	20·4	6·0	1·7
1960	72·6	20·5	5·9	1·0

* A slight decline in the use of Romansh and a slight increase in foreign speech has occurred.

EXERCISE 6:

Following a study of an atlas map and Figures 39, 40 and 41, select from the statements given below only those which are correct and arrange them to make a short explanation of the social geography of Switzerland.

(*a*) *The French-speaking Swiss are mainly Roman Catholic.*

(*b*) *The population which has Romansh as its mother-tongue is located in Canton Graubünden.*

(*c*) *Ticino is the only canton in which Italian is the principal speech.*

(*d*) *The French-speaking area is located in western Switzerland north and east of Lac Léman (Lake Geneva).*

(*e*) *Canton Berne has mainly a Protestant population, the majority of whom are German-speaking.*

(*f*) *It is the eastern cantons which are mainly the French-speaking areas and also Protestant.*

(*g*) *The Italian-speaking majority is located south of the chief Alpine watershed.*

(*h*) *The linguistic zones of Switzerland appear to owe as much to the influence of history as to physical geography.*

(*i*) *The social geography maps of Switzerland demonstrate the religious tolerance and the mixing of the Swiss peoples.*

(*j*) *The variety of languages spoken is due to the influx of European refugees.*

THE SAAS VALLEY COMMUNES

The age composition, numbers of each sex and the migration of young people have a striking effect upon housing, schools and work force available in a community.

AGE STRUCTURE

Age data can be analysed in at least four different ways, by using:

1. Triangular graphs to give a generalized picture of population structure.
2. Indices.
3. Cumulative frequency graphs.
4. Age pyramids.

1. Triangular Graphs

Triangular graphs are used where three variables, individually expressed as total percentages, need to be illustrated diagrammatically. Kosiński divides a population on a basis of its working potential into a pre-productive

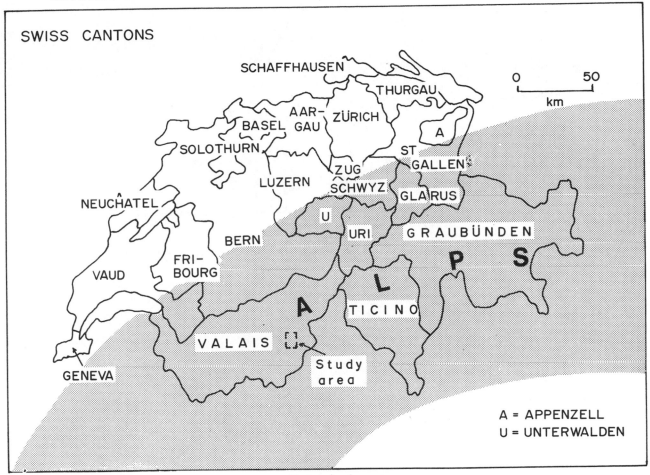

FIG. 40. Switzerland: cantons.

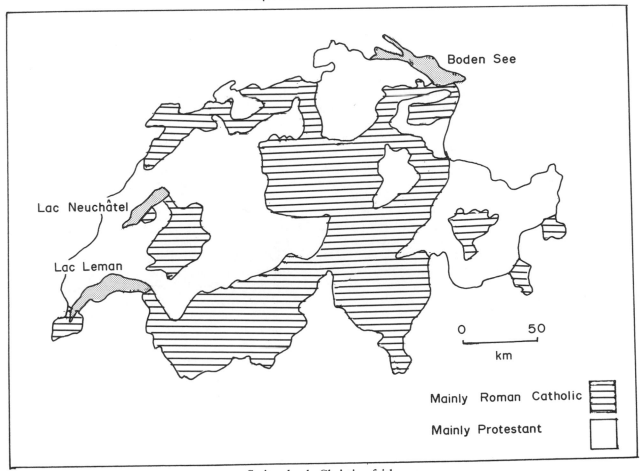

FIG. 41. Switzerland: Christian faith, 1973.

S = SAAS GRUND 1970
K = KOBLENZ 1970
P = PUY DE DÔME 1968
V = VALAIS 1970

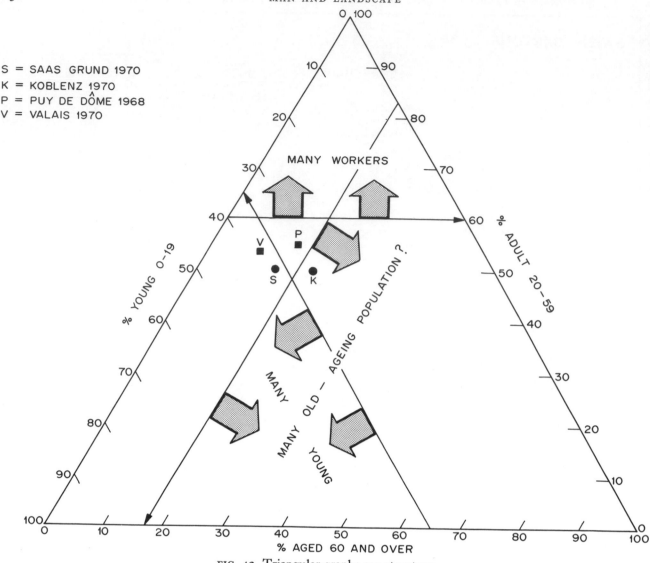

FIG. 42. Triangular graph: age structure.

(o–14 years), productive (15–59 years) and a 'retired' or post-productive age group of the 60s and over. Other scholars take 18 or 21 as the upper limit of the 'young' but all are agreed that the age group 20–59 is the most economically important class. A high proportion of children and 'young' people ensures a potentially large labour force. The adage that the 'country with many children has a promising future' is, however, by no means true if there is insufficient wealth to support them. A low percentage of adults may be a result of war or emigration. If it merely results from a high birth rate, then it could imply that there is a heavy financial burden upon the existing adult population.

An ageing population requires considerable social and financial aid and can bring problems to a country carrying an increasing percentage of old citizens. Where there is an advanced technology and a region is supplied with excellent social services there could be a large number of old people.

Method of construction
1. The making of triangular graphs of population is extremely easy. In our example, Figure 42, we begin by adding up all the people in one village whose ages are within three separate groups: o–19, 20–59 and 60 and over.
2. Calculate for each age group the percentage of the total population that is found within each.

3. Draw an equilateral triangle (each angle is 60°) and divide each side into ten equal parts, or use printed graph paper with a triangular net.
4. Each side of the triangle represents 100 per cent and thus each subdivision is a 10 per cent interval. Commence at the apex with the value o and with the left-hand side relating to percentage of young people allocate values to each subdivision. Complete the scales by working anti-clockwise round the graph as shown in Figure 42.
5. In our example, 36 per cent of the population are young persons, 50 per cent are adults, and therefore a dot is positioned where these two lines meet. The reading on the base line scale gives a value of 14 per cent, and this can be checked by calculation. Hence it is usually sufficient to mark only the position of the intersection of any two scale lines. Obviously the three variables, which add up to 100 per cent can be represented by only one dot or point. Our example compares two types of data, one concerning an alpine village (Saas Grund), and a central place in Germany (Koblenz), and the other relating to a Swiss canton and a French commune

EXERCISE 7:
Examine Figure 42 and use an atlas to study the location of the settlements and areas illustrated on the graph. Write a brief, generalized account of the age structure and its implications for each of these types.

2. Age Indices

Another generalized impression of the population structure is given when age indices are calculated for specified groups. Such an index gives a single quantitative value that can be used when comparing two settlements or two regions.

The Dependency Ratio =

$$\frac{\text{Percentage of Children} + \text{Percentage of Aged}}{\text{Percentage of Adults}}$$

or the Old Age Ratio $= \dfrac{\text{Percentage of Aged}}{\text{Percentage of Adults}}$

are both useful when studying social geography.

3. Cumulative Frequency Graphs

Another means of handling population data is by the construction of a cumulative frequency graph. This differs from the histogram depicting frequency distributions (as discussed in Chapter 1) in that it is the accumulated frequencies which are plotted by this method. Not only does this particular type of graph produce another visual impression of the distribution of the data but it also provides us with a simple 'tool' which has one outstanding asset—it can be read directly. The cumulative frequency graph can be applied to many types of geographical data, but for the underlying principles of the construction and reading of such graphs the population by age groups of Saas Fee will be considered.

POPULATION OF SAAS FEE

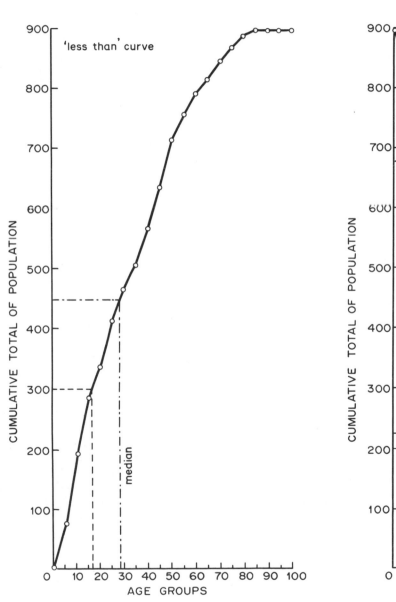
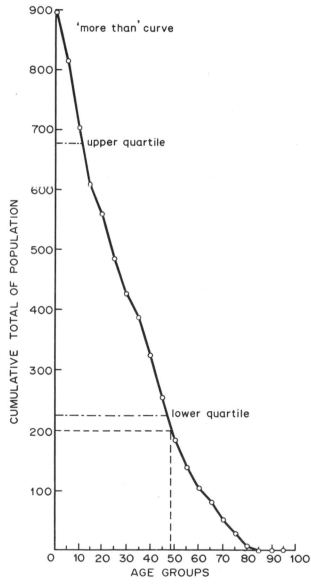

FIG. 43. Types of cumulative frequency graph: (a) 'less than' curve; (b) 'more than' curve.

Method of construction

For each age group calculate the total number of persons in each class and tabulate. Find the cumulative total class by class, e.g. in the 0–4 age range there are 78 persons. Enter this in the cumulative total column along the row corresponding to this class. Between 5 and 9 there are 114 and so in the two classes combined there are 192 people. To this total add 93, the number of persons in the 10–14 age range. Continue in this way until column (1) in the table below is completed. The final total must agree with the total population figure of Saas Fee for 1970, namely 895. These figures represent the frequencies and are plotted on the vertical or *y*-axis, while the age groups are the classes and are plotted along the horizontal or *x*-axis. (Compare the histogram mentioned earlier.)

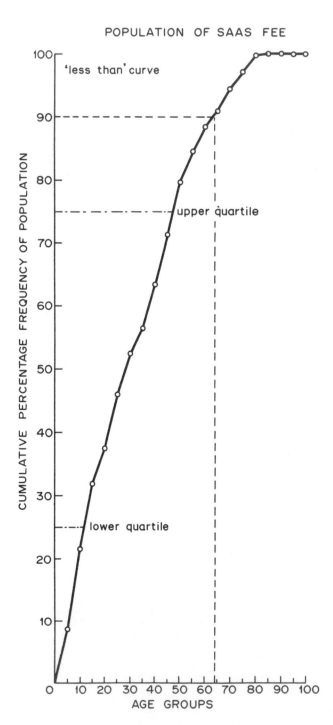

POPULATION OF SAAS FEE

FIG. 44. Cumulative percentage graph.

Construct the cumulative total graph by using the figures calculated in column (1). It is important to remember that as 78 represents *all* the people in group 0–4 the point on the graph is plotted at the *upper* boundary of the class which in practice is 5. Likewise there are 192 children between the ages of 0 and 9 and the 192 point is therefore marked at the 9 boundary edge of the class (line 10). Thus a graph drawn by this method always begins at 0.

Population by Age Groups of Saas Fee, 1970

AGE GROUP	TOTAL POPULATION	CUMULATIVE TOTAL		% TOTAL POPULATION	CUMULATIVE %	
		(1)	(2)		(3)	(4)
0–4	78	78	895	8·7	8·7	100·1
5–9	114	192	817	12·7	21·4	91·4
10–14	93	285	703	10·4	31·8	78·7
15–19	49	334	610	5·5	37·3	68·3
20–24	77	411	561	8·6	45·9	62·8
25–29	56	467	484	6·3	52·2	54·2
30–34	39	506	428	4·4	56·6	47·9
35–39	62	568	389	6·9	63·5	43·5
40–44	70	638	327	7·8	71·3	36·6
45–49	73	711	257	8·2	79·5	28·8
50–54	44	755	184	4·9	84·4	20·6
55–59	35	790	140	3·9	88·3	15·7
60–64	23	813	105	2·6	89·9	11·8
65–69	30	843	82	3·4	94·3	9·2
70–74	24	867	52	2·7	97·0	5·8
75–79	19	886	28	2·1	99·1	3·1
80–84	9	895	9	1·0	100·1	1·0
85–89	0	895	0	0·0	100·1	0·0
90–94	0	895	0	0·0	100·1	0·0
95+	0	895	0	0·0	100·1	0·0

From the completed graph (Figure 43(*a*)) it can be seen that there are 300 persons *less than* seventeen years of age; hence the name 'less than' graph for this diagram. There are 448 people, the median figure, less than twenty-eight years old. Thus half the population is under this age.

The 'less than' graph is the cumulative frequency graph in most common use, but by calculating the cumulative totals from the highest class and proceeding through exactly the same stages but this time remembering that it is the *lower* boundary edge of the class which is used for plotting the points (see Figure 43(*b*)) the 'more than' cumulative frequency graph can be constructed. If a line is projected from the 200 mark on the vertical axis on Figure 43(*b*) to the graph curve and then projected to the base line it will be seen that 200 people are more than forty-nine years old.

By converting the cumulative totals to percentages of the total population (columns (3) and (4), in the table above) both a 'less than' and a 'more than' cumulative percentage frequency graph can be constructed. These are read in a similar manner to those above and have a further advantage in that they make possible direct comparison between two or more sets of data. These types of graphs can also be very readily used for information relating to any given individual percentage of the data. These are the *percentiles* and are read directly from the graphs. Thus, in Figure 44 the upper 10 per cent of the population living in Saas Fee are more than sixty-four years of age.

The 75 per cent line of the distribution is the *upper quartile* and the 25 per cent line the *lower quartile*. These are particularly important points in a distribution, for lying between these two values is 50 per cent of the distribution. Thus half the population of Saas Fee is between eleven and forty-seven and a half years of age and it may be concluded that it is a young and vigorous one as befits a tourist centre. It is not necessary always to construct a percentage graph to find the quartiles. These can be found from any graph distribution simply by finding the value in the frequency corresponding to $\frac{1}{4}$ and $\frac{3}{4}$ of the data. There are 895 individual items in the distribution and if plotted in a dispersion diagram it will be seen that the median corresponds to the 448th item. But this is long and tedious so a very simple formula can be used, namely $(n + 1)$ where n is the number of items in the distribution. The position of the median is given by $\frac{(n + 1)}{2}$ that is $\frac{896}{2} = 448$ (item).

The position of the upper quartile is at the $\frac{3(n + 1)}{4}$ item, that is 672, and the lower quartile at the $\frac{(n + 1)}{4}$ which is the 224th item. At these points lines are drawn to the graph curve and projected to the base line to read off the respective ages corresponding to the upper and lower quartiles.

EXERCISE 8:

(a) *Construct two 'less than' cumulative frequency graphs, one for Saas Grund and one for Saas Almagell, using the data given in Document D, page 56.*

(b) *What percentages of each of the populations may be classed as adult workers?*

(c) *State whether there are any significant differences in the population structures of the two settlements.*

(d) *Find the median age of both groups of people.*

(e) *Use figures obtained from (a) to (d) above to aid the making of a comparison of the structures of the populations of Saas Grund and Saas Almagell.*

4. Age Pyramids

Age pyramid diagrams are a series of horizontal bars arranged on either side of a central vertical axis which is commonly graduated in groups of years. One set of bars relates to the males and the other to the females. The lengths of each of the bars is proportional to either the total or the percentage of each sex in that category. If class totals are used then the five-year census group is the common unit, for example 0–4, 5–9 and so on. For comparative purposes it is essential to use percentage values rather than actual numbers, as shown in Figure 45.

In the alpine village of Saas Grund the surplus of women is strikingly portrayed when one side of the graph is superimposed on the other. The excess percentage of men or of women can be visualized if the difference in the lengths for each column is shaded in.

This mirror-image comparison is most useful for an examination of the population structure of any European country or settlement. Losses were high in both world wars and the impact on national fertility and mortality was tremendous. In Europe losses and subsequent imbalance of the population are also accounted for by migration or emigration due to race persecutions, movements of prisoners of war and forced labour, or to invasion by hostile forces.

Value of age pyramids to the geographer

1. They highlight one cause of some of the social problems that arise due to imbalance of the sexes.
2. They can be used to indicate the varying percentages of the working population within each age group for any community.
3. They could reflect the percentage of the foreign-born element in the society.
4. They may reflect mass migration, as during the period prior to and after the building of the 'Berlin Wall'.

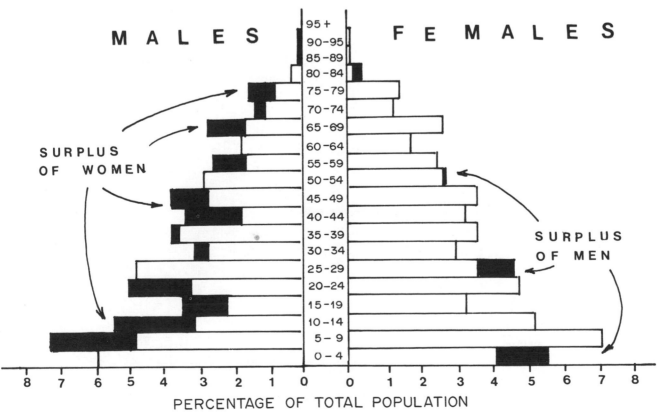

FIG. 45. Saas Grund: age pyramid, 1970.

5. The process of resettlement is demonstrated as when New Towns are constructed.

6. Long-term trends in mortality and fertility can be studied.

7. Contrasts between rural and urban populations are demonstrable.

8. They show short-term trends which can affect plans for economic and social development.

9. Results of continual migration, such as the depopulation of mountain areas, can be shown.

10. The impact of the social services upon a population, such as those which prolong life or reduce infant mortality, can be reflected in the age pyramid.

EXERCISE 9:

(a) *Using the data given in Document D, page 56, construct an age pyramid for Saas Fee. Compare this pyramid with that for Saas Grund, Figure 45.*

(b) *With the aid of the topographical map and the pyramids, write a reasoned account of the similarities and differences in the age structure of the two villages.*

MIGRATION

Migration is the permanent or semi-permanent change of residence and is sex selective, but so are events. During the last century large numbers of European men, some with their families, migrated to the American continent or to the world-wide empires created by Europeans. Today there are within Europe migrations of Italians, Spaniards and Portuguese who move into hotels and catering establishments and into the building industries. At times men dominate the migrations, but at others women who, today, are seeking work in offices or hotels. Internal migrations reflect the degree of urbanization and industrialization of Europe and thus are becoming less sex selective. In the country areas loss of women, because of inadequate opportunities for employment, also affects the fertility rate, for it is the young, usually under the age of thirty, who are migrants. Many industrial suburbs display high masculinity due to a preponderance of young migrant men seeking accommodation near their work.

Alpine areas of Switzerland have for a long time experienced rural depopulation but the table below shows that where tourism is important to the economy, as at Saas Fee and Saas Grund, there have been increases in population during the past decade. Where the economy is still largely based on agriculture, migration occurs as at Saas Almagell and Saas Balen.

The Communities of the Upper Saas Valley

	COMMUNE			
	SAAS ALMAGELL	SAAS BALEN	SAAS FEE	SAAS GRUND
Population				
No. of all resident inhabitants				
1960	359	457	739	614
1970	350	451	895	774
% change '60–'70	−2·5	−1·3	+21·1	+26·1
Swiss nationals				
1960	305	334	553	502
Swiss nationals born in same commune as now resident in 1960	277	293	456	444
Place of birth for all residents (1960)				
(i) In same commune	304	385	526	506
(ii) Other communes in Canton Valais	48	61	141	88
(iii) Other cantons	6	3	43	17
(iv) Foreign	1	8	29	3
Religion (1960)				
Protestant	0	0	19	3
Roman Catholic	359	456	719	611
Anglo-Catholic	0	0	0	0
Jewish	0	0	0	0
Others or atheist	0	1	1	0
Mother-tongue (1960)				
German	351	440	728	611
French	8	9	7	2
Italian	0	8	4	0
Romansh	0	0	0	1
Others	0	0	0	0
Employment (1960)				
Agriculture and forestry	14	46	19	39
Industrial	67	105	88	141
Commerce, hotels and transport	36	16	120	45

EXERCISE 10:

Why do people migrate—change their residences? Make a list of the circumstances that would compel you to migrate. Try to distinguish between those factors which would cause you to consider short and long distance migrations as a solution to your problems.

Everett Lee summarized the factors which enter into decisions to migrate under four considerations:[1]

1. Factors associated with the area of origin.
2. Factors associated with the area of destination.
3. Intervening obstacles.
4. Personal factors.

There are many circumstances which attract people to an area or cause them to leave it and these can be conceived by the use of + and − signs, as weights on a balance. Some factors are not 'heavy' enough to cause movement, or the major part of the population has no strong feelings about

---

[1] E. S. Lee, 'A Theory of Migration'. *Demography*, Volume 3 (1966), pp. 47–57. Reprinted in *Population Geography: A Reader*, ed. Demko, Rose and Schnell (1970), pp. 288–98.

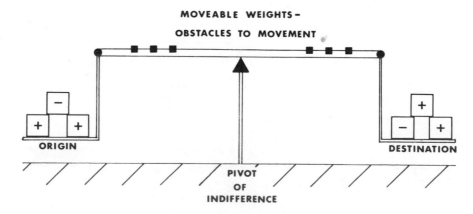

MOVEABLE WEIGHTS –
OBSTACLES TO MOVEMENT

ORIGIN

DESTINATION

PIVOT
OF
INDIFFERENCE

FIG. 46. Migration balance.

them or is not aware of them. Clearly what is attractive to one person is repulsive to another, but even so there are major factors which cause an important part of a population either to remain in or to move out from a settlement.

The number of positives must be greater than the number of negatives and the intervening obstacles must be neither too numerous nor too formidable to tip the balance in favour of migration. Would you or could you migrate to an alpine village?

POPULATION DECLINE IN THE ALPS

EXERCISE 11:

Form a committee to discuss and investigate the problem of rural depopulation in alpine Switzerland. Appoint a chairman and a secretary to take minutes. Speeches or reports should be brief. All members of the committee should study the documentary evidence which follows and make proposals for a course of action that will help mountain areas retain a larger population of all ages. A report should be issued which is a summary of the decisions made and the reasons underlying them.

DOCUMENTARY EVIDENCE FOR STUDY

Documents A and B are partly based on information given in *Exode rural et dépeuplement de la montagne en Suisse* which is a report on a project undertaken by the Swiss National Commission of UNESCO and published in 1968. Document D presents data made available by the Federal Bureau of Statistics at Berne and is based upon the census of 1970. Document E has as its foundation a field survey of social conditions in the valley in 1971.

DOCUMENT A
Causes of Rural Depopulation in the Alps

1. Decline in meat and milk supplies due to a recession in alpine agriculture, and thus the inadequate cash returns from farming cannot be used to provide those amenities in mountain areas that are found in lowland regions.
2. Social life is more attractive in lowland towns than in remote mountain villages.
3. Few employment opportunities for young men and the presence of too many older people of traditional outlook encourages young people, especially men, to leave the villages.
4. Limited capital resources only are available in alpine communities—a result of the decline in the numbers of animals kept. Formerly 60 to 90 per cent of agricultural revenue came from animal farming on alpine pastures.
5. Industrial work in urban regions is better paid than farm work in alpine villages.
6. With a decline in cultivation, shrubs and coarse grasses have invaded the field areas with the ultimate result of a breakdown in the interrelationship between mountain and lowland farming.
7. There are few employment opportunities for married women in alpine village communities.
8. Considering the trend towards a 'leisure society', the work in most mountain areas is arduous and associated with long hours.
9. Income from tourism has benefited only a few, since some of the facilities may be owned by those living outside the village. The income may also be seasonal.
10. Industrialization has created the demand for household products that are more easily obtainable by residents in lowland towns.

DOCUMENT B
Suggested Remedies and Solutions to the Problem of Rural Depopulation in Mountain Areas

1. Create special work for mountain areas.
2. Develop model farms and build agricultural research stations to improve mountain farming.
3. State provision of cheap or free transport of potatoes, for sale and for seed.
4. Establish cheese factories in the alpine villages.
5. Large discounts on sale of agricultural machinery for mountain farmers.
6. Establish petrol stations and improve roads in mountain regions.
7. Cheaper fares on postal motor coaches (village buses) for residents.
8. More telephones and rural bus services.
9. Encouragement of light industry which will fit the environment.
10. Stimulation of tourism.
11. Conversion of old property into 'second homes' for town-dwellers.
12. Introduction of work suitable for married women.
13. Higher wages for professional and technical staff in alpine regions than in lowland regions.
14. Cheap loans for building hotels and chalets.
15. A fixed higher price for milk.
16. Amalgamation of small holdings into larger farm units.
17. Plant forests and develop timber and wood-product industries.
18. Creation of more National Parks.

DOCUMENT C
Local Emigration

Number of persons emigrated into another canton in thousands in 1960

Canton	Emigration	Immigration	Excess of immigrants	Number of immigrants per 100 emigrants
Berne	212·3	129·8	−82·5	61
Geneva	16·5	89·7	73·2	544
Graubünden	43·3	21·7	−21·6	50
Uri	12·1	5·8	−6·3	48
Valais	36·6	13·4	−23·2	37
Vaud	60·4	102·5	42·1	170
Zürich	123·7	293·0	169·3	237

Source: *La Vie Economique*, January 1965, p. 5.

DOCUMENT D

Age Structure of the Resident Population in the Saas Communes 1970

AGE	SAAS ALMAGELL		SAAS BALEN		SAAS FEE		SAAS GRUND	
Group	Male	Female	Male	Female	Male	Female	Male	Female
0–4	18	19	19	17	39	39	46	32
5–9	25	23	29	30	58	56	37	56
10–14	16	20	21	24	49	44	24	41
15–19	7	11	16	18	20	29	18	25
20–24	12	6	14	15	35	42	26	37
25–29	7	9	10	20	27	29	37	28
30–34	14	13	16	17	20	19	21	23
35–39	6	8	12	12	29	33	27	28
40–44	14	14	13	13	32	38	14	25
45–49	18	8	12	14	31	42	21	28
50–54	7	11	12	7	26	18	22	21
55–59	9	8	11	21	16	19	13	19
60–64	13	8	15	14	13	10	14	14
65–69	5	6	5	5	8	22	13	21
70–74	3	2	1	6	12	12	9	10
75–79	1	5	3	4	7	12	6	11
80–84	1	2	0	2	4	5	3	2
85–89	1	0	0	2	0	0	0	1
90–94	0	0	0	1	0	0	0	1
95+	0	0	0	0	0	0	0	0
TOTALS	177	173	209	242	426	469	351	423
	350		451		895		774	

GRAND TOTAL: 2470

Source: *Tableau Général* (Census 1970), Bureau Fédéral de Statistique, Bern.

DOCUMENT E
A Survey of the Human Geography of the Saas Communes 1971

The older inhabitants are still farmers but agriculture plays a declining part in the economy today. The younger generation is employed in the tourist industry while some of their parents work the land and tend the animals. It is doubtful if any families in Saas Fee and Saas Grund now live entirely from agriculture.

Before the recent development of tourism in this valley menfolk left the district to find work elsewhere, leaving the women to rear the family, till the land and move the animals to the alp.

The plots of potatoes, rye, barley, root vegetables and hay on the valley floor are so subdivided that any reorganization of farming would be difficult. Property, land and businesses are handed down within families and therefore hoteliers, ski-instructors and shopkeepers are almost without exception local people.

Family ties are strong and marriages between local people are common. The traditional belief in Christianity is a powerful force in the valley. The quality and originality of religious art is seen in fifteen chapels on the Kapellen Weg— a mule track from Saas Grund to Saas Fee—and in the numerous wayside crucifixes, one of which dates from 1763. Modern ones are still carved in the old style. The present is linked to the past but the future rests in the hands of God. When devastation in the form of floods or avalanches affect the population these disasters are seen by the older inhabitants as evidence of divine displeasure. Two peasant women, aged about sixty, in Saas Grund suggested that the present prosperity of the valley would end in 1977. In a valley with a long history of natural disasters more misfortune is fatalistically awaited in a year with two sevens in it.

Many of the animal stalls and hay barns are now empty and there has been a considerable decline in the number of cows kept. In fact milk is now imported into the valley from Visp. There has been a similar decrease in the number of sheep. Last year the local school-teacher spent his summer holiday working as a shepherd! At Saas Grund in 1971 there were less than 60 cows whereas twenty years ago there were 200. Similarly the numbers of sheep have been reduced to 300 from a figure more than double this present one. The goat population has also declined from 140 to 20 during the same period.

Transhumance has almost collapsed. Previously cows were ceremoniously taken each summer up to the Trift alp from Saas Grund but now they are mainly restricted to the low pastures during the period July to September. At Saas Almagell cattle do not now go to permanent summer pastures but sheep are still temporarily transferred to the pastures at Mattmark from Saas Fee, since sheep are easier to look after than cows. A few old women still take about seven cows each up to the Trift alp where they remain for two or three months, and one old resident still makes cheese which is used only for consumption by the families concerned.

Although all the communes have clearly defined grazing rights on the high alps these meadows are not fully utilized and there is a lack of interest by the younger generation both in transhumance and in peasant agriculture.

EXERCISE 12:

Draw a street plan or map of your 'ideal' mountain village showing how you have developed it to attract new residents and to keep its population in employment.

EXERCISE 13:

Your aim is not merely to slow down the rate of rural depopulation but to improve living and economic conditions in the Swiss Alps. Write an essay in which you outline the present economy and discuss the kind of future developments that you would permit in this alpine environment.

TOURISM AND INDUSTRIALIZATION

Tourism stimulates the growth of local trade, banking and insurance and provides employment in catering, transport and in the building industry. After the end of the Second World War (1939–45) tourism developed rapidly and with the completion of a metalled road surface in 1952 villages such as Saas Fee received a new lease of life. In 1920 there was a resident population of 317 at Saas Fee, whereas now, (1970), there are 895 people and tourists more than treble that number for much of the year.

In 1950 Stalden had a population of 810 but after the construction of its power stations there were 1121 residents.

Visp (Viège) is a developing market town lying at the confluence of the Rhône and Vispa (Visper) that has become industrialized, with a strong interest in chemicals and the production of agricultural fertilizers. The neighbouring area to Visp is now a commuter belt.

All this has occurred in a region where rural depopulation has taken place on a continuous and considerable scale during the past fifty years. Is the cure for the economic problems that beset remote alpine villages more tourism or industrialization?

The effect of this modernization can be seen when a map of population change is constructed as suggested below.

EXERCISE 14:

(a) On a copy of the map of the communes of the Saaser Vispa valley (Figure 47) represent these statistics by means of located proportional bars[1] which should be placed above or below a base line to indicate increase or decrease.

ADMINISTRATIVE DISTRICT (COMMUNE)	PERCENTAGE CHANGE IN POPULATION 1960–70
Eisten	−27·3
Saas Almagell	−2·5
Saas Balen	−1·3
Saas Fee	21·1
Saas Grund	26·1
Stalden	11·3
Stalden-Ried	−1·6
Visp	43·6
Visperterminen	23·0
Zeneggen	0·9

(b) Use the above table and an atlas map to examine the positions of these cantons with respect to their physical geography. Comment on your observations.

The traditional agriculture of the valley has been eroded, not merely by the loss of population during this century, but rather by the force of tourist development. Rock climbing, winter sports and the influx of mobile summer visitors provide a substantial source of income and the younger generation prefer gay tourists to prosaic pastures.

Although Schmid wrote some thirty years ago, his script needs little revision. Some rural depopulation had to occur to permit a better life for those who remained. Psychological resistance to change is a characteristic of the old but the population of the Saas communes has a large young element as seen in the age pyramid and triangular graph. Where tourism is queen the economic foundations are safe but where peasant agriculture reigns supreme ominous cracks have occurred. Urban amenities and income may even come to this alpine community who follow their own eternally 'strange' way of life.

---

[1] The use of bar graphs is discussed and explained in the author's *Advanced Practical Geography*, pp. 66–72.

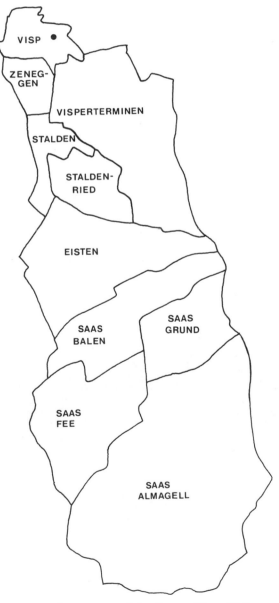

FIG. 47. Communes of the Saaser Vispa Valley.

VISP

ZENEGGEN

VISPERTERMINEN

STALDEN

STALDEN-RIED

EISTEN

SAAS BALEN

SAAS GRUND

SAAS FEE

SAAS ALMAGELL

4. A City Region in the Leisure Age—Clermont-Ferrand and the Volcanoes Nature Park

La ville se transporte à la campagne. *Alphonse Allais*

IN THE heart of France a historical, cultural and economic capital is situated in a shallow basin of an obscure stream which rises amid a chain of famous but extinct volcanoes.

This town, Clermont-Ferrand, lies under the shadow and reflects the glory of that queen of volcanoes, the Puy de Dôme, and that monarch of modern industrial firms, Michelin. At the core of the city stands the cathedral built upon a small knoll of volcanic rock rising about fifty metres (164 feet) above its surroundings. It was a dry point and a defensive settlement site superbly chosen by the Romans, and the town of Augustonemetum subsequently became known as Clermont. On the rich black earth soils of the Limagne Plain to the north-east, Montferrand was founded and the two settlements united to create Clermont-Ferrand in 1731.

EXERCISE 1:
(a) *Study the oblique air photograph (Plate X) and on a copy of the street plan based on the analytical sketch, Figure 48, mark the approximate limits of the old town which is still recognizable by the closely packed dwellings around the cathedral.*
(b) *Compare the old street pattern with that of the modern, and older building styles with those of the new.*

Photograph IX *Le Puy de Dôme.*

Photograph X *The centre of Clermont-Ferrand.*

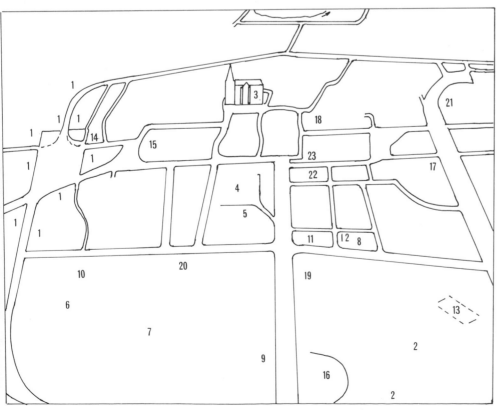

FIG. 48. Principal features of Clermont-Ferrand.

KEY
 1. Main banks and shops, department stores and tourist hotels
 2. Botanical Gardens
 3. Cathedral of Nôtre Dame
 4. Central Post Office
 5. City Finance Offices
 6. Clinic
 7. General Hospital
 8. Library
 9. Maternity Hospital
10. Municipal Laboratory
11. Museum
12. Museum of Natural Sciences
13. Open-air Theatre
14. Opera House
15. Prefecture (Office of the Central Government)
16. Rose Gardens
17. Savings Bank
18. Town Hall
19. University of Clermont-Ferrand—Administration buildings
20. University of Clermont-Ferrand—School of Dentistry
21. University of Clermont-Ferrand—School of Fine Art
22. University of Clermont-Ferrand—School of Commerce
23. University of Clermont-Ferrand—School of Music

A local industrialist, who had married MacIntosh's niece, established in 1830 his factory for making rubber balls. This Michelin firm now has 26 000 workers on its pay-roll and has played a vital part in the recent rapid growth of the city and its suburbs.

In the mid-nineteenth century although Clermont-Ferrand covered an area of 43 square kilometres a great part of this large administrative area was devoted to agriculture. The change from a former wine market town to a 'rubber capital' has been closely linked to the brisk expansion in demands for car tyres and for engineering products, a phenomenon particularly of the mid-twentieth century. In 1911 the city had a population of some 65 000, and in 1954 106 000, but in 1968 it had risen to 146 000. The urban expansion of the past ten years has embraced the vineyard villages and small towns not only along the foothills but, even more strikingly, on the Limagne plain, resulting in some 202 000 people living in this enlarged urbanized zone. On the map extract only the foot-hill zone can be examined, and here Durtol and Nohanent are typical examples of the way in which this urbanization process had affected small settlements, by stifling their agricultural functions and turning them into commuter-based settlements.

EXERCISE 2:

Study the information in the table below and on a copy of Figure 49 distinctively shade the communes which have (a) the highest; (b) the lowest percentages of their working populations engaged in agriculture. Suggest geographical reasons for the location of these contrasting areas.

Percentage of Working Population Engaged in Agriculture in 1962

A: HIGHEST PERCENTAGES	
COMMUNE	%
Orcet	25
Les Martres-de-Veyre	25
La Roche-Blanche	25
Veyre-Monton	23
Sayat	20
Lempdes	15

B: LOWEST PERCENTAGES	
COMMUNE	%
Chamalières	0
Royat	1
Beaumont	1·5
Aubière	2·5
Aulnat	3
Ceyrat	4

Source: *Census, Puy-de-Dôme*, INSEE, Paris.

Chamalières, the largest and oldest suburb, not physically separated from Clermont and inextricably linked to it economically, has completely eliminated agricultural employment.

FIG. 49. City region of Clermont-Ferrand.

AGGLOMERATION, CONURBATION OR CITY REGION?

The French census authorities classify this cluster of towns around Clermont-Ferrand as an agglomeration, since settlement growth has arisen from this single centre. The fact that the city had, at its earliest stages, a double centre is of little real significance since the Clermont element has always dominated the urban scene.

Urban geographers have always argued that if towns remain administratively distinct yet physically a part of a *large* group, then the term conurbation is most appropriate, as for example the Birmingham conurbation in Britain. The strict application of this definition would result in the London region also being determined as an urban agglomeration rather than a conurbation for the administrative development of the two regions has been different. T. W. Freeman, no doubt wishing to simplify the position or to clarify confused terminology, has described a conurbation as an accumulation of industrial towns, and thus no distinct class is accorded to Birmingham and London. It seems highly desirable therefore to adopt Dickinson's descriptive City Region concept, since this best relates to a cluster of small towns and urbanized villages which have been drawn into the functional orbit of a major city. Their mutual interest must lie in the major industries and services which provide work for inhabitants of these urban areas. Such individual settlements, bound together by social and economic links, form a city region.

Factors in Location

The interesting way in which chance and personal initiative have operated has led to the growth of substantial settlement at the foot of the Auvergne mountains in the heart of France. This chance factor is perhaps the last to recall to mind when considering such principal reasons for the development of towns as:

1. Central Place function, e.g. administration and distributive trades.
2. Communications centre, e.g. route junctions.
3. Local resources, e.g. ironstone, wool.
4. Religious centre, e.g. cathedral, abbey.
5. Defensive function.
6. Chance, e.g. initiative of a local manufacturer or a dynamic personality.

In reality, it is usually a combination of these factors which ensures the success of a town, although site geology should not be underestimated. Favoured sites would include gravel terraces, sandy heaths, chalk and limestone bedrock and, as in the case of Clermont, a knoll of volcanic rock. Areas of marsh, damp clay and fragile shale are clearly to be avoided although advanced technology can overcome site limitations but may be thwarted by the magnitude of the physical obstacles.

Restrictions on Suburban Growth of Clermont-Ferrand

To the west of the city is the high plateau of the Auvergne, crowned by the Puy de Dôme rising to a height of 1464 metres. When, some nine thousand years ago, this acidic, viscous péléan-type volcano erupted there also appeared to the north of it other secondary uprisings of lava which are now recognizable on the map extract as 'Dômes'. From these volcanic craters, comprised of scoriae (cinders and slag), lava flowed from the plateau down pre-existing river valleys into the down-faulted basin of the Limagne. The north–south border fault is prominent on the geological map (Figure 50) and its effect clearly visible on the topographical map.

EXERCISE 3:
  Using the map extract and Figure 50:
(a) *Calculate the mean height of the plateau.*
(b) *List the puys by name, state their heights and calculate the mean value. Give the difference between the two mean values.*
(c) *Name the volcano (puy) along the actual line of the border fault.*
(d) *Calculate the mean distance of the easterly line of puys from the fault line.*
(e) *What effect have the puys on the present communications of the region?*

The Limagne was also affected by vulcanity for it contains many dykes, sills and lava flows together with remnants of volcanic cones and knolls, on one of which, as we have seen, was founded the present city.

EXERCISE 4:
(a) *Draw a sketch map outlining the built-up areas of high and medium density of Clermont-Ferrand.*
(b) *Insert the position of the cathedral.*
(c) *Outline the chief areas of urban expansion within the area of the map extract.*
(d) *With the aid of the sketch map and the account given below comment upon the recent growth of urban areas.*

The nearness of the border scarp is a powerful, physical restraint to the westward urban expansion of the city but, fortunately, this feature forms a narrow but attractive 'Green Belt' in which new housing is prohibited or placed under severe restrictions. This recreation belt is also free from atmospheric pollution and the scarp summit is free from the temperature inversions which plague the Limagne. Since the steep scarp slopes are unstable, the presence of landslip material and gullies are also restraints on housing expansion. 'High rise' buildings near the scarp foot are only possible on steel pile foundations.

The dry climate and the more or less permeable rocks of the Limagne imply that there is little ground water available for domestic and industrial use. The importance of piped water and streams coming from the plateau cannot be overestimated as supply sources, but the urbanization of the scarp foot zone has increased the risk of storm floods, since between 25 and 50 mm of rain per hour can fall during a short but intensive summer storm. Most of this runs off roofs and down streets, for little can be absorbed into the ground.

Old property in the scarp foot settlements, when occupied by commuters, needs conversion and modernization, since these solidly-built houses were formerly the homes of peasant farmers who used the ground floors for fermenting grapes and the first floors, with their attractive balconies, for their residential quarters. Some of these wine-cellar homes have been turned into garages and shops and the vineyard suburbs, such as Sayat, have become dormitory settlements. But the pressure on agricultural villages is greatest to the east and south of Clermont-Ferrand since here there are fewer physical and human restraints, in spite

METAMORPHIC

 METAMORPHIC SANDSTONE

GNEISS

IGNEOUS

GRANITE & DIORITE

VOLCANIC CONES

MANTLE OF VOLCANO

FRAGMENTAL VOLCANIC PRODUCTS

LAVAS

FAULT

SEDIMENTARY

 DETRITUS

BLACK EARTH

RECENT ALLUVIUM

LOWER TERRACE } OF ALLIER & ITS
MIDDLE TERRACE } TRIBUTARIES

M MIOCENE

OLIGOCENE

FIG. 50. Geological map of the region west of
Clermont-Ferrand.

SCALE 1:50000

Arrivals and Departures During the Period 1962–68

I	2	3	4	5	6	
	INCREASE	LOCAL	LOCAL	NATURAL CHANGE	MIGRANTS†	
	OR DECREASE	NUMBER OF	NUMBER OF	(i.e. column		
COMMUNE	IN POPULATION.	BIRTHS	DEATHS	3 − 4 = 5)	NUMBER	PERCENTAGE
Aubière*	+1 024	769	387	+382	+642	+9·4
Beaumont*	+641	624	374	+250	+391	+6·2
Blanzat*	+520	179	119	+60	+460	+39·1
Cebazat*	+1 007	391	194	+197	+810	+28·6
Ceyrat	+631	250	157	+93	+538	+24·2
Ceyssat	−25	22	42	−20	−5	−1·3
Chamalières*	+2 878	1 535	853	+682	+2 196	+14·9
Chanat La Mouteyre	+15	39	22	+17	−2	−0·5
Clermont-Ferrand*	+20 672	14 213	7 113	+7 100	+13 572	+10·8
Cournon	+2 390	442	210	+232	+2 158	+68·8
Durtol*	+307	111	59	+52	+255	+26·8
Nohanent	+152	110	77	+33	+119	+12·6
Orcines	+245	186	104	+82	+163	+10·4
Royat*	+218	522	263	+259	−41	−1·0
St Genes Champanelle	+193	150	73	+77	+116	+9·6
St Ours	−32	84	94	−10	−22	−2·1
Sayat	+177	113	69	+44	+133	+12·8
Greater Clermont-Ferrand‡	+31 950	19 735	9 841	+9 894	+22 056	+12·9

NOTES
* Part of Greater Clermont-Ferrand (Unité Urbaine).
† Migrants include those from neighbouring communes as well as from other countries. The percentage is that of the total population of 1962.
‡ Communes other than those marked * are Gerzat, Lempdes and Aulnat.

Source: *Census, 1968*, INSEE, Paris.

Airport of Clermont-Ferrand, Aulnat (Limagne Plain)

(Altitude 329 metres)

1931–60

MONTH	MEAN PRESSURE IN MILLIBARS	MEAN DAILY TEMPERATURES		MEAN PRECIPITATION IN MM	NUMBER OF DAYS WITH THUNDER-STORMS	MEAN CLOUDINESS IN OKTAS	MEAN SUNSHINE IN HOURS
		Mean °C	*Range* °C				
Jan	987·0	2·7	7·8	25	0	7·2	82
Feb	977·6	3·5	9·1	25	0·1	6·7	108
Mar	976·1	7·3	11·2	29	0·1	6·2	167
Apr	976·5	10·1	11·4	43	1·1	6·3	190
May	976·3	13·7	11·8	67	4·1	6·1	215
June	978·5	17·2	11·8	72	5·6	6·4	221
July	978·7	19·2	12·5	51	4·9	5·5	259
Aug	978·1	18·8	12·5	68	5·9	5·6	235
Sept	979·1	16·1	11·4	61	2·3	5·7	197
Oct	978·4	11·0	10·4	49	0·4	6·2	158
Nov	977·3	6·7	8·1	40	0·4	7·3	86
Dec	977·7	3·5	7·2	33	0·2	7·3	72
Annual	977·7	10·9	10·5	563	25·1	6·4	1990

of a relatively unfavourable microclimate. At Cournon, in the south-east of the city region, for example, the population has doubled in six years with an increase of migrants (68·8 per cent) that is highest in the city region, as shown in the table opposite.

EXERCISE 5:
   Study the map extract and the geological map, Figure 50.
(*a*) *Describe the geographical situation and site of each of the settlements of Aubière, Royat and Beaumont.*
(*b*) *Draw simplified street plans of the main streets for these three settlements.*
(*c*) *List the assumed restrictions on the growth of Royat.*

The flat floor of the Artière river valley has been easy to cultivate and easy to build over, and Aubière, once physically separated from the city, is now linked to it, but local industry still survives in the confectionery and building trades. Royat, on the other hand, is an old spa town with some 19 000 annual summer visitors. In winter the accommodation is taken over by students. Between Royat and Aubière is Beaumont which typifies the changes that accrue from urbanization. The old village and the new housing area is clearly defined on the map extract. Situated on a large basaltic lava flow, Beaumont is a residential suburb of importance.

Microclimate and Man in the City Region

EXERCISE 6:
(*a*) *Construct temperature and precipitation graphs for Clermont-Ferrand and the Puy de Dôme using continuous lines for temperature and column bar graphs for precipitation.*
(*b*) *Contrast the climate of the Limagne Plain with that of the adjacent plateau with special reference to its influence upon the human geography of the map extract region.*

Summit of the Puy de Dôme
(Altitude 1464 metres)

MONTH	MEAN DAILY TEMPERATURE °C	MEAN PRECIPITATION IN MM
Jan	−2·2	157
Feb	−1·9	141
Mar	−0·5	163
Apr	1·2	155
May	6·5	141
June	9·0	141
July	10·9	129
Aug	11·0	126
Sept	8·8	127
Oct	5·0	137
Nov	0·9	138
Dec	−1·3	165

The Limagne is virtually a closed basin as far as meteorological conditions are concerned and under stable anticyclonic situations air masses stagnate. The burning of rubber debris from factories can therefore create air pollution resulting in smog. This, together with land haze, hinders the operation of the airport. On the other hand the mountain region is breezy and although free from atmospheric pollution can experience frequent and severe winter snowstorms.

CORRELATION

Existing in space and time are many factors which are interrelated and which serve to produce the existing distributions found today on the earth's surface. Some of these factors or variables are more closely interrelated than others and it is the degree of interrelationship with which geographers have more recently been concerned. For example, the angle of slope of a hillside will be the result of the hardness of rock which will control its rate of disintegration, the angle of dip, the aspect of the slope, the intensity of the precipitation, the extreme temperatures experienced and the vegetation cover. In the field of human geography the acreage of a certain crop grown by a farmer may vary from year to year and this variation could be closely interlinked with the type of soil, angle of slope of the fields, the amount of sunshine or precipitation available, distance from markets, prevailing prices for that crop or even government control of farm products and prices. In either of these cases the variables do not comprise an exhaustive list but they serve to show some of the complex interrelationships between man and his environment. All these variables do not play the same role of importance in influencing the 'end' product, and it is this relationship with which we are now concerned, that is the correlation between variables. Although relationships do exist this should not suggest that one factor is a *cause* of the other variation.

Not all relationships are as complex as those mentioned above and in its simplest form we shall consider only two variables which appear to affect each other.

There are several ways in which an investigation of correlation may be undertaken and here we shall study three of them:
1. Scatter Graph (Scatter Diagram).
2. Spearman Rank Coefficient of Correlation.
3. Pearson Product-Moment Coefficient of Correlation.

Scatter Graph (Scatter Diagram)

The simplest method of correlation is to construct a scatter graph of the two variables. To do this plot the independent variable on the *x*-axis and the dependent variable on the *y*-axis. In Figure 52 it is seen that sunshine hours are dependent upon cloud amount. The more closely the points tend to fall on a straight line, the greater the degree of interdependence of the two variables. When all points form a straight line then there is a perfect correlation. However, as one variable increases the other may also increase, in which instance there is a positive correlation. But this is not always the case for as one variable increases the second may decrease, thus giving a negative correlation (Figure 51(*a*), (*b*)). More frequently points will be distributed within a 'band' rather than on a single straight line, again showing either a positive or negative gradient. But it is in these circumstances that the problems of defining the degree of correlation, by eye, become critical, for should the points lie in a narrow 'band' there is a high degree of interrelationship. But the interpretation of the graph now rests with the observer to determine the meaning of 'narrow'. In these graphs where points are scattered widely a very low degree of correlation exists or in the ultimate no correlation whatsoever, i.e. a change in one variable does not produce a change in the other.

Thus, although this is a simple construction and gives an indication as to whether a relationship appears to exist, it gives no measure of that relationship, and the interpretation is entirely that of a single observer. To overcome this subjective approach a numerical value of the interdependence, i.e. the coefficient of correlation, should be calculated.

Spearman Rank Coefficient of Correlation

This method is especially useful when the 'order of merit' of the data is known but not the numerical values of individual items, or where a quick assessment of the degree of correlation is required, for it is a simple method giving a numerical answer.

The coefficient of correlation for Spearman Rank is given by the formula

$$R_s = 1 - \frac{6 \Sigma d^2}{n(n^2 - 1)}$$

where $d =$ difference between the rankings of the same item in each series and $n =$ number of pairs of items. R_s varies from $+1$ to -1 both these values showing complete correlation but when $R_s = 0$ there is total lack of correlation.

Using the figures for the number of hours of sunshine and cloud amount, in oktas, for the Aulnat Meteorological Station (see table on page 67), the correlation coefficient has been evaluated in the table below.

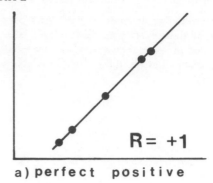

a) perfect positive

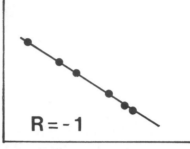

b) perfect negative

Spearman Rank Coefficient of Correlation
Sunshine/Cloud, Clermont-Ferrand

MONTH	SUNSHINE		CLOUD			
	NUMBER OF HOURS	RANK	OKTAS	RANK	d	d^2
Jan	82	11	7·2	3	+8	64
Feb	108	9	6·7	4	+5	25
Mar	167	7	6·2	7·5	−0·5	0·25
Apr	190	6	6·3	6	0	0
May	215	4	6·1	9	−5	25
June	221	3	6·4	5	−2	4
July	259	1	5·5	12	−11	121
Aug	235	2	5·6	11	−9	81
Sept	197	5	5·7	10	−5	25
Oct	158	8	6·2	7·5	+0·5	0·25
Nov	86	10	7·3	1·5	+8·5	72·25
Dec	72	12	7·3	1·5	+10·5	110·25
						$\Sigma d^2 = 528$

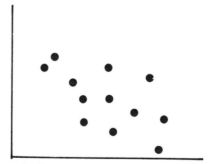

c) high positive

$$R_s = 1 - \left(\frac{6 \Sigma d^2}{n(n^2 - 1)} \right)$$

$$= 1 - \left(\frac{6 \times 528}{12(12^2 - 1)} \right)$$

$$= 1 - \frac{3168}{12 \times 143}$$

$$= -\frac{1452}{1716}$$

$$= -0·85$$

Three points should be noted:

1. When ranking data number 1 is always given to the highest value and an 'order of merit' created through 1, 2, 3 etc. The rank for sunshine is evaluated independently of that for cloudiness.

2. When items in the data have the same numerical value their positions in the table are added together and averaged between the items. Thus under cloudiness the first and second places have an equal value of 7·3 oktas.

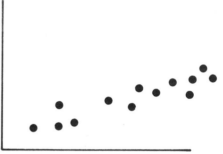

d) little negative

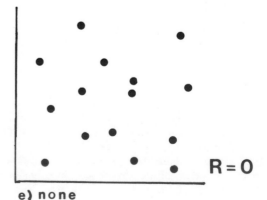

e) none

FIG. 51. Types of correlation.

Thus the value of the first two places is 3 and there are two items occupying these places, thus $3 \div 2 = 1.5$, and this is the rank value accorded to *each* of the 7.3 items.

3. The sign, indicating the direction of correlation, is given in the value of R_s.

Whereas the Spearman Rank Coefficient of Correlation is quick and easy it only gives an indication of the closeness of the correlation but the Pearson Product-Moment Coefficient of Correlation gives an accurate mathematical result. However, it does involve long and tedious mathematical calculation.

Pearson Product-moment Coefficient of Correlation

This method is based on the deviations of the individual values of the two variables from their means and is expressed as

$$r \text{ (or } rho) = \frac{\frac{1}{n}\Sigma(a - \bar{a})(b - \bar{b})}{\sigma_a \sigma_b}$$

where $(a - \bar{a})$ = deviations from the mean in the 1st variable

$(b - \bar{b})$ = deviations from the mean in the 2nd variable

n = number of pairs of items

σ_a and σ_b = standard deviations of a and b

In the calculation of r all results should be tabulated. Proceed in the following order:

1. Find the mean $\bar{a}$ of the hours of sunshine (Column 1).
2. Calculate the deviation $(a - \bar{a})$ of each month's sunshine from the mean, working consistently in the same direction, this involving the use of a + or − sign.
3. Square the individual deviation values and calculate the mean (Column 3).
4. Repeat these three processes, in the same order, for cloudiness (Columns 4, 5 and 6).
5. Multiply columns 2 and 5 together to find the product-moment (Column 7), taking account of the signs and tabulating in two columns—a positive and a negative one.
6. Find the value of the positive items and subtract the total value of the negative items, noting the sign. This is necessary as it indicates the direction of the correlation.
7. Substitue the values from the table in the formula to calculate r noting that the standard deviations are the square roots of the mean values given in Columns 3 and 6. As in the case of the standard deviation the formula

$$r = \frac{\frac{\Sigma ab}{n} - \bar{a}.\bar{b}}{\sigma_a . \sigma_b}$$

can be used in the place of the one given above to simplify the calculations.

From the Pearson Coefficient of Correlation, the Coefficient of Determination can be obtained by squaring its

Pearson Product–Moment Coefficient of Correlation

	SUNSHINE			CLOUD			
	1	2	3	4	5	6	7
	(a)	$(a - \bar{a})$	$(a - \bar{a})^2$	(b)	$(b - \bar{b})$	$(b - \bar{b})^2$	$(a - \bar{a})(b - \bar{b})$
Jan	82	−83·83	7027·47	7·2	+0·82	0·67	−68·74
Feb	108	−57·83	3344·31	6·7	+0·32	0·10	−18·51
Mar	167	+1·17	1·37	6·2	−0·18	0·03	−0·21
Apr	190	+24·17	584·19	6·3	−0·08	0·01	−1·93
May	215	+49·17	2417·69	6·1	−0·28	0·08	−13·77
June	221	+55·17	3043·73	6·4	+0·02	0·00	+1·10
July	259	+93·17	8680·65	5·5	−0·88	0·77	−81·99
Aug	235	+69·17	4784·49	5·6	−0·78	0·61	−53·95
Sept	197	+31·17	971·57	5·7	−0·68	0·46	−21·20
Oct	158	−7·83	61·31	6·2	−0·18	0·03	+1·41
Nov	86	−79·83	6372·83	7·3	+0·92	0·85	−73·44
Dec	72	−93·83	8804·07	7·3	+0·92	0·85	−86·32
	$\Sigma a = 1990$ $\bar{a} = 165.83$		$\Sigma = 46\,093.68$ Mean = 3841·14	$\Sigma b = 76.5$ $\bar{b} = 6.38$		$\Sigma = 4.46$ Mean = 0·37	$(a - \bar{a})(b - \bar{b}) =$ 2·51 − 420·06 = −417·55

$$\sigma_a = \sqrt{\frac{\Sigma(a - \bar{a})^2}{n}} = \sqrt{3841.14} = 61.98$$

$$\sigma_b = \sqrt{\frac{\Sigma(b - \bar{b})^2}{n}} = \sqrt{0.37} = 0.61$$

$$\therefore r = \frac{\frac{1}{n}\Sigma(a - \bar{a})(b - \bar{b})}{\sigma_a.\sigma_b} = -\frac{\frac{417.55}{12}}{61.98 \times 0.61}$$

$$= -\frac{34.80}{37.80}$$

$$= -0.92$$

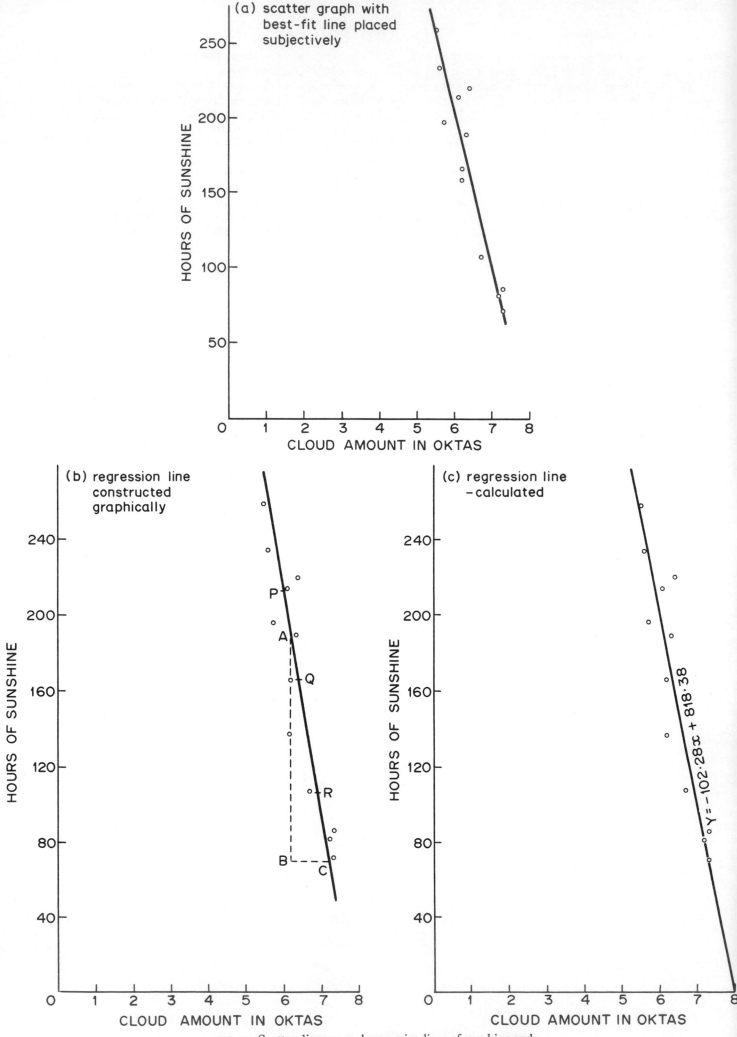

FIG. 52. Scatter diagram and regression lines of sunshine and cloud for Aulnat, Clermont-Ferrand airport.

value and multiplying by 100 per cent. This coefficient has a value —0·92 in the worked example. Thus the Coefficient of Determination is

$$(0·92)^2 \times 100\%$$
$$= 84·6\%$$

The determination coefficient is a measure of the percentage of the variation in one variable being explained by the variation in the other. Thus for Aulnat 84·6 per cent of the variation in the sunshine is due to variation in cloud cover. Hence we immediately ask ourselves what other factors are influencing the amount of sunshine recorded. Is it haze that has produced insufficient burning for it to be registered on the Campbell-Stokes sunshine recorder chart or is it the difficulty of not being able precisely to read the burning recorded when the angle of the sun's rays is low? More probably it is a combination of both aspects.

In any set of data there is always the possibility that 'chance' or human behaviour could have influenced the correlation and thus it is necessary to determine whether or not your calculated value of a correlation coefficient has validity, i.e. is statistically significant. There are several tests that can be utilized for this purpose, but they lie beyond the scope of this book. However, by using the extract from statistical significance tables below, it is possible to read directly whether your relationship can be accepted as a valid relationship or should be rejected because of too great a chance element.

In reading the table below, the calculated product-movement coefficient of correlation must exceed the stated minimum value to be significant at the 1 per cent level. This means that only 1 per cent of the correlation of the two variables will be uncertain due to chance, i.e. 1 in every 100 observations, and that the other 99 per cent will be truly correlated.

It should be noted that the number of degrees of freedom used in the tables is always 2 *less* than the number of pairs of variables being correlated, and relates to the number of items in an array of data which can be assigned *any* value (hence the name). The remaining values, however, are pre-determined since the two variables are related by specific values of both the mean and the standard deviation.

Extract from Table 5, Heinemann's Statistical Tables

Number of degrees of freedom v	Minimum value of r for the correlation to be significant
1	0·9995
2	0·9800
3	0·9343
4	0·882
5	0·833
6	0·789
7	0·750
8	0·715
9	0·685
10	0·658
11	0·634
12	0·612
13	0·592
14	0·574
15	0·558
16	0·543
17	0·529
18	0·516
19	0·503
20	0·492
25	0·445
30	0·409
35	0·381
40	0·358
45	0·338
50	0·322
60	0·295
70	0·274
80	0·257
90	0·242
100	0·230

To use the tables, twelve pairs of items were correlated and the product–moment coefficient of correlation was calculated to have a value of 0·92. In the tables, along the row of 10 degrees of freedom, i.e. (12–2), the minimum value of r is given as 0·658, which is less than the computed figure of 0·92. Thus we can say that our two variables are significantly correlated at the 99 per cent level.

EXERCISE 7:
(a) *Draw a scattergraph to indicate the degree of correlation between either rainfall and cloudiness or temperature and cloud cover for Clermont-Ferrand.*
(b) *Calculate the Spearman Rank and Pearson Product–moment Coefficients of Correlation for items chosen in part (a).*
(c) *Determine whether or not the latter result is significant.*
(d) *Calculate the Coefficient of Determination.*
(e) *What other factors influence the relationship?*

REGRESSION

We saw in Figure 52A that in plotting a scattergraph of the relationship between cloud cover and the number of sunshine hours at Aulnat airport, the points on the graph lay in a narrow band. It is now possible to draw, by eye, a line which shows the trend of the relationship, and in doing this, almost subconsciously, the analyst will construct the line to pass through some points, leaving an equal number of points 'free' on either side of it—thus acknowledging the line to represent the average of all the points. This is a purely subjective method but it is possible to show the trend of the relationship by a 'best-fit' line, which when calculated mathematically is known as the *regression line*. Depending on the relationship of the two variables this may be of a linear or curvilinear form.

Method

Here we shall only discuss the simpler form—the linear relationship. The simplest method for establishing the position of the regression line is a graphical one (see Figure 52B).

1. Calculate the mean values of x and y (see Table, page 70). These are $\bar{x} = 6·38$; $\bar{y} = 165·83$. Mark this point Q (6·4, 165·8) on the scattergraph. Q is known as the *mean of the array of points.*
2. There are now seven points above Q, namely:

x	6·2	6·3	5·7	6·1	6·4	5·6	5·5
y	167	190	197	215	221	235	259

And their mean values are 5·97 and 212 plotted as the point P (6·0, 212).

3. Below point Q are five points:

x	6·2	6·7	7·3	7·2	7·3
y	158	108	86	82	72

whose mean values are 6·94 and 101·2 represented by point R (6·9, 101·2).

4. The regression line is drawn through Q and as nearly as possible through P and R.

Using the right-angled triangle ABC, BA represents an increase of 120 hours of sunshine with a decrease of 1·0 oktas of cloud (CB). Thus $\dfrac{BA}{CB} = -120$. This ratio of the vertical to the horizontal component is the *slope* or *gradient* of the regression line and is known as the *regression coefficient*.

In drawing the line through points P, Q and R it is seen that the line does not pass through all three points and hence this method produces only a good estimate. So it becomes necessary to adopt the mathematical method of establishing the best-fit line of the data, independent of any graphical method. To calculate the equation of the regression line, the formula will be of the standard form for any line

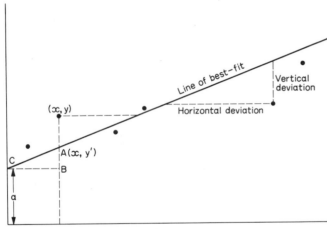

To find the value of y'

Slope of line = $b = \dfrac{AB}{BC}$

$AB = (y' - a)$

$BC = x$

$\therefore b = \dfrac{(y' - a)}{x}$

$y' = bx + a$

i.e. $y = mx + c$

where m is the slope or gradient of the line and c is a constant equal to the intercept cut off along the y-axis by the regression line. By using $y = mx + c$ where m and c are both numerical values, for any known value of x y can be calculated. Thus x is the independent variable and y the dependent variable. In our example for Aulnat the cloud amounts are the independent variable and the sunshine hours are the dependent variable.

Although $y = mx + c$ is the standard *mathematical* formula for a straight line, the statisticians use a modified form, namely $y = bx + a$. It is this form which we will use in our calculations.

To find the equation of the regression line it is necessary to calculate the value of b and a. Since the line of best-fit is an average line it immediately implies that the sum of the deviations round the arithmetic mean must be zero, i.e. $\Sigma d = 0$ where $d =$ deviation. But there are many lines which would satisfy this condition and thus a second criterion is used.

When calculating the standard deviation of a set of data the sum of the squares of the deviations is used. There is a position for the line of best-fit where the sum of the deviations squared is at a minimum, i.e. Σd^2 is a minimum. This concept, as the second criterion to fix a particular line, gives rise to the method of least squares being used to identify this regression line for a single array of data.

To evaluate the two equations noted above

i.e. (1) $\Sigma d = 0$
　　　(2) $\Sigma d^2 =$ minimum

where $d =$ the deviation. This is expressed as the y value of the point less the y' value on the regression line for the same x value.

i.e. $\quad d = y - y'$
$\qquad d = y - (bx + a)$　(see diagram above)
$\qquad \Sigma d = \Sigma[y - (bx + a)] = 0$
$\qquad \Sigma d^2 = \Sigma[y - (bx + a)]^2 =$ minimum.

By the use of differential calculus these two normal formulae for the calculation of the equation of the regression line can be shown to be

(1) $\Sigma y = b\Sigma x + na$ where n is the number of pairs
(2) $\Sigma xy = b\Sigma x^2 + a\Sigma x$

Dividing equation (1) by n

$$\frac{\Sigma y}{n} = \frac{b\Sigma x}{n} + a$$

(3) i.e. $\bar{y} = b\bar{x} + a$. This shows that the line passes through the mean point $(\bar{x}, \bar{y})$ of the array.

By direct substitution in equations (2) and (3) for Σx, Σx^2, Σxy, $\bar{x}$ and $\bar{y}$ the values for b and a can be calculated.

AULNAT AIRPORT

CLOUD			SUNSHINE	
x	x^2	xy	y	y^2
7·2	51·84	590·4	82	6 724
6·7	44·89	723·6	108	11 669
6·2	38·44	1 035·4	167	27 880
6·3	39·69	1 197·0	190	36 105
6·1	37·21	1 311·5	215	46 221
6·4	40·96	1 414·4	221	48 841
5·5	30·25	1 424·5	259	67 085
5·6	31·36	1 316·0	235	55 229
5·7	32·49	1 122·9	197	38 804
6·2	38·44	979·6	158	24 964
7·3	53·29	627·8	86	7 396
7·3	53·29	525·6	72	5 184
$\Sigma x = 76·5$ $\bar{x} = 6·38$	$\Sigma x^2 = 492·15$	$\Sigma xy = 12\ 268·7$	$\Sigma y = 1\ 990$ $= 165·83$	$\Sigma y^2 = 376\ 102$

To calculate the equation of the regression line of y on x using the vertical deviations of the points.

$$\bar{y} = b\bar{x} + a \qquad\qquad (1)$$

$$\Sigma xy = b\Sigma x^2 + a\Sigma x \qquad\qquad (2)$$

From equation (1) $a = \bar{y} - b\bar{x}$

Substituting in (2) $\Sigma xy = b\Sigma x^2 + \Sigma x(\bar{y} - b\bar{x})$
$\qquad\qquad\quad \Sigma xy - \bar{y}\Sigma x = b(\Sigma x^2 - \bar{x}\Sigma x)$
$$b = \frac{\Sigma xy - \bar{y}\Sigma x}{\Sigma x^2 - \bar{x}\Sigma x}$$

Substituting numerical values from the table above:

$$b = \frac{12\ 268\cdot7 - 165\cdot83 \times 76\cdot5}{492\cdot15 - 6\cdot38 \times 76\cdot5}$$

$$= \frac{12\ 268\cdot7 - 12\ 686\cdot00}{492\cdot15 - 488\cdot07}$$

$$= -102\cdot28$$

$$a = 165\cdot83 + 102\cdot28 \times 6\cdot38$$

$$= 818\cdot38$$

Having calculated the values of b and a, the equation of the regression line for y on x can now be written

$$y = -102\cdot28x + 818\cdot38$$

To construct the regression line on the graph select two values of x near the extreme ends of the range given and calculate the respective values of y.

For $\quad x = 8 \quad y = -818\cdot24 + 818\cdot38 = 0\cdot14$

and $\quad x = 6 \quad y = -613\cdot68 + 818\cdot38 = 204\cdot7$

Mark the two points (8, 0·14), (6, 204·7) and the mean of the array $(\bar{x}, \bar{y})$, i.e. point (6·38, 165·83) on the graph and draw the straight line. Mark on it the equation of the line (see Figure 52C).

To calculate the equation of the regression line of x on y. Using again the method of least squares but on this occasion evaluating the horizontal distances of the points from the regression line, it is possible to construct a second regression line which is the line of x on y. This is a line quite distinct from y on x and only when there is perfect correlation of the data will the two coincide. The regression of x on y has been omitted on Figure 52C as the regression lines are almost coincident. However it can be shown that the greater the degree of correlation and the smaller the angle between the two regression lines. Conversely the lower the degree of correlation and the greater the angle between the two lines.

Using similar arguments as for the regression line y on x then it can be shown that for the regression line of x on y the two equations are:

$$\bar{x} = b\bar{y} + a \qquad (1)$$

$$\Sigma xy = b\Sigma y^2 + a\Sigma y \qquad (2)$$

Substituting the values directly from the table above

$$b = \frac{\Sigma xy - \bar{x}\Sigma y}{\Sigma y^2 - \bar{y}\Sigma y}$$

$$= \frac{12\ 268\cdot7 - 6\cdot38 \times 1990}{376\ 102 - 165\cdot83 \times 1990}$$

$$= \frac{12\ 268\cdot7 - 12\ 696\cdot2}{376\ 102 - 330\ 001\cdot7}$$

$$= -0\cdot0093$$

$$a = \bar{x} - b\bar{y}$$

$$= 6\cdot38 + 0\cdot0093 \times 165\cdot83$$

$$= 6\cdot38 + 1\cdot54$$

$$= 7\cdot92$$

And thus the equation of the regression line x on y is

$$x = -0\cdot0093y + 7\cdot92$$

The construction is as for y on x. Select two values of y near the extreme values of the array and calculate the respective values of x.

If $\quad y = 0 \quad x = 0 + 7\cdot92 = 7\cdot92$

and $\quad y = 200 \quad x = -1\cdot86 + 7\cdot92 = 6\cdot06$

Mark the points (7·92, 0) and (6·06, 200) on the graph and draw the line joining them and passing through the point $(\bar{x}, \bar{y})$. Mark on it the equation of the line.

There are many instances in geography where two variables appear to be related and thus correlation gives a measure of the relationship (but *not* the cause of the relationship), and regression shows the trend of that variation. It should be noted, however, that outside the observed area of the relationship the same linear trend may not be continued, and thus it is not justified to assume the same regressions beyond either the extreme upper or lower ends of the relationship.

By constructing the y on x regression line it is thus possible to see the trend of the relationship between sunshine hours and cloud cover and to estimate the sunshine hours for any value of cloud cover within the given range of values. Likewise the regression of x on y relates the cloud cover to the number of sunshine hours and allows for the estimate of cloud cover at intermediate values of sunshine hours.

Where semi-log relationships are being plotted then the form of the equation of a line becomes $\log y = bx + a$ and all calculations involving 'y' values are made by using the log values.

In the case of log-log relationships the form is

$$\log y = b \log x + a$$

and both the 'x' and the 'y' values must be made using log values. (See Appendix for an explanation of log graphs.)

THE CITY AND ITS FUNCTIONS

The advantages and disadvantages of the local physical environment pale into insignificance when the role of Michelin is considered as a force for urbanization. The several Michelin factories, employing 26 000 people, may appear to dominate the scene, but there are many varied services and other industries in the city. In 1962 the major class of employment was indeed manufacturing, but in 1968 the service sector claimed dominance, as seen in the table below.

THOUSANDS OF ACTIVE WORKERS
EMPLOYED IN THE CITY
BY CLASS

	1962	1968
Primary	0·8	0·5
Secondary	36·7	42·2
Tertiary	34·4	44·4

Source: *Census 1968.*

If the functions of the city, listed below, are studied, then the significance of this change can be appreciated.
1. Aircraft and servicing
2. Biscuit manufacture
3. Building construction
4. Chocolate manufacture
5. Confectionary products
6. Electrical engineering

7. Furniture making
8. Jams, preserves and food pastes production
9. Metallurgy
10. Milk products
11. Paint works
12. Pharmaceutical and other chemical production
13. Printing (especially for the Bank of France)
14. Rubber manufacturing
15. Service industries—storage depots, warehousing and distribution, banking, administration, retail shops and professional services
16. Sugar refining
17. University services

EXERCISE 8:

Use the air photograph (Photograph X) and its accompanying diagram to create a sketch map to illustrate the urban land use of central Clermont-Ferrand. Differentiate, by areas of contrasting shading, explained in a key, the zones in which some or all of the following functions are dominant:

Main shopping area	*Area cleared for*
Administrative	*redevelopment*
Public services and	*Cathedral precinct*
institutions	*Residential area*
University zone	*Industrial*
Open space and parks	*Undifferentiated*

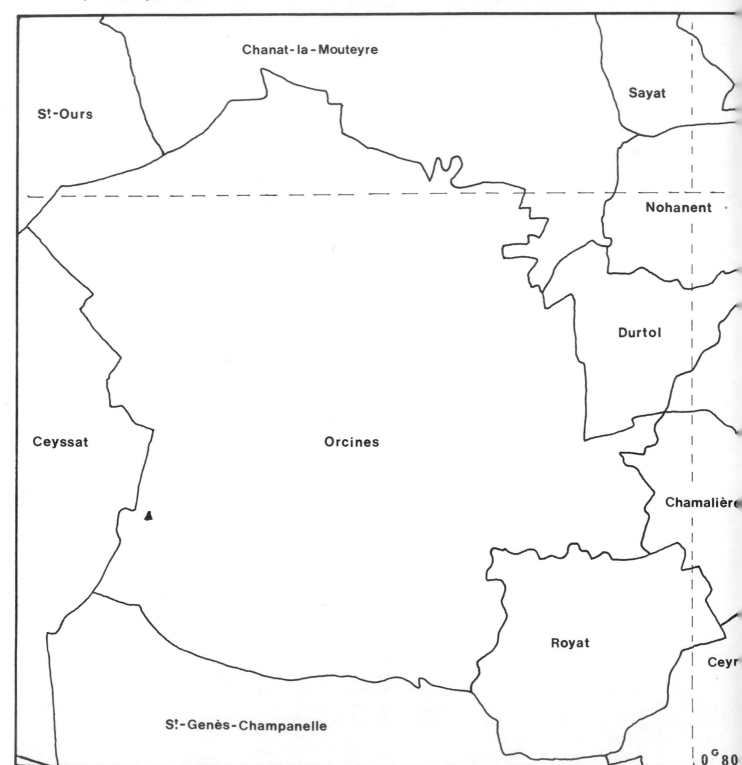

FIG. 53. Communes west of Clermont-Ferrand.

SPATIAL PATTERNS IN RURAL POPULATION DISTRIBUTION

Within an hour the city motorist can be among the heavily wooded volcanic mountains of the Parc de Volcans. Income from tourists and from small interspersed sheep and cattle pastures has, until now, been limited. The use of the high pastures ('estives') for cattle rearing has declined here as it has in the Saas Valley of Switzerland. Transhumance has almost died out too as the economic life in the villages has changed. However, with the encouragement of tourism in the Nature Park, the enlargement of farm holdings and the increased mechanization of farming portends a brighter

future. Ranching has developed where the 'estives' have been fenced in and re-seeded with nutritious grasses. Farmers who retire early have received financial benefits if their land has been made available for the enlargement of existing near-by farms. The old subsistence agriculture, based on stock rearing and the growing of rye and potatoes is therefore declining, although there is still a small out-migration of population as indicated in the table below.

Census of 1968
Puy de Dôme Département

COMMUNE	POPULATION†		PERIOD 1962–68 % VARIATION
	1968	1962	
Aubière*	7 844	6 820	+15·0
Beaumont*	6 930	6 289	+10·2
Blanzat*	1 696	1 176	+44·2
Cebazat*	3 837	2 830	+35·6
Ceyrat	2 850	2 219	+28·4
Ceyssat	348	373	−6·7
Chamalières*	17 578	14 700	+19·6
Chanat La Mouteyre	392	377	+4·0
Clermont-Ferrand*	146 643	125 971	+16·4
Cournon	5 525	3 135	+76·2
Durtol*	1 259	952	+32·2
Nohanent	1 096	944	+16·1
Orcines	1 814	1 569	+15·6
Royat*	4 380	4 162	+5·2
St Genes Champanelle	1 406	1 213	+15·9
St Ours	1 011	1 043	−3·1
Sayat	1 215	1 038	+17·1
Total	205 824	174 811	
Total Greater Clermont-Ferrand‡	202 306	170 356	+18·8

NOTES
† Population 'Municipale', March 1968.
‡ Communes marked * form part of the conurbation of Clermont-Ferrand, other communes being Gerzat, Lempdes and Aulnat.

Source: *Census de 1968*, INSEE, Paris.

EXERCISE 9:

(a) *By means of located proportional circles illustrate the distribution of the 1968 population in the communes shown in Figure 53. (A method of drawing these comparative pie diagrams is explained in the author's* Advanced Practical Geography, *pp. 76–7.)*

(b) *Describe briefly the geographical distribution of the population mapped.*

NEAREST NEIGHBOUR ANALYSIS

This technique, first used by botanists, measures the amount and the way in which the distribution of individuals in a statistical population in a given area departs from that of a random distribution.[1]

But it is a method which has both physical and human applications. This analysis compares the observed (existing) spatial distribution with that which would exist if all points or individuals were randomly distributed.

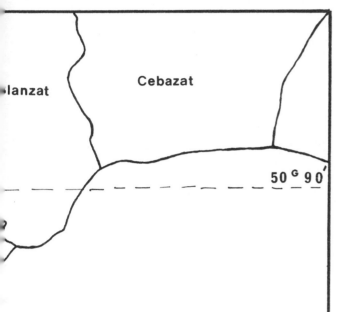

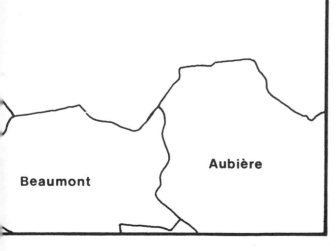

Cebazat · Blanzat · 50 G 90' · Clermont-Ferrand · Beaumont · Aubière

[1] P. J. Clark and F. C. Evans, 'Distance to Nearest Neighbours as a Measure of Spatial Relationships in Populations', *Ecology* (1954), Vol. 35, no. 4, pp. 445–53.

Method

1. Within a defined study area, such as that of the settlements shown on the Clermont-Ferrand map, decide which size of settlements are to be considered and mark on tracing-paper a dot to represent the centre of each. In the case of linear settlements establish the centre at, for example, a road junction or a church.
2. Define the boundary of the study area. This may be a rectangular map area when settlements within contrasting regions are compared or it may be formed by joining all the peripheral dots by straight lines. However, this analysis has a wider application to all forms of spatial distributions and in some circumstances the boundary may be irregular, as for example, when the distribution of springs on a particular rock outcrop, drumlins on a lowland region or hotels in a holiday resort are under consideration.
3. Number the dots consecutively within the chosen boundary.
4. Measure in millimetres the direct distance from point 1 to its nearest neighbour; then from point 2 and so forth for each dot numbered. All measurements must be taken within the boundary of the study area. Calculate the mean. Scale distances can be used to avoid the long calculations involved in converting these to actual distances, since the end result is an index independent of units. Care must be taken, however, to calculate the area in the same units.
5. Tabulate the values as suggested below.

POINT NUMBER	DISTANCE IN MM TO NEAREST NEIGHBOUR
	$\Sigma =$
	$\bar{d} =$

6. Use the formula:

$$Rn = 2\bar{d}\sqrt{\frac{n}{A}}$$

where Rn is the nearest neighbour index, $\bar{d}$ is the mean distance between points, n is the number of settlements considered within the area. A is the area studied.

7. The calculated value will lie between 0, which indicates that all points are placed at the same locality and 2·15, which is the value for points distributed at the vertices of a regular hexagon, and would therefore represent maximum regular spacing. As we have seen earlier, each individual in a hexagon is equidistant from six other individuals.
8. The answer to this formula gives a value which enables the distances measured to nearest neighbours to be compared to those which would occur if the points were randomly distributed, as indicated on the Rn scale below.

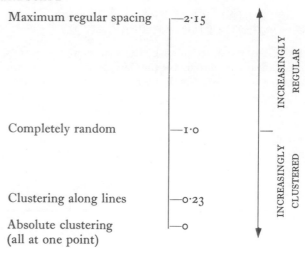

Maximum regular spacing — 2·15

Completely random — 1·0

Clustering along lines — 0·23

Absolute clustering (all at one point) — 0

INCREASINGLY REGULAR

INCREASINGLY CLUSTERED

The value of this type of analysis is that it is possible to compare two or more spatial distributions of populations with respect to ascertaining how far they depart from randomness. Thus the settlement pattern of the plateau can be analysed mathematically. The problem for geographers is in the recognition of those 'elements of regularity in what seems to be a totally irregular spatial pattern. We have long sought to identify these regularities intuitively by staring at the map and hoping that what we think we see is really there. We now possess objective ways of measuring pattern.'[1]

EXERCISE 10:

(a) *On tracing-paper placed over the map extract insert the border fault from the geological map and locate, by means of a dot, all the settlements west of that fault line. Number these consecutively. For each settlement (i) state its height in metres and tabulate the results; (ii) measure in metres the direct distance to its neighbour. (The centre of the settlement should be determined and used as the points of origin and destination of your measured distances.)*

(b) *Calculate the mean values for (i) the height of settlements and (ii) the distances between them. Using the nearest neighbour statistic, describe how far the settlement pattern departs from randomness.*

The area of the map extract can be divided into three contrasting settlement zones. On the east there is part of the city region, the central area is one of plateau village settlement and to the west there is a negative area where the aligned cinder cones and the Puy de Dôme occupy much of the territory. On the extensive Auvergne mountains the majority of the plateau settlements are at 'water-seeking' sites located on the gentle back slopes of the lava plateaux and are frequently found within the altitudinal range of 760 to 860 metres.

EXERCISE 11:

(a) *Construct a dispersion diagram to show the altitude of the settlements on the plateau zone as depicted on the map extract.*

(b) *Give reasons, which could be deduced from the geological and topographic maps for any locational preferences.*

(c) *Describe other techniques that could be employed to analyse the altitude and location of these settlements.*

---

[1] D. Harvey, *Explanation in Geography* (1969), p. 385.

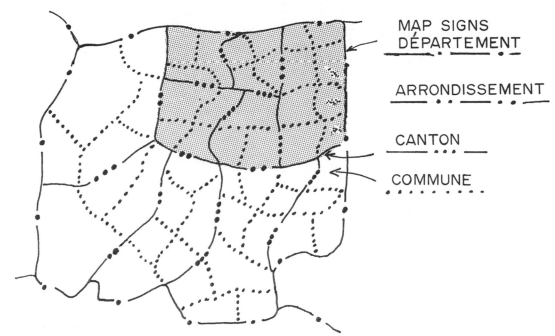

FIG. 54. Diagrammatic map of administrative divisions within a département.

FIG. 55. Areas of small and large communes in France. Small communes have a mean area of under 15 km². Large communes have a mean area of over 15 km². The shaded département is Puy de Dôme. The highland areas of France could be superimposed on a copy of this map (*after Meynier*).

SPATIAL PATTERN OF COMMUNES

France is administratively divided into ninety-five 'départements' in each of which is an important settlement with its 'préfecture', or administrative centre, responsible to the national government. Each department is divided into 'arrondissements' and these are subdivided into cantons. In each canton are about twelve communes each with its own 'central place'. In medieval times the farthest part of the commune was no more than a day's journey to the central place. The 37 708 present communes are basic elements of local government under the influence of mayors. Since 1959 some of the smaller communes have been grouped into districts, but the size and boundary shapes of communes reflect both the historical and physical factors which have exerted their influence through historic time. Large communes are located in urban areas and in forested and mountainous country, while the smaller network is seen in the lowlands of north and north-east France as shown on the generalized map, Figure 55. The map extract area illustrates the validity of these generalizations.

EXERCISE 12:

Compare the map of the communes, Figure 53, with those of geology and topography for the same area.

(*a*) *Name the two largest communes. Suggest reasons for their size.*

(*b*) *Discuss the extent to which the boundary fault and the puys have influenced the size and shape of the communes.*

(*c*) *In 1962 the communes of France had a mean area of 1428 hectares. Draw a rectangle on the same scale as the map to represent this size. Which commune in the study region is nearest to this size?*

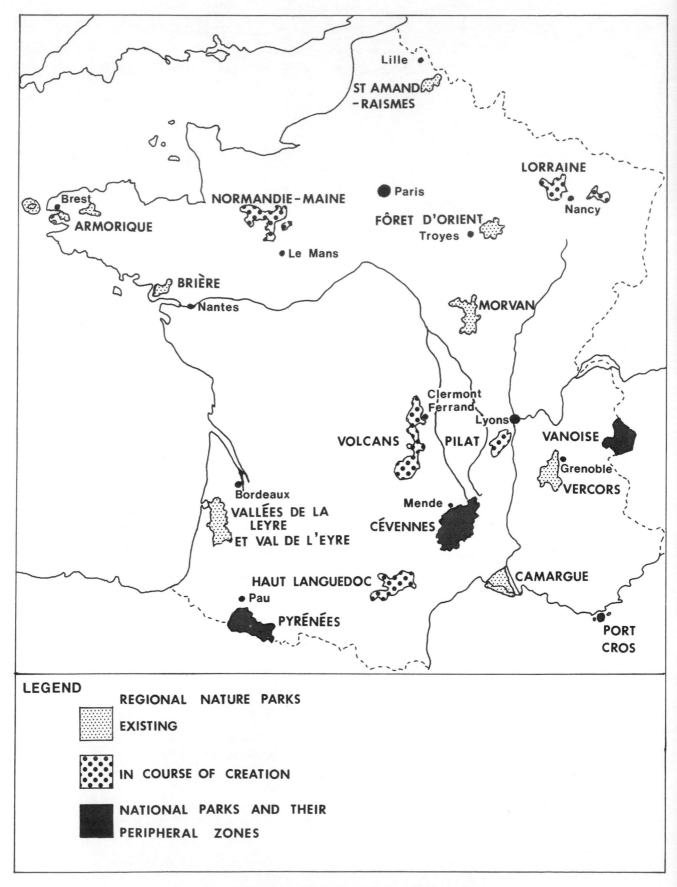

FIG. 56. National and Regional Nature Parks in France.

BRITISH AND FRENCH NATIONAL PARKS

In December 1949 the National Parks and Access to the Countryside Act was passed by the British Parliament. The land that was to be included in these parks was partly unoccupied and relatively wild, and partly farmed and forested. Life in the villages within these rural areas would continue to function, for the land was not to be solely devoted to public recreation as in America where the world's first national park (Yellowstone) had been established as long ago as 1872.

The aim in Britain was both to preserve the natural beauty of England and Wales (presumably Scotland had its full share of beauty since it was excluded from the Act), and to encourage the development of facilities for open-air enjoyment. As Darby pointed out in his address to the British Association in 1963 one type of recreation is gregarious and another type is solitary, thus roads, television masts, car parks and caravan and camping sites co-exist with riders, walkers, rock climbers and naturalists.[1]

In France the aim of the creators of National Parks was to reconcile these basic conflicts by devising a zonal system. The inner zone has entry restricted to scientists since rare species of plants and animals must be safeguarded, and the ecosystem left relatively undisturbed by invasions of tourists. The second zone, with open entry, is devoted to sport and recreation, while in the outer periphery economic development, 'rural renovation', has priority.

The first French National Park was the Vanoise in Savoy, having received its charter on 6 July 1963. In the same year the Mediterranean island of Port Cros was designated a National Park in order to conserve its unique maquis vegetation. In 1967 an area of the central Pyrenees was selected as a park and in 1970 the National Park of the Cévennes safeguarded karstic landscape from exploitation. Since then other parks have been or will be opened as shown in Figure 56.

In addition to the chain of National Parks, France has designated many of its most beautiful areas as Regional Nature Parks. Here the aim is the harmonious development of town and countryside. These parks have an administration that is strongly rooted in the locality of the park. The administrative 'syndicat' comprises representatives from the local communes and local public establishments as well as Département and national officials. The boundaries of the areas chosen and the way economic development takes place is thus strongly controlled both by the inhabitants of the included settlements and by those of its adjoining urban area, which in the case of the Volcanoes Regional Park is the city region of Clermont-Ferrand.

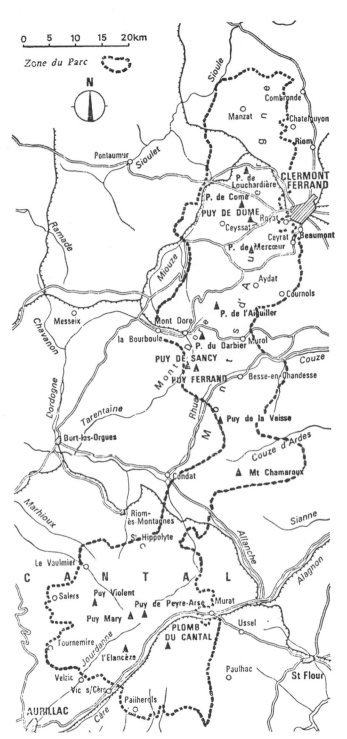

FIG. 57. Parc Régional des Volcans.

GEOGRAPHY OF LEISURE

A new aspect of human geography is the study of the economic influence of holidays-with-pay and of the almost universal use of the private car. The movement of population thus involved has its effect upon both city and rural area, for the leisure-migrant includes the week-ender as well as the family on holiday and those who retire from work or business. In all West European countries the leisure-migrant category is continually increasing its numbers. In France, in 1961, some 35 per cent of the total population were involved but in 1970 these 'migrants' formed 53 per cent of the population. This suggests that now some 25 million persons per annum are seeking a change of environment. To this 'native' element must also be added a considerable number of foreign tourists.

The frequency of holiday or leisure journeys is as significant as the duration of the main annual holiday. In 1960, for example, the average French annual holiday lasted for more than 20 days as compared with 15 days for the

---

[1] H. C. Darby, 'British National Parks', *The Advancement of Science* (1963), Vol. XX, pp. 317–18.

Germans and 10 for most other West Europeans, but for all countries these values are increasing year by year. Clearly, especially in France, the long summer holidays adversely affect the economic life of the permanent home areas. This migration also plays a significantly beneficial role in the economy of mountain regions, sea-side resorts and those birth-place areas to which returning city dwellers, especially Parisians, come each summer. This movement has created a demand for rural second homes by city house or flat occupiers. With increasing wealth and leisure 8 per cent of the population have been able to buy their second homes. The 1968 census lists 1 230 000 second homes in France, and in the Volcans region of the Puy de Dôme there were 1564 such properties in 1969.[1] This local survey shows an increase of 245 per cent in nineteen years for this category of property, and this is in an area of former depopulation. These vacation homes, mainly for an urban population, are frequently located in villages that were being part abandoned by country dwellers. The newcomers may temporarily revitalize old, remote settlements and if retirement takes place to these homes a permanent social contribution will result. There is, as Clout indicates, a sentimental attachment to one's birth-place and many Parisians can claim to be born in the villages of the Massif Central.

In the area of the map extract the commune of Orcines has 174 second residences and has profited by the arrival of this migratory population. Settlements near to Clermont-Ferrand which have received an influx of second-home seekers may grow into suburbs of that city. Will the town invade the countryside?

In Britain a similar situation has developed since second homes are being sought in the coastal settlements of Devon, Cornwall and in East Anglia and in the mountain villages of Wales and the Lake District.

In the inner Lake District a village such as Patterdale has a high percentage (33 per cent) of its property classified as second homes.[2] In Wales, Denbighshire County Planning Authority state that a figure of 12 per cent represents 'saturation point' for this type of property in any one village, which suggests that demand has outstripped supply when this figure is exceeded. However, it should be remembered that the cause of departure of most young people from villages is the shortage of local employment rather than of houses.

EXERCISE 13:

Margaret Capstick suggests six solutions to the problems arising from the purchase of holiday 'second homes' in English Lake District villages suffering depopulation.
(a) *Tax such homes at a high level.*
(b) *Limit ownership of 'second homes' to houses above a certain rateable value.*
(c) *Improvement grants to be limited to people intending to live permanently in the houses.*
(d) *Increase the building of local authority houses.*
(e) *No restrictions on the building of 'second homes'.*
(f) *Raise local incomes to the point at which local people could outbid potential 'second-home' owners for houses.*
Discuss each of these and suggest which one is the most likely to restrict ownership of second homes in rural surroundings.

[1] H. D. Clout, 'Second Homes in the Auvergne', *The Geographical Review* (1971), Vol. LXI, pp. 530–53.
[2] Margaret Capstick, *Some Aspects of the Economic Effects of Tourism in the Westmorland Lake District* (1972), Section 5, pp. 75–81.

EXERCISE 14:
(a) *Suggest reasons (i) for the existence of British farm guest-house type of accommodation; (ii) for your acceptance of an invitation to stay at one for a holiday.*
(b) *List other types of tourist enterprises in such areas as Devon and Cornwall or any National Park.*

EXERCISE 15:
Write an essay on 'Agriculture and Tourism'.

EXERCISE 16:
(a) *Compare the tourist accommodation facilities for the inner English Lake District as tabulated below, with that for the department of the Puy-de-Dôme seen below.*
(b) *Suggest which type of enterprise seen only in France could be established in the Lake District.*
(c) *By means of divided proportional circles illustrate these two sets of figures.*

TOURIST ACCOMMODATION IN THE WESTMORLAND LAKE DISTRICT 1971	
TYPE	NUMBER OF ENTERPRISES
Licensed hotels	72
Unlicensed hotels	32
Guest houses	88
Bed and breakfast (only) accommodation	310
Farm guest-houses	32
Caravan and camp sites	24
Furnished flats	120
Hostels and youth hostels	18

Source: M. Capstick.

EXERCISE 17:
Debate the motion that 'this house deplores the existence of "second homes" and proposes that the purchase of such property should be prohibited by law.'

In France the needs of the leisure age are met by the provision of such new types of employment as building, constructing garages and car parks, operating ski-lifts, staffing information bureaux (Les Syndicats d'Initiative) and organizing tours as well as stimulating the older type catering industry. In the department of the Puy-de-Dôme there was, in 1972, the following accommodation for the holiday-maker:

500	Furnished rural cottages for hire
60	Inns (Auberges)
313	Tourist hotels
8	Holiday villages
3	Youth hostels
60	Authorized camping and caravan sites

This is in addition to the numerous 'second homes' already acquired.

EXERCISE 18:
Select any one British National Park or Forest Park other than the Lake District, as shown in Figure 58.
(a) *Investigate its geography and discuss its attraction for tourists.*

(b) *Using a reference library consult AA or RAC hotel guides and other holiday guide-books together with official publications. Describe and assess the accommodation offered within the park for holiday-makers or 'leisure-migrants'.*

EXERCISE 19:

(a) *Using an atlas and the two maps of National Parks, Figures 56 and 58, state, for both the United Kingdom and France:*
  (i) *Which parks are most easily accessible to tourists?*
  (ii) *Which parks are nearest to major urban areas (agglomerations, conurbations or city regions)?*
(b) *For either south-eastern or eastern England suggest one area for which you would like to see a National Park*

designated. Give reasons for your choice. (If you do not know the region study an atlas and appropriate geography textbooks to help you make your choice.)

The differences between city life and rural life are slowly disappearing. The availability of power, sewage and social security applies to all—countrymen or townsmen. Central heating and other domestic comforts are no longer restricted to suburban households. Occupiers of 'second homes' and tourists bring urban influences into rural surroundings and the creation of a Nature Park is largely due to the pressure of an urbanized population. 'La ville se transporte à la campagne.'

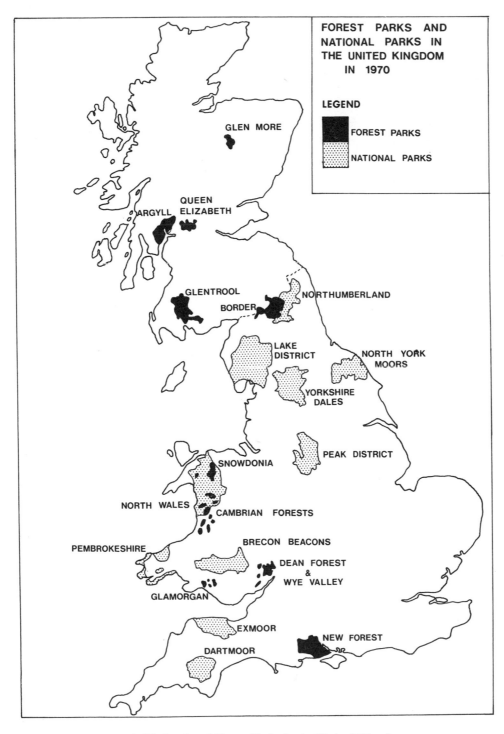

FIG. 58. National and Forest Parks in the United Kingdom.

5. Industrial Change—Development Areas, Overspill and New Towns

Yesterday and tomorrow join hands in the midst of a lively present. *Sir William Beach Thomas*

CHANGES IN industry and technological development in the last forty years have created variations in the amount and type of work in individual regions of Britain. This had important consequences for population migration which is reflected in the age structure of a region's work force. At the same time the rate of urban growth has accelerated resulting in expensive congestion within major city regions and conurbations.

New Towns have been a major instrument of government policy when faced with the dual problem of economic imbalance between regions and overcrowding in cities. Governments have attempted to avoid wasting physical and human resources by creating or stimulating new employment in areas of slow economic growth, and by restricting urban overcrowding with the designation and planning of New Towns. Linked to these plans in Britain is improvement in communications through the construction of motorways, and road bridges across such wide, deep estuaries as the Humber, Tay and Bristol Channels. Encouragement is also given to local authorities to build houses outside their territory to rehouse residents who were living in substandard dwellings or who were required to move because of road widening and other redevelopment schemes.

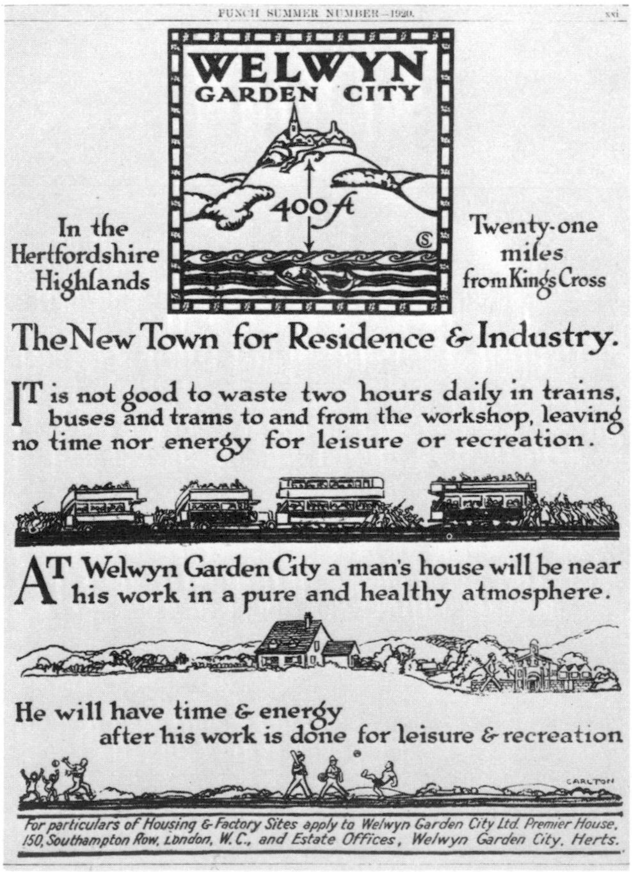

New Towns, powerful instruments of development, are not as new a concept as their name implies, for it was in the green fields of Hertfordshire that Ebenezer Howard created in 1903 the first garden city, Letchworth, which was followed in 1919 by his Welwyn Garden City. 'A man's house will be near his work in a pure and healthy atmosphere' said the Welwyn advertisement of 1920 (Photograph XI). Even before the twentieth century it was 'the healthy environment' which was foremost in the mind of Sir Titus Salt when, in 1852, he created the first English-planned 'village' at Saltaire, near Shipley in Yorkshire, to house his three thousand textile workers. George Cadbury, another enlightened factory owner, established in 1879 Bournville, Birmingham, for his chocolate and cocoa workers. Undoubtedly it was Howard's precepts that determined the basic structure of the twentieth-century New Towns. Letchworth was to be a self-contained settlement with ample open space and with gardens to each house. The residential areas would be separated from industrial and shopping zones and all would be surrounded by a belt of rural England. The interrelationship between factory provision, and house construction was the fundamental basis of this new concept which marks a tremendous advance in the planning of settlements.

Today even the most grudging visitor to Letchworth admires the breadth of the roads and avenues lined with almond, acacia, birch, poplar and maple trees. The variety of the housing types, the interestingly devised street patterns, the verdant parkland and the segregation of industry must have served as guidelines for the planners of near-by Stevenage.

Photograph XI *A 1920 advertisement for Welwyn Garden City.*

STEVENAGE, THE FIRST BRITISH POST-WAR NEW TOWN

Thirty miles north of London is situated the first of a series of towns designated under the New Towns Act of 1946. The revised master plan, Figure 59, shows the town divided into seven residential neighbourhoods, two industrial zones and a main shopping and administrative centre. This latter area, restricted to pedestrians, has numerous car parks located on its periphery. Here also is the core area of amenities including the swimming pool, dance hall, parish church, central library, railway and bus stations.

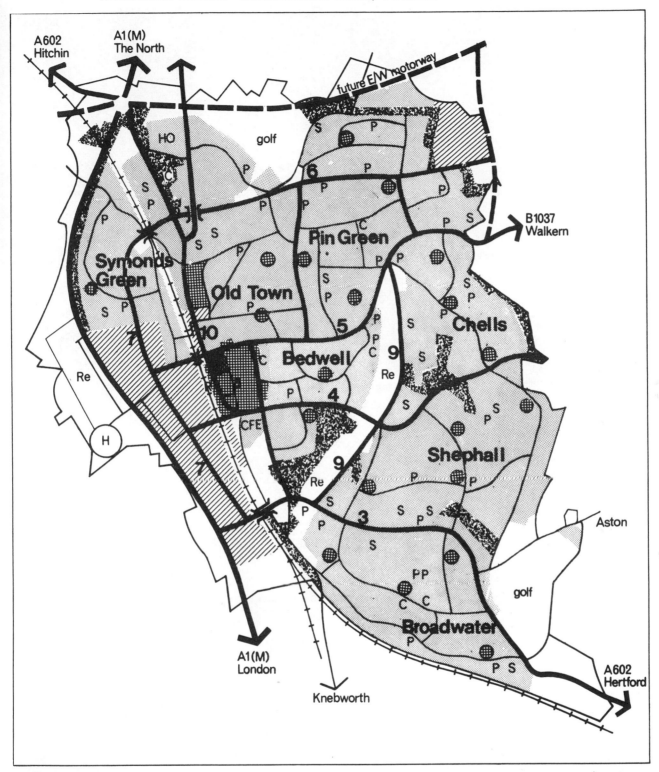

A602
Hitchin

A1(M)
The North

future E/W motorway

HO

golf

S

P

C

S

P

6

P

P

P

P

C

S

Pin Green

B1037
Walkern

Symonds
Green

S

P

C

Old Town

S

P

P

S

P

S

P

Chells

S

P

S

P

S

P

Re

5

P

P
P
C

9

Re

S

Bedwell

4

P

S

CFE

Shephall

P
S

P

P

9

Re

S
S

P

Aston

P

3

S

S

P
S

P

golf

H

Re

S

PP

C

C

Broadwater

A1(M)
London

P

Knebworth

P
S

A602
Hertford

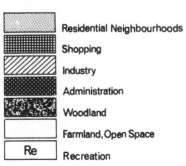

	Residential Neighbourhoods	B	Bus Station
	Shopping	H	Helicopter landing ground
	Industry	C	Community and Youth Uses
	Administration	HO	Hospital
	Woodland	P	Primary School
	Farmland, Open Space	S	Secondary School
Re	Recreation	CFE	College of Further Education
R	Railway Station		

Stevenage
Master Plan 1966

N

0   ¼   ½   ¾   1 mile

FIG. 59. Stevenage Master Plan, 1966.

Photograph XII *Air view of Stevenage New Town centre.*

EXERCISE 1:

   Study both the air photograph (Photograph XII) and the Town Centre plan of Stevenage (Figure 60), noting their differing orientations, and draw a simplified sketch map to show the varied urban land use of the area shown in Photograph XII. Use, in a slightly modified form, the same classification which was employed for your study of Clermont-Ferrand (Chapter 4, Exercise 8) and distinguish zones by a variety of shadings.

Main shopping area	*Parish Church precinct*
Administrative area	*Residential area*
Public services and institutions	*Industrial zone*
College zone	*Undifferentiated areas*
Open space and parks	

EXERCISE 2:

   Write a comparison between

(a) *the layout and*

(b) *the urban land use of the central areas of Clermont-Ferrand and Stevenage New Town. (Consult relevant plans and Photographs X and XII.)*

In each of the neighbourhoods are located primary schools, churches, public houses and local shopping parades. This network of units can be compared to the basic concept of sets as found in modern mathematics. Since a set is a collection of well-defined objects thought of as a whole, then a New Town neighbourhood is a set with a 'tree structure'; that is, no one set overlaps another. Critics of the neighbourhood concept have argued that a town's 'unit' structure should form a semi-lattice which occurs when

Photograph XIII *Stevenage New Town centre—pedestrian precinct shopping area.*

there are overlapping sets of elements. However, the mobile residents of New Towns may create their own overlapping sub-sets, such as the catchment areas of the youth club, college, sports club, or friends in the same office. The amenity advantage of having distinct neighbourhood areas outweighs this objection to theoretical separateness, for today 'the basic social unit is the separate transportable family not the old ramified family clan'.[1] The neighbourhood offers privacy without isolation, and the road network is used to link one unit area to another as the need arises— neighbourhoods are back in favour with planners!

The New Town main roads also link neighbourhoods to the town centre and to the industrial zones where most of the residents work. The results of a 1962 survey showed that only 2·8 per cent of Stevenage residents were daily commuters to the Greater London region. New Towns, such as

Stevenage, are, in this respect, largely self-contained, but as growth points they attract shoppers and commuters from near-by settlements.

Daily Journey to Work

A study of the daily journey to work undertaken by the population of a region or settlement indicates the degree of mobility and thus the economic independence of that element of the population. Therefore such a survey of journey to work patterns can be used to:

1. Define the region from which a town draws its labour.
2. Assess the degree of success enjoyed by satellite centres or New Towns in reducing the time spent on journeys to work.
3. Analyse the various modes of transport used, such as cars or suburban trains, and their effect on the urbanization of rural areas.

[1] N. Fairbrother, *New Lives, New Landscapes* (1972), p. 57.

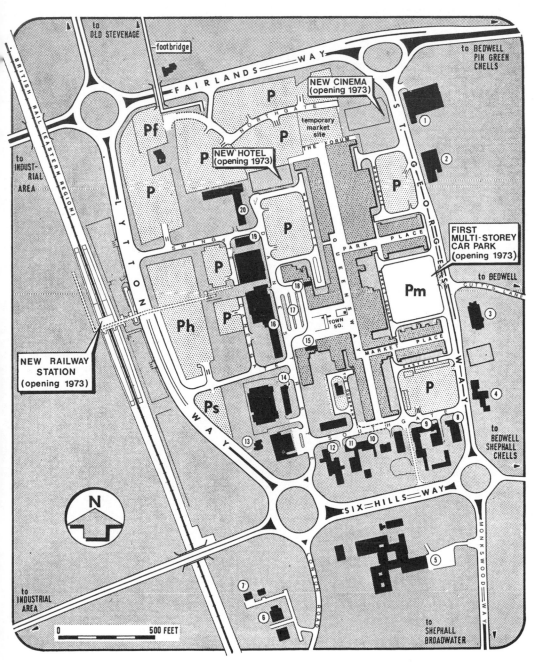

1. Swimming Pool
2. Bowes Lyon House
3. St. Georges Church
4. Fire & Ambulance Brigade
5. College of Further Education
6. Temporary Arts Centre
7. Women's Royal Voluntary Services
8. Southgate House (Stevenage U.D.C.)
9. Police
10. Health Centre
11. Central Library
12. Health Centre
13. Museum
14. Bus Enquiries
15. Post Office
16. Daneshill House (S.D.C.—Information)
17. Bus Station
18. Family Centre
19. Swingate House (S.D.C. Head Office/Housing)
20. Brickdale House

▨ Pedestrian Shopping Centre

P Car Park (Pf-Free Sun. to Thurs.)

Pm Multi-Storey Car Park/Market

Ps Short-Stay Car Park (Free - Max. Duration of 20 minutes)

Ph Heavy Vehicle & Car Park

Prepared in the Social Relations Department, Stevenage Development Corporation, by Nick Scott.   August 1972

FIG. 60. Stevenage Town Centre Plan, 1972–73.

4. Study the work opportunities for people of various ages, if the survey includes such data and it is classified into age groups.
5. Ascertain how age affects the distances to which people will travel to work.
6. Investigate movement into the Central Business District of a city which in turn would indicate the degree of inter-dependence of the various parts of a city region. (The Central Business District is the 'retail heart' or commercial core of a city.)

The collection of data for journey to work surveys is obtained either from the workplace and residence tables of census reports or preferably by 'field study' involving questionnaires.

EXERCISE 3:
(a) *Using bar graphs illustrate the following data:*

Daily Journey to Work at Glenrothes

RADIAL DISTANCES AND MODE OF TRANSPORT

MILES	CAR DRIVER	CAR PAS-SENGER	BUS	CYCLE	MOTOR CYCLE	WALK	TOTAL
0–1	74	23	27	15	7	82	228
1–2	38	37	32	8	3	5	123
2–3	11	4	28	0	2	1	46
3–4	9	4	13	0	0	0	26
4–5	12	10	19	1	4	0	46
5–6	20	16	24	0	1	0	61
6–7	6	3	7	0	0	0	16

Source: M. Barke, *Field Survey* (1967).

(b) *Collect and illustrate similar data for your own locality.*
(c) *State which type of bar graph would enable a comparison to be made between the two sets of data.*

Although the development of New Towns, especially in the Greater London area, has had the effect of reducing the length of the journey to work for thousands of their inhabitants, the Scottish New Towns have not yet been as successful in this respect. Nevertheless the incidence of commuting has been minimized. At Livingston in 1971, for example, 53 per cent of its employees lived within the town, 56 per cent within the Greater Livingston area and only 11 per cent commuted from outside the region, the majority of these travelling from near-by Edinburgh.

In general, New Towns may be regarded as trend-setters in terms of amenity provision and in traffic separation. In this respect, Cumbernauld New Town has achieved complete segregation of motor traffic and pedestrians, by a system of interconnecting footpaths linking schools, churches and local shops, and linking them to the town centre itself.

New Towns are also powerful trend-setters with the establishment of new industry being linked simultaneously to new house construction. The decentralization of industry has created better living conditions for families moving from old and crowded urban centres.

A study of the United Kingdom distribution of New Towns and of those with overspill arrangements, can be made by an examination of Figures 61 and 62, and their dramatic growth will be seen in the exercise below.

EXERCISE 4:
(a) *Illustrate, diagrammatically, the following statistics:*

Twelve Early New Towns

	POPULATION		
	1951	1961	1971
Aycliffe	594	12 101	20 190
Basildon	24 661	53 707	77 154
Bracknell	5 143	20 380	33 953
Corby	16 743	35 880	47 713
Crawley	10 707	54 065	67 709
Cwmbran	13 656	30 043	46 400
Harlow	5 825	53 496	77 684
Hatfield	9 256	20 504	25 211
Hemel Hempstead	21 976	54 816	69 966
Peterlee	298	13 792	21 836
Stevenage	7 311	42 422	66 975
Welwyn Garden City	18 804	34 944	40 369
TOTAL	134 974	426 150	595 160

Source: Census data.

(b)
  (i) *Suggest and describe an alternative cartographic method for illustrating the same data.*
  (ii) *Discuss the advantages and disadvantages of the two methods chosen.*

CHARACTERISTICS OF BRITISH NEW TOWNS

1. New Towns have attracted a large middle-class population. They possess a cross-section of most United Kingdom occupational and income groups but with a broader middle-class representation than is usually seen elsewhere.
2. These towns are largely, but not entirely, self-contained. Over 80 per cent of the employees of firms located in them live in the New Town itself, hence long-distance commuting to work is minimized but not prevented.
3. For the short daily journey to work it is possible for employees to cycle or walk using specially constructed paths.
4. New Towns are frequently divided into residential districts termed 'neighbourhoods' each of which is separated from another by open spaces but linked to each other, to the town centre and to the industrial areas by the main road system. Neighbourhoods have their own shopping, educational, cultural and sports facilities. (At Cumbernauld and Skelmersdale there is a concentration of residential areas around the town centre and this neighbourhood structure is less clearly defined.)
5. Industrial zones are physically distinct from residential neighbourhoods and may be located in the north-east of the urban area so that any noise or fumes are carried away by the prevailing westerly winds.
6. The density of houses, or persons per hectare, is medium or high, as shown in the table below.

Photograph XIV *Open area in the Pitteuchar precinct, Glenrothes New Town.*

Photograph XV *Aerial view of Kildrum housing area, Cumbernauld New Town. A variety of housing types can be seen, ranging from low-cost rented housing to executive and private developments. The Muirhead/Braehead road interchange is seen to the left centre and in the background is the Wardpark industrial area.*

FIG. 61. United Kingdom New Towns, 1973.

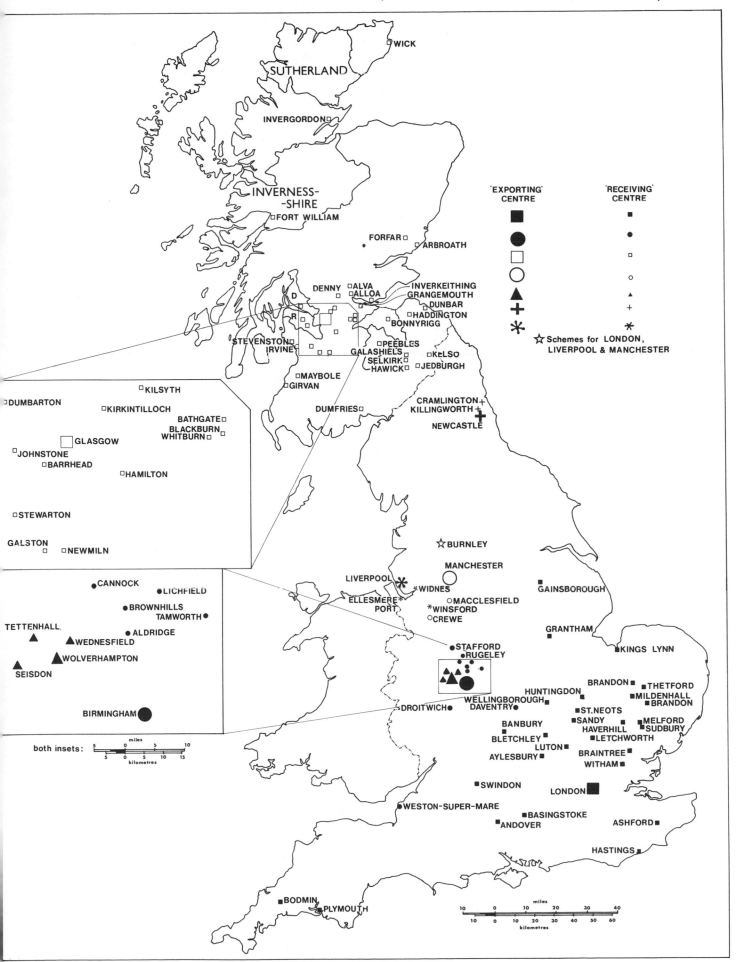

FIG. 62. United Kingdom overspill town development schemes, 1973.

Population Density Within Total Designated Area
of Early New Towns in England and Wales

NEW TOWNS DESIGNATED PRIOR TO 1962	DENSITY (1972) HECTARES PER 1000 PERSONS
Aycliffe	40·1
Basildon	38·6
Bracknell	35·1
Corby	35·8
Crawley	33·8
Cwmbran	30·4
Harlow	32·4
Hatfield	36·4
Hemel Hempstead	32·7
Peterlee	44·1
Skelmersdale	49·0
Stevenage	34·9
Welwyn Garden City	41·9
Average	37·3

These figures, however, do not give a true picture of the density of housing since there is much open space of amenity value within designated areas. Hence New Towns 'do not exemplify "low" densities of development for actual *residential* densities are frequently high.'[1]

7. The principal shops, offices and public buildings are in the planned Town Centre which, as at Stevenage and Crawley, may have limited or prohibited access for cars.

8. The construction of residences and the growth of new industry are closely associated. Employment is automatically available for new residents who initially come with firms establishing factories or offices which were formerly in congested urban areas such as in Central London, Glasgow or Birmingham. (The new factory or office units may be either purpose-built or standard units which can then be adapted by the individual firms to suit their purpose.)

9. Residences are built either for sale or to rent and are usually erected by the Development Corporation, although private builders are able to purchase land and construct dwellings. In the London ring of New Towns especially encouragement is given to residents to purchase their own homes.

10. New Towns, except for Aycliffe and Basildon, are constructed around existing urban centres which are then 'rejuvenated' and their existing road pattern revised and integrated into that of the new structure.

FRENCH DOMINOES AND NEW CITIES

When driving to Paris from the French Channel ports or when looking out of the railway carriage windows on approaching the city, groups of high-rise flats, 'grandes ensembles', dominate the skyline. Each group of these 'domino-style' apartments house about 50 000 people, and since these units are close to the railway stations they are within easy commuting distance of the centre of Paris.

[1] R. H. Best, *Land for New Towns* (1964), p. 49.

This typically French solution to modern housing problems is far different from the British answer as seen in their New and Expanding Town schemes.

The absence of industrial estates and office blocks and the lack of local recreational or amenity areas in the 'grandes ensembles' has now led French planners to partly adopt the New Town principle. In the master plan for Greater Paris, Figure 63, eight New Towns are proposed and the decayed and congested city areas are to be 'renewed': the New Towns will be situated on the plateaux surfaces and the incised meandering valleys will be developed as recreational amenity areas.

The New Town of Cergy-Pontoise is typical of these. It is within 25 kilometres (16 miles) of the centre of Paris and on a fast inter-city rail route. Its existing population was over 40 000 but it will, after development, house at least 130 000. The proposed maximum size of Basildon, Essex, will be 134 000, but it is more than likely that the French New Towns or Cities, will be much larger than their English counterparts and may each house from 300 000 to 1 000 000 people by the year 2000.

EXERCISE 5:
EITHER
(a) Draw simplified town plans for Stevenage and Pontoise. (Figures 59 and 64.)
(b) With the aid of your sketches, an atlas and this text, compare and contrast their sites, structures and functions.
OR
'The path to visual hell is frequently paved with sound economic intentions' (R. H. Best). To what extent is this statement a fair comment upon the appearance of our towns? Study the photographs in this chapter and also refer to any new urban developments known to you.

It will be noticed that the lack of industrial estates at Pontoise suggests that the prime aim of the French planners is housing. Le Vaudreuil, situated within a meandering reach of the River Seine between Rouen and Paris, will, however, have a zone for light manufacturing industries and thus this settlement is likely to be the first, British-style New Town in France.

INDUSTRIAL EXPANSION AND OVERSPILL AGREEMENTS

Where towns are attractive to industrialists and where diversification of industry is desirable, local councils have made agreements with their counterparts in the conurbations that the cost of moving factories and workers is to be subsidized by the 'exporting' area. Expanding Towns, such as those marked on Figure 62, are, together with the New Towns, normally the only locations outside the Development or Intermediate (Assisted) Areas for which the Government permits manufacturing industry to occupy new units with a floor space exceeding 3000 square feet.

Under overspill agreements the receiving or 'importing' town develops the industrial estates and builds the houses while the 'exporting' town nominates the tenants. Overspill schemes favourably affect the 'importing' town since improved central shopping areas result and internal communications may be improved. The ideas brought by the new residents are valuable and since the typical overspill family is one in which the parents are in their twenties or

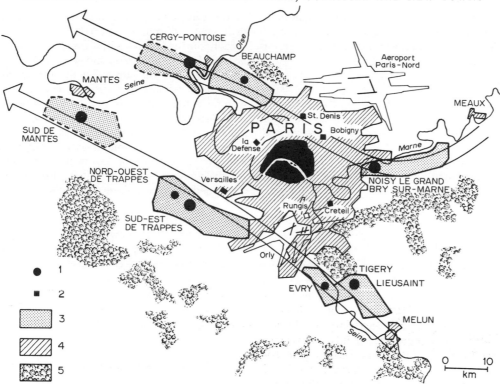

MASTER PLAN OF THE PARIS CITY REGION

1. New urban centres. 2. Important urban centres for renewal or development within existing agglomeration. 3. Sites for eight new towns. 4. Areas covered by the existing urban agglomeration. 5. Woodland
The arrows show direction of preferred development

FIG. 63. Master plan of the Paris City Region.

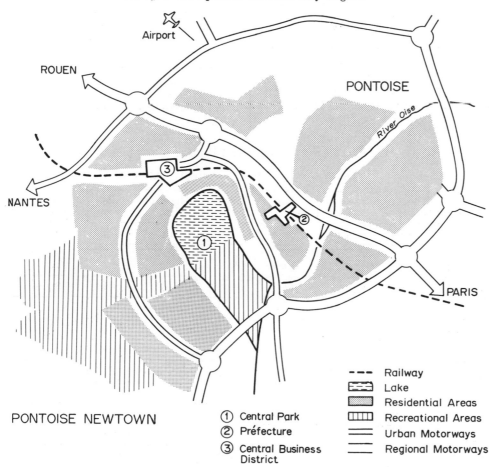

PONTOISE NEWTOWN

① Central Park
② Préfecture
③ Central Business District

- - - Railway
Lake
Residential Areas
Recreational Areas
Urban Motorways
Regional Motorways

FIG. 64. Pontoise New Town, Paris Basin.

thirties, with a young family, the existing community is given new vigour. The 'exporting' area benefits in that space is available for redevelopment and life is better for those remaining in less crowded conditions.

EXERCISE 6:
EITHER   Visit one of the overspill towns (see Figure 62) and describe your impressions of the development and changes resulting from the agreement made between 'exporting' and 'importing' towns.
OR   Read the case study that is to be found in the East Midland Geographer *(1969), vol. 4, no. 32, of King's Lynn, as an overspill town for Londoners.*

YOUNG MAN, DON'T GO SOUTH!

When a First Division football team is constantly winning matches through attractive play, the crowds are attracted to its ground. The team itself receives publicity, its members are well paid and morale is high. On the other hand if relegation to the Second Division is a certainty, apathy sets in, and the crowd dwindles in numbers. So it is with regions and the towns within them, for a 'first-class' region has successful firms, morale within the workforce is high, and the towns are attractive places in which to live. Stagnating old industrial regions may experience little growth, have few opportunities (hence high unemployment rates) and morale is low in obsolete factories and offices and thus population dwindles. Professor A. J. Brown (1972) brilliantly sums up this situation when he discusses the connection between this loss of population and regional decline. 'The selective nature of migration—the greater responsiveness of the younger, more enterprising, better educated and more skilled to the pull of opportunity elsewhere (and perhaps also to the push of poor opportunity at home)—may mean that, other things being equal, places with sizeable rates of net emigration are felt by many to be less interesting and stimulating to live in than those with substantial net immigration.'[1] The truth of this statement can be seen by an examination of the table below. This phenomenon of the drift south of population is not, however, confined to Britain, for the Germans in the Ruhr have moved to Munich in considerable numbers, and workers in Northern France have escaped to the sunny Mediterranean coastland towns for similar reasons to those given by British northerners who migrated to the Surrey hills or to glorious Devon.

In Britain this migration is clearly seen in the following table, and the resulting imbalance between regions must provide central governments with strong reasons for interfering in the location of new factories and offices.

Governments, whether British, French or German, are concerned with correcting the social problems created by declining northern regions and with modernizing old coal, steel and textile industrial areas so that national productivity will rise and exports flow into an expanding affluent European market of some 290 million people. The way governments try to achieve these aims is usually described as their 'regional policy'. The European Community also uses its Social Fund as an instrument of regional policy, although its chief function is to help areas where action taken by the community has created unemployment.

BRITISH REGIONAL POLICY

The need for a regional policy is created by the existence of one or more of the following problems:
1. Substantial numbers of people and firms are in the wrong place with reference to materials used and markets available. Firms no longer need coalfield locations.
2. There is a surplus of population in traditional industry. Much of modern industry needs skilled labour.
3. There is an excess of population in relation to the work that is available or vice versa. In other words there is a maladjustment between labour and capital, perhaps due to the effects of population migration or reorganization within individual industries.

[1] A. J. Brown. *The Framework of Regional Economics in the United Kingdom* (1972), p. 14.

Net migration between regions in Great Britain, 1961–66 in thousands

(excluding overseas emigration and immigration)

TO → ↓ FROM	North	Yorks and Humberside	North West	East Midlands	West Midlands	East Anglia	South East	South West	Wales	Scotland
North	—	+4·4	+2·7	+9·4	+11·2	+1·3	+18·3	+2·5	+1·4	−2·9
Yorks and Humberside	−4·4	—	+1·9	+9·3	+1·6	+3·0	+8·4	+4·9	+0·5	−8·5
North West	−2·7	−1·9	—	+3·6	−1·9	+2·7	+11·6	+8·3	+8·7	−10·7
East Midlands	−9·4	−9·3	−3·6	—	−5·3	+2·9	−8·9	+2·1	−0·2	−12·1
West Midlands	−11·2	−1·6	+1·9	+5·3	—	+0·8	+12·3	+17·8	−0·8	−8·5
East Anglia	−1·3	−3·0	−2·7	−2·9	−0·8	—	−37·7	+0·2	+0·4	−1·7
South East	−18·3	−8·4	−11·6	+8·9	−12·3	+37·7	—	+53·5	−4·9	−27·7
South West	−2·5	−4·9	−8·3	−2·1	−17·8	−0·2	−53·5	—	−6·5	−4·9
Wales	−1·4	−0·5	−8·7	+0·2	+0·8	−0·4	+4·9	+6·5	—	−1·6
Scotland	+2·9	+8·5	+10·7	+12·1	+8·5	+1·7	+27·7	+4·9	+1·6	—
NET TOTAL	−48·3	·16·7	−17·7	+43·8	−16·0	+49·5	−16·9	+100·7	+0·2	−78·6

Source: Sample Census, 1966.

4. Types of industry are unevenly distributed throughout a nation and certain firms are more dynamic than others creating uneven demands for labour. Capital will therefore be drawn into one region at the expense of another.

5. The growth of the tertiary sector (work in offices and in the service industries) has been greater than growth in primary (provision of raw materials), and secondary (manufacturing) industries.

If the problem is to revitalize an industrial and urbanized nation and to create a better economic balance between its regions, then it is reasonable to assume that the basis of any regional policy is to take work to the workers and also to encourage mobility. In the 1970s government aid given to United Kingdom manufacturing industries amounted to some £300 million per annum and, as seen in Figure 65, the extent of the areas now receiving help is considerable.

Cynics, realists, pessimists, call them what you will, may question the effectiveness of such a policy. With profound apologies to John Hall for mutilating his verse, it could be said in their defence that

Industry grows where the grass is greener
Where the sun shines bright and the rain is sweeter.
Managers know what their wives want most
Not slums, smog or old industrial cities
But shops, schools, friends and amenities.

Nevertheless, without cash and tax incentives the imbalance between regions would become worse rather than better. If unemployment is declining and industrial output increasing in the old coal and steel areas then regional policy is working but wonders aren't worked overnight. This influence of government directive can be demonstrated in the next exercise.

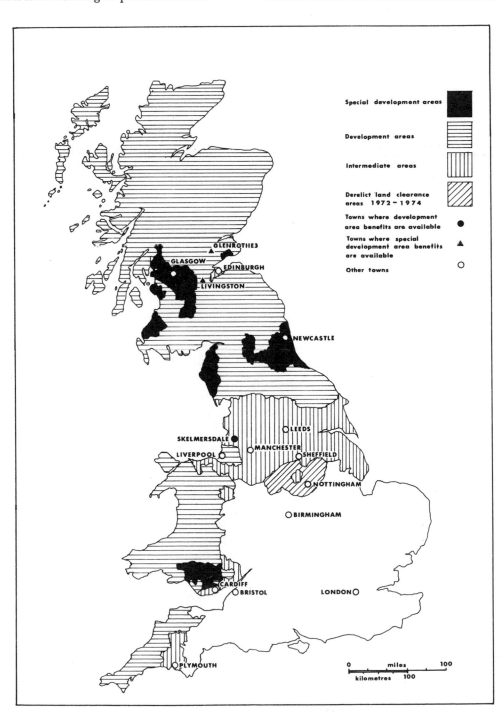

FIG. 65. Assisted areas, 1973.

EXERCISE 7:
Study the table below and
(a) *State for the period 1952–66 which three regions have been most successful in creating additional work in manufacturing.*
(b) *Why has the South East failed to increase the flow of this type of employment during the same period?*
(c) *On a copy of Figure 66, illustrate the data by means of superimposed located bar graphs.*

Movement of Manufacturing Jobs Into or Out of the Regions

NET FLOW OF NEW AND BRANCH FACTORIES
(IN THOUSANDS)

	1952–59	1960–66
North	+1·5	+2·5
Yorks and Humberside	+0·7	−0·8
North West	+2·3	+7·4
East Midlands	+0·7	−0·1
West Midlands	−1·5	−6·3
East Anglia	+0·2	+1·6
South East	−3·0	−14·3
South West	+1·0	+2·5
Wales	+0·5	+2·6
Scotland	+2·2	+6·0

Source: Board of Trade.

This data, however, gives only a partial view of the changes taking place in the regions.

Many aspects of regional economic differences are discussed in the Hunt Report and the table used to illustrate changes in floor space, over a three-year period, for factories, offices and shops is most revealing. (See table below.) The statistics for floor space growth in commercial offices does not provide evidence for the success of government direction of offices to development areas, although these areas were not as extensive before the Report as they can be seen to be now. (Figure 65.)

EXERCISE 8:
Construct located pie diagrams (divided circles) to illustrate the regional data concerning percentage changes in the floor space of offices, shops and industrial premises for the period 1964–67. (A method is explained on page 75 in Advanced Practical Geography *and a base map is available as Figure 66 in this chapter.)*

Percentage Change in Floor Space 1964–67 in England and Wales

REGION	COMMERCIAL OFFICES		SHOPS AND RESTAURANTS		INDUSTRIAL PREMISES	
	%	Ranking	%	Ranking	%	Ranking
Northern	+7·7	7	+3·6	8	+10·7	2
Yorkshire and Humberside	+8·5	6	+5·1	5	+2·6	8
North West	+7·6	8	+2·7	9	+1·8	9
East Midlands	+15·8	1	+5·5	3	+5·8	4
West Midlands	+10·1	5	+6·9	1	+4·3	7
East Anglia	+10·6	2	+5·2	4	+10·9	1
South East	+10·5	3	+4·5	6	+5·5	5
South West	+10·3	4	+5·8	2	+6·9	3
Wales	+7·2	9	+3·8	7	+5·3	6

Source: The Hunt Report.

EXERCISE 9:
(a) *Explain the following terms, with the aid of a named example for each:*
  (i) *'New Town'.*
  (ii) *Overspill town.*
  (iii) *Quasi-satellite town.*
  (iv) *Dormitory town.*
(b) *Which two English conurbations are not within the Assisted Areas? Why is this so?*
(c) *Explain what is meant by the term 'Regional Policy'.*

Assisted Areas 1972

THE NEW INVESTMENT INCENTIVES
TAXATION ALLOWANCES COUNTRYWIDE

All plant and machinery (new and second-hand—other than passenger cars), for use in both services and manufacturing	First-year allowance 100 per cent.
New industrial building and structures	Initial allowance 40 per cent. and writing down allowance 4 per cent.

REGIONAL DEVELOPMENT GRANTS IN ASSISTED AREAS

	Plant, machinery and mining works	Buildings
Special Development Areas ..	22 per cent.	22 per cent.
Development Areas	20 per cent.	20 per cent.
Intermediate Areas	—	20 per cent.
Derelict Land Clearance Areas (for two years only) 1972–74	—	20 per cent.

Source: Economic Progress Report (C.O.I.) Oct. 1972.

As suggested earlier and as pointed out in the Report it is too early 'to assemble meaningful information about the effects of our latest development area policies'.[1]

Whether it is too early or not, it is possible to attempt a small-scale examination of part of Tayside, Scotland, with a view to discovering how a traditional textile area has welcomed and attracted new industry, and how government policies have played a vital role in developing the region and changing its employment structure.

DUNDEE AND THE TAY ROAD BRIDGE

A new road bridge across the estuary of the Tay was opened in August 1966. At the first glance of the map (Figure 68) the bridge appears to be remote from the main motorway artery from Edinburgh to Perth, but once the economic importance of Dundee to its region is understood then clearly local rather than national considerations were paramount in deciding upon its construction. It should be said that Glenrothes New Town is a growth point and this is now along the new alignment Dundee to Kirkcaldy, via the Tay Bridge.

The volume of traffic which crosses the bridge is as yet modest, since it is mainly local commuter and shopping traffic from Fifeshire into Dundee, but as seen in Figure 69 it increases considerably at holiday times. Heavy commercial vehicles during the period 1966–68 constituted only 7 per cent. of the total bridge traffic even though the sphere of interest of Dundee includes all Fifeshire, which incidentally had a declining rural population. On a basis of

[1] The Hunt Report, p. 33.

FIG. 66. United Kingdom Planning Regions.

time and distance many small villages and towns in Fife are as near to the shopping centre of Dundee as are parts within the city boundary.

The bridge, coming into the heart of Dundee, has played a major role in the redevelopment of the city, for a former obsolete dock site was filled in to give access to it and to permit development of the inner ring road. (See Photographs XVI and XVII.)

Industry—Ancient and Modern

Rural cottage industry disappeared as an economic force during the Industrial Revolution but Dundee and similar industrial areas in Britain, depending heavily on textiles, have a legacy of eighteenth- and nineteenth-century mills, factories and terrace housing.

EXERCISE 10:

For the rectangular area enclosed by Northings 34 and 47 and Eastings 32 and 36 construct a sketch map of the Dighty Valley.

(a) *Insert the 46, 61, 76 and 91-metre contours.*

(b) *Draw in all streams, lakes and reservoirs.*

(c) *By means of appropriate symbols, mark the positions of works and mills.*

(d) *Mark, by symbols, the small-scale river gorges.*

(e) *Insert the location of greenhouses (glasshouses).*

(f) *Shade in the urban areas (new housing estates at Fintry and Downfield).*

The early industrial history of Dundee and its growth to city status is related first to the prosperity and expansion of the Scottish linen industry (1821–81) and then to the jute

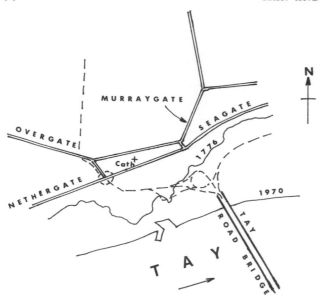

FIG. 67. City centre, Dundee: reclamation and redevelopment. The pecked line is the new inner ring-road. The extent of reclaimed land on the left bank of the Tay, originally used for docks, is now used for access to the road bridge and is shown by comparing the coastlines of 1776 and 1970.

industry (1881–1951). The Dighty Valley, with its water driven and steam-powered mills was the cradle of the linen industry, for the ponds, seen at Balmuir, are adjacent to a former linen bleach field—today greenhouses are built over it. The eighteenth-century flax-spinning Mill of Mains (Grid Square 4133) is now (1972) disused and the valley is being invaded by the bricks and mortar of new housing estates. There are numerous ruined mills, disused mill-races (lades) and ponds in the valley. The Claverhouse Jute Mill 'Works' (Grid Square 4033) also began its life in the eighteenth century and became the most important linen mill in the Dighty Valley.

Restructuring Industry in Dundee

In 1871 over half the population of Dundee worked in textiles, mainly jute, and the associated linoleum works, but the number of textile workers fell from 40 000 in 1901 to about 18 000 in 1971. Clearly Dundee faced several problems:

1. A serious decline in employment in textiles.
2. Modernization of the jute industry to meet competition from new wrapping materials and new types of floor coverings.
3. The need to diversify the industrial structure of the city and its region.
4. Modernization of housing.

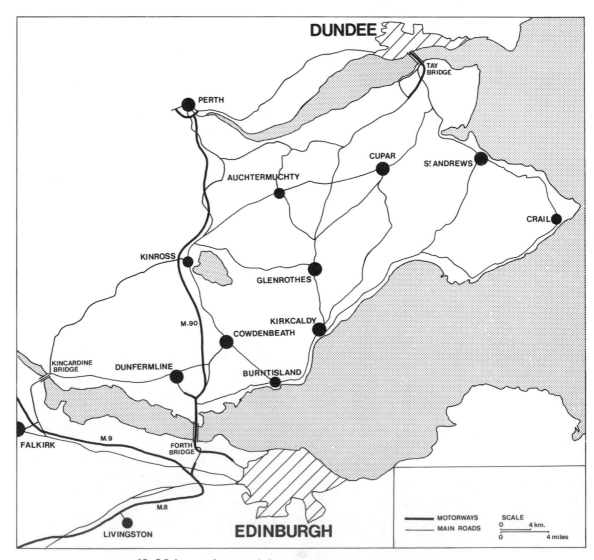

FIG. 68. Major road network between Dundee and Edinburgh, 1972.

Photograph XVI *The Tay bridges and the situation of Dundee, 1969.*

Photograph XVII *A view of the city of Dundee, looking NNE, July 1969. The university district is on the extreme left north-wards of the railway area but west of the inner ring road. The Dighty valley is visible in the north-east corner.*

FIG. 69. Tay Road Bridge traffic: weekly totals, 1971.

The jute industry invested in machinery to extrude and weave plastics, and new Board of Trade factory estates were established on the north perimeter of the city. One of these is clearly shown in grid square 3732 south of the outer ring road. These factory estates provide employment, and through the building of new factories since 1972 have rehoused existing industry in modern premises. The diversification of industry has been successful with some 4000 new jobs created and industry modernized and re-structured as seen in the table below.

Some Major New Developments in Dundee

FIRM	TYPE OF INDUSTRY	SQUARE FEET
National Cash Register	Computers	403 000
London Rubber Co.	Contraceptives	60 000
Caledonian Cold Storage Co. Ltd.	Food processing and freezing	54 500
Veeder Root Ltd.	Counting mechanisms	50 000
Yorkshire Imperial Metals Ltd.	Non-ferrous fittings	46 000
Ferranti Ltd.	Electronic valves	38 200
Timex Ltd.	Watch and camera parts	37 000
Filtrona Textile Products Ltd.	Plastic tapes, yarns and sheets	30 000
National Cash Register (Mfg) Co. Ltd.	Accounting machines	27 500
Dundee Tool and Gauge Co. Ltd.	Press tools, etc.	24 000

Source: D. C. Thomson & Co. Ltd, Dundee, 1969.

EXERCISE 11:
  Study the air photograph of Dundee (Photograph XVII) and fully describe what evidence can be deduced for urban renewal, urban expansion and improvement to communications.

EXERCISE 12:
  Using the table illustrating type of employment given below, describe and explain the industrial structure of Dundee, and compare it with that of the New Town of Glenrothes.

Employed Residents by Type of Employment

STANDARD INDUSTRIAL CLASSIFICATION	TOTAL NUMBER OF PERSONS DUNDEE 1968	GLENROTHES 1969
Agriculture, forestry, fishing	1 244	36
Mining and quarrying	0	424
Food, drink and tobacco	3 278	284
Chemicals and allied industries	497	30
Metal manufacture	258	44
Engineering and electrical goods	14 081	2 187
Shipbuilding and marine engineering	1 065	51
Vehicles	0	10
Metal goods (not elsewhere specified)	1 042	169
Textiles	18 098	95
Leather, leather goods and fur	140	0
Clothing and footwear	671	112
Bricks, pottery, glass and cement	286	36
Timber, furniture	1 022	59
Paper, printing and publishing	3 332	735
Other manufacturing industries	502	259
Construction	6 857	1 045
Gas, electricity and water	1 570	126
Transport and communication	4 444	432
Distributive trades	11 837	673
Insurance, banking and finance	1 762	105
Professional and scientific services	11 729	839
Miscellaneous services	6 094	409
Public administration and defence	2 694	643
Industry not stated	367	38
TOTAL	92 870	8 841

Sources: Department of Employment and Productivity and Planning Research, Glenrothes Development Corporation.

This broad survey, with specific examples of industrial and population changes, can only hint at some of the factors affecting future development in Britain and Europe. Surely one of the most influential factors for change in Scotland will be the availability of new sources of power in the form of North Sea natural gas and petroleum, as electrical power changed local industrial opportunities at an earlier date. Regional variations in the supply and quality of labour also play their part in development, but the powers exercised by governments are ever increasing and these work both positively by aiding independent firms to expand in development areas and negatively by prohibiting expansion elsewhere.

  Our survey has also provided a glimpse of Stevenage New Town, and it is suggested that New Towns are powerful growth centres. The changes on Tayside are small, but significant in that they illustrate the type of changes that are occurring in the landscape.

EXERCISE 13:
  Selecting areas of rural, urban, industrial and wild landscapes known to you, write an essay in explanation of the contention that 'landscape is the natural habitat manipulated by man' (Nan Fairbrother).

6. Real and Unreal Worlds

It is only by simplifying reality that science has made any great progress in dealing with the complex.   *D. M. Smith*

WE ALL live in a complex world and Europeans live as members of a Community (the E.E.C.) which is in itself a complex economic giant. We are also intellectually curious about life so it is not surprising that in our attempt to simplify reality down to its essentials we use maps, models and theories to twist space, shorten time-spans and explore relationships of cause and effect.

As long ago as 1886 it was recognized that physical phenomena was arranged in a series of components or in 'chains of necessary sequence'. 'In such a chain', wrote Gilbert, 'each link is the necessary consequent of that which preceeds it and the necessary antecedent of that which follows'.[1] How can we examine such components in the realm of human geography? One answer is to devise a theory which attempts to analyse a regional series of settlements to explore any relationship that exists between them in terms of population size and order of magnitude. If a sequence exists what does it signify?

Rank-Size Rule

Felix Auerbach first noticed a relationship between size and rank when he plotted the population sizes of a set of settlements on ordinary (linear) graph paper using decreasing order or rank on the x-axis and size on the y-axis. He joined a series of plotted points by a curved line and demonstrated the fact that the size of the settlements appeared to be inversely proportional to their rank.[2] In other words the size of the second settlement in such a list was half that of the largest or rank 1 settlement, the primate 'town'. Hence the size of the third settlement was but one-third of that of the first and so on. London, according to the 1971 census, had 7·4 million inhabitants and therefore the second city of Great Britain, Birmingham, could according to Auerbach's concept, be expected to have a population of 3·7 million. Thus a basic formula evolves which is

$$P_r = \frac{P_1}{R}$$

P_r = Population of a given town in a ranked list.

P_1 = Population of the primate town.

R = Rank-size of that given town in the set.

According to the same rule Derby, the twentieth town, would have an expected population of 343 thousand. The census records Birmingham and Derby as having 1 013 366 and 219 582 inhabitants respectively. The rank-size rule pattern for the United Kingdom, when plotted on log-log graph paper as shown in Figure 71, indicates a rapid fall-off in population number after London which reflects the dominance of London within the country. Hence the pattern is described as a primate one (see Figure 70).

Rank-size rule patterns prompt enquiry into whether urban boundaries are realistic or whether there are strong physical, economic or political causes for deviations from the ideal theoretical relationships between settlement size and rank. Theoretically all settlements on a uniform landscape have an equal chance of attracting settlers if complete freedom of action is possible. This presupposes that no special barriers or incentives are operating, but this may seem to be unrealistic. The concept must not be rejected because of this, for we all realize that order is achieved when constraints are placed upon our freedom—the classroom or lecture theatre would be in a state of anarchy if this were not so! Obviously a study of the nature and working of such constraints is of real value. In other words the rank-size rule is a model created to simplify the complex relationships existing between a sequence of settlements and their environment and it also enables a prediction to be made on the future pattern of settlement sizes for any given system of urban centres.

Method

1. Using population data arrange a set of settlements in descending order of magnitude, i.e. in rank size.
2. Plot a series of points using the x-axis of log-log (3 cycle × 3 cycle) graph paper for the magnitude or rank value and the y-axis for the population size.
3. Calculate the regression line as explained on page 69. Mark this best-fit line on the graph.

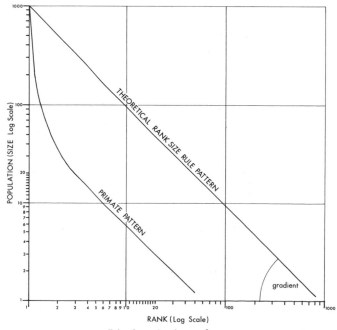

FIG. 70. Ideal rank-size rule patterns.

[1] G. K. Gilbert, 'The Inculcation of the Scientific Method by Example', *American Journal of Science* (1886), 3rd Series, Vol 31, p. 286.
[2] F. Auerbach, 'Das Gesetz der Bevolkerungskonzentration', *Petermann's Mitteilungen* (1913), Vol 59, pp. 74–6.

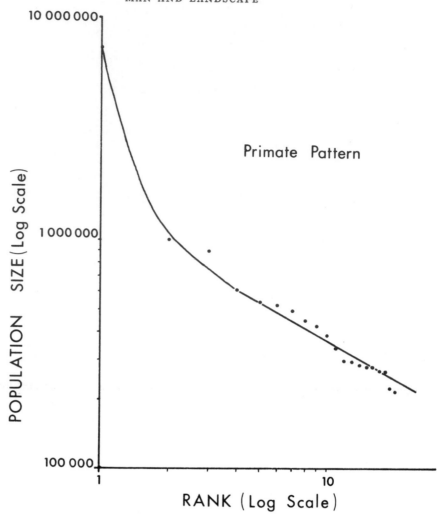

FIG. 71. Cities of the
United Kingdom
according to rank-
size 1971.

EXERCISE 1:

Plot the data given below relating to the population of the chief towns of the United Kingdom using (a) ordinary graph paper; (b) semi-log graph paper; (c) log-log (2 cycle × 2 cycle) graph paper. Examine your graphs and state the advantages and disadvantages of each of the methods employed.

RANK	URBAN CENTRE	POPULATION 1971
1	London	7 379 014
2	Birmingham	1 013 366
3	Glasgow	897 848
4	Liverpool	606 834
5	Manchester	541 468
6	Sheffield	519 703
7	Leeds	494 971
8	Edinburgh	448 895
9	Bristol	425 303
10	Belfast	383 600
11	Coventry	334 839
12	Nottingham	299 758
13	Bradford	293 756
14	Kingston-upon-Hull	285 472
15	Leicester	283 549
16	Cardiff	278 221
17	Wolverhampton	268 847
18	Plymouth	239 314
19	Newcastle-upon-Tyne	222 153
20	Derby	219 582

EXERCISE 2:

(a) *'Above a population of about one thousand the rank-size rule appears to fit normally, but for smaller sizes the distribution changes completely.' (Haggett.)[1] Test this hypothesis by drawing two similar log-log graphs to illustrate the relationship between rank and magnitude for (i) the cities of West Germany and (ii) the towns of Kent, England. (See Tables opposite.)*

(b) *Draw the regression lines of each data set (see pages 69–71).*

(c) *Measure and compare the angles of slope of the regression lines concerned and comment upon the significance of the gradient differences.*

[1] P. Haggett, *Geography: A Modern Synthesis* (1972), p. 285.

Chief Towns of Germany, 1969

RANK	TOWN	POPULATION
1	Berlin	2 134 256
2	Hamburg	1 817 122
3	München (Munich)	1 326 331
4	Köln (Cologne)	864 754
5	Essen	702 615
6	Düsseldorf	666 118
7	Frankfurt	673 091
8	Dortmund	649 006
9	Stuttgart	625 888
10	Bremen	607 184
11	Hannover (Hanover)	523 874
12	Nürnberg	477 108
13	Duisburg	458 916
14	Wuppertal	415 345
15	Bochum	356 447
16	Gelsenkirchen	352 152
17	Mannheim	330 077
18	Bonn	299 376
19	Kiel	267 890
20	Wiesbaden	260 828

Source: Statistisches Jahrbuch, 1971.

Chief Towns of Kent, 1971

RANK	TOWN	POPULATION
1	Gillingham	86 862
2	Maidstone	70 987
3	Chatham	57 153
4	Rochester	55 519
5	Gravesend	54 106
6	Margate	50 347
7	Dartford	45 705
8	Royal Tunbridge Wells	44 612
9	Folkestone	43 801
10	Ramsgate	39 561
11	Ashford	35 615
12	Dover	34 395
13	Canterbury	33 176
14	Tonbridge	31 016
15	Sittingbourne	30 913
16	Whitstable	25 449
17	Deal	25 432
18	Herne Bay	25 198
19	Broadstairs	20 048
20	Sevenoaks	18 247

Source: Census 1971, Kent.

Christaller's Central Place Theory, as outlined in Chapter 2, implies that larger towns offer more services than smaller centres; hence settlements of differing population size are likely to attract different numbers of shoppers or visitors. The larger of any two sizeable neighbouring towns could offer more and more varied facilities and would have a larger 'pull' or force of attraction upon people living in the intermediate areas. This idea is developed in the gravity model.

GRAVITY MODEL

This concept is based on Newton's law of universal gravitation which states that the force of attraction between any two bodies is directly proportional to the product of their masses and inversely proportional to the square of their distances apart, i.e. the force of attraction

$$F = \frac{m_1 \times m_2}{d^2}.$$

In Geography this law can be used to demonstrate how two places interact with one another. Journeys made by people to major towns are related to the amenities or opportunities that are available in them. Other aspects influencing people are the time taken on the journey and the cost of travel.

In the mid-Trent valley are two competing centres, Derby and Nottingham, with 1971 populations of 219 582 and 300 630 respectively. Between them is Long Eaton with its population of 33 714. In terms of straight-line distances the two major centres are 15·5 miles (25 kilometres) apart with Long Eaton 6·5 miles (10 km from Nottingham) and 9 (14·5 km) from Derby. The force of attraction (F) exerted between either of these two centres on Long Eaton varies as the product of the populations or masses (m) and inversely as the square of the distance between them (d²). This latter variable need not be considered as an actual distance but may be taken as the time or cost involved when travelling from the intermediate town to either of the major attracting centres. As stated earlier, in physics the formula

$$F = \frac{m_1 \times m_2}{d^2}$$

expresses this relationship but in Geography the same concept can be represented by this modified equation:

$$M_{ij} = \frac{P_i P_j}{d_{ij}^2}$$

in which i and j are the two settlements, M is the force of attraction, P is the population (mass), and d is the distance between i and j.

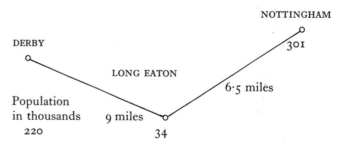

To calculate the theoretical attractive force of Derby (i) upon Long Eaton (j)

$$M_{ij} = \frac{220 \times 34}{9^2}$$
$$= \frac{7480}{81}$$
$$= 92 \cdot 35$$

The theoretical attractive force of Nottingham (i) upon Long Eaton (j) is

$$M_{ij} = \frac{301 \times 34}{6 \cdot 5^2}$$

$$= \frac{10\ 234}{42 \cdot 25}$$

$$= 242 \cdot 18$$

Thus the relative attraction of Nottingham and Derby in drawing to themselves the population of Long Eaton is in the ratio of 242·18 to 92·35 which is approximately 3 to 1 (the actual value is 2·6). In interpreting this result we would suggest that for every three persons visiting Nottingham from Long Eaton only one could be expected to visit Derby. Is this so in reality? A survey of the number of visits made during the period of the Christmas holidays by 150 pupils living in Long Eaton showed that 284 were made to Nottingham but only 63 to Derby—a ratio of 1 to 4·5. This answer prompts an enquiry into why there is a more strongly marked preference for Nottingham than that to be expected from the theoretical consideration. Are there cheaper fares, a more efficient bus service, a better panto-mime, more attractive illuminations or better shopping facilities and other opportunities in Nottingham? The majority of the pupils did in fact state that they preferred the shops and entertainments in Nottingham to those in Derby. Another popular reason given referred to cheaper travel to the nearer city of Nottingham, but the 'pull' of football (Derby County) was revealed as the main factor which stimulated visits to Derby! If this major reason of 'cheaper bus fares' be isolated for further consideration then the attractive force of Nottingham becomes 68·75 and that for Derby 22·41 and the ratio of the greater attractiveness of Nottingham to Derby becomes more than 3 to 1. When considering the ratio of 4·5 found in favour of Nottingham it is suggested that the opportunities afforded by Nottingham do exert a major influence upon young people. Other factors can be isolated and similarly investi-gated and discrepancies explored such as that given above (4·5:1 for stated reasons and 3:1 for measurable travel cost reason).

EXERCISE 3:

Collect travel data from your own class or student group and use it to construct a gravity model which will show, for your own locality, the relative attraction of two major towns in drawing the population of an intermediate town or village.

ISOTROPIC SURFACES

We have already seen an example of the simplifications that Geographers make in looking at the real world when we examined Christaller's Central Place Theory. This type of view is common in Economic Geography and is met once again in theories concerning industrial and farming activities. Such a view of the world allows us to make simplifying assumptions such as suggesting that the cost of certain

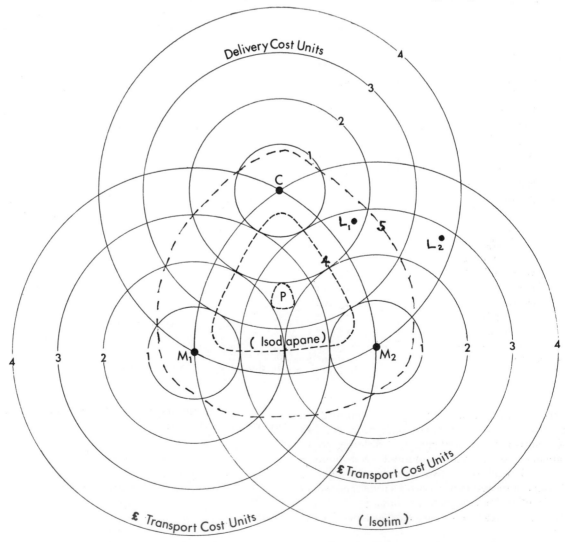

FIG. 72. Weber's analysis leading to the least-cost location for a manufacturing firm.

resources is everywhere the same. Alfred Weber and Johann Heinrich von Thünen were two German economists who used this type of theory. They were aware that they were simplifying reality and that variations in costs occur in real life, but such statements were necessary to allow them to develop idealized patterns of industrial and agricultural land use. Geographers thus are not saying that the isotropic or uniform surface is the real world any more than the physicists are saying that the laboratory bench truly represents the physical world.

An example of the value of the concept of a uniform surface can be seen in the work of Weber who studied the location of manufacturing industry placing strong emphasis on the cost of supplying raw materials.

WEBER'S INDUSTRIAL LOCATION THEORY

Weber's belief was that industrialists primarily wish to find a location for their manufacturing plant at which total costs of assembling raw materials and transporting products to consumers would be at a minimum.

Weber, as locational theorists are apt to do, commenced his enquiry by making assumptions. His include:

1. The entire area or land surface has uniform physical, cultural, technological, political and economic conditions.
2. Fuels and industrial raw materials are only found in specific localities—such materials being described as 'sporadic'.
3. Transport costs increase in direct proportion to distance; hence transport costs are equal to weight multiplied by distance (i.e. ton-miles or tonne-kilometres).
4. Each firm sells only to one market (i.e. one consumer) but demand at that market is unlimited.
5. Labour occurs in unlimited amounts at predetermined fixed prices in certain specific localities.

Under these assumed conditions transport costs are the primary determinant of factory location; hence the first task is to find the least-transport-cost location for a factory or manufacturing plant. We can find this position in two ways; firstly, as shown in Figure 72; by creating a geometrical cost-surface diagram on which lines are drawn to join places with equal transport costs per unit weight, or secondly by using a mechanical model which employs the concept of resolution of forces and is represented by the 'weight triangle', Figure 73.

On the cost-surface diagram lines of equal transport costs (isotims), radiate out from specified raw material centres (M_1 and M_2 on Figure 73) and from the point of consumption (C). By a close study of such a diagram the position of the minimum total-transport-cost-location for the manufacturing plant (P) can be discovered, as explained below. On the cost-surface isotims have been drawn but a further set of lines, isodapanes, can be constructed to join places which show equal *total* transport costs, which are the sums of the values of the isotims at particular points. In Figure 72 the plant (P) is located where the total values of the isotims is four since elsewhere any total value would be greater than that and this obviously is the most advantageous position for the plant. This concept is also developed in the 'weight triangle' (Figure 73), in which each corner is thought to exert a pull on the least-cost location (P) as suggested by the arrows marked on this diagram. The manufacture of one unit of production would require x tons of raw material M_1 and y tons of raw material M_2

which are to be transported to the market at C. As stated earlier the problem is again where to locate P which theoretically is free to move to come to rest finally at the position of compromise between the forces acting upon it of which C is the resultant of forces a and b.

How did Weber introduce modifying factors into his analysis? Assume, for example, that if cheaper labour could be found at a specified locality would a firm be attracted to that location? The least-cost surface diagram can be used to provide an answer, as shown in Figure 72, in which L_1 is the proposed location of the plant which is sited in response to the pull of cheap labour. If this plant moved to this resource at L_1 it would save £5 per unit of production. This £5 isodapane represents the same value as the savings in labour cost. Outside this isodapane at, say, L_2 costs would rise and therefore there would be no saving in diverting the factory from the least-transport cost location (P). In this instance the £5 isodapane is termed the 'critical isodapane'—so called because it plays a vital part in the decision-maker's choice of location.

A second modification was the effect of agglomeration upon site location but in an introductory survey such as this the above example is sufficient to show the type of approach that Weber adopted when analysing the location of industry.

From highly simplified location models of individual manufacturers we can now turn to the study of regional patterns on uniform surfaces, the best known example of which is the theoretical land-use rings of von Thünen.

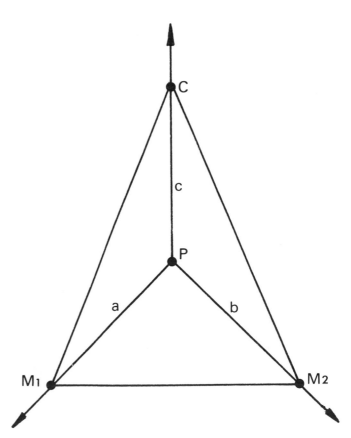

C = Point of Consumption (Market)

M_1
M_2 } are deposits of necessary materials

FIG. 73. Weberian weight-triangle.

VON THÜNEN'S LAND-USE RINGS

This theory starts with the following five assumptions:

1. The farming is dominated by a single town which is situated on a broad featureless plain of equal fertility and is isolated from the rest of the world.
2. All produce (outputs) from the farms on this plain are sold at this single market town and all farm requirements (inputs) are purchased there.
3. The farmers themselves cart their own produce to market along lanes of equal quality.
4. Only one form of transport is available to all the farmers.
5. The aim of the farming is to obtain the maximum profits.

On the basis of these assumptions von Thünen considered how farmers would compete for equally fertile plots of land. Since there was no advantage to be gained from differences in fertility then a farmer's preference for one piece of land as opposed to another would be based on proximity to the market, as transport costs are proportional to the distance travelled. Land nearest the town would be in greatest demand and would be more expensive than that further away. For farming to be profitable revenue must exceed expenditure so that high value crops would be grown on land nearest the market. Obviously different forms of agriculture incur different transport costs. Since net profit is gross profit minus the cost of transport then farmers have every incentive to choose the crop which gives them maximum return per hectare. As returns would vary with distance there comes a point where it is uneconomic to market one type of product and a different farming system would then be employed. The cost of a location therefore becomes *the* major factor in deciding land use. This cost may be termed *Locational Rent* and can be found by using the formula

$$L = Y(P - C) - YD(F)$$

where L = Locational Rent in £ per km²
Y = Crop yield in tons/km²
P = Market price of crop in £ per ton
C = Production cost of the crop in £ per ton
D = Distance to market in km
F = Transport rate in £ per ton per km.

The manner in which Locational Rent operates can best be seen by using a hypothetical example. Suppose only one crop is grown, for example, vegetables. The market price for production from one hectare of land is £75. If there were no transport costs products from every hectare throughout the area would earn £75. Suppose transport costs are £5 per kilometre then vegetables would only be grown on land within 15 kilometres from the market (i.e. 15 × £5 = £75). At greater distances than this the farmer could earn nothing by vegetable production. If there were other agricultural activities that could be adopted he would change to an alternative crop. Figure 74 illustrates the situation when there is a competing land use. The lines drawn on this graph have different slope angles which reflect the different cost-characteristics of these crops. The position P marked on this figure is the point where the two lines intersect. This point is called 'the margin'—that is the limit of profitability for a particular crop. As Figure 74 shows it is

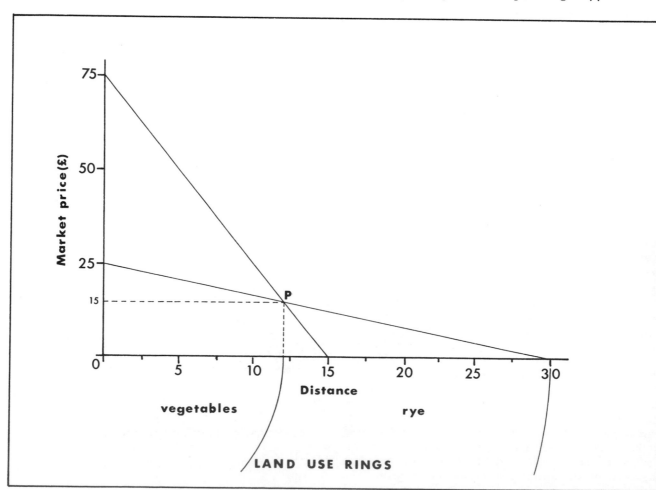

FIG. 74. The concept of locational rent as a basis for determining land-use.

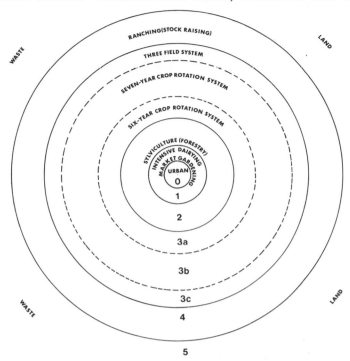

FIG. 75. Von Thünen's land-use rings.

more profitable to grow rye than vegetables at a distance of approximately 12 kilometres from the market. It follows that nearer the market than this vegetables are the most profitable crop. A study of this diagram illustrates the method which von Thünen used to develop rings of agricultural land use around a town. Our example has shown how it can be done when considering two crops but with a wider range of agricultural activities a more complete system of rings can be established as seen in Figure 75. The concept can also be examined by a study of the more detailed information given in the table below.

von Thünen's land-use 'rings' (1826)

ZONE	AREA, PER CENT, OF STATE AREA	RELATIVE DISTANCE FROM CENTRAL CITY IN KM	LAND-USE TYPE	MAJOR MARKETED PRODUCT	FARMING SYSTEM
0	Less than 0·1	Less than 0·1	Urban–industrial	Manu-factured goods	—
1	1	0·1–0·6	Intensive agriculture	Milk; vegetables	Intensive dairying and market gardening; heavy manuring; no fallow
2	3	0·6–3·5	Forest (Sylvi-culture)	Firewood; timber	Forestry
3a	3	3·4–4·6	Extensive agriculture	Rye; potatoes	Six-year crop rotation: rye (2), potatoes (1), clover (1), barley (1), vetch (1), no fallow; cattle stall-fed in winter
3b	30	4·7–34	Extensive agriculture	Rye	Seven-year crop rotation system: pasture (3), rye (1), barley (1), oats (1), fallow (1)
3c	25	34–44	Extensive agriculture	Rye; animal products	Three-field arable system: rye, etc. (1), pasture (1), fallow (1)
4	38	45–100	Ranching	Animal products	Mainly stock-raising, some rye for use on farm
5	—	Beyond 100	Waste	None	None

(After Haggett)

EXERCISE 4:

Using the concepts of von Thünen and the data given below construct a diagram to show a pattern of concentric rings of land use.

DISTANCE IN KILOMETRES FROM MARKET	TRANSPORT COSTS OF PRODUCTS IN £ PER HECTARE		
	MARKET GARDENING	FORESTRY	RANCHING
10	5	10	4
20	10	20	8
30	15	30	12
40	20	40	16
50	25	50	20
60	30	60	24
70	35	70	28
80	40	80	32
Production costs per hectare	25	10	5
Market price per hectare	125	100	75

We conclude this brief excursion into the theoretical world by remembering Chorley's analogy. 'Theories,' he suggests, 'are like torches of varying size and intensity shining in different directions and each illuminating some novel aspect or relationship of reality.'[1] We have briefly examined four different theories. The first, Rank-size rule, threw light upon the nature of a set of urban centres and stimulated enquiry into those forces which disturb an orderly succession. The second theory in the form of a gravity model examined the relative force of attraction exerted by important neighbouring towns. The third and fourth theories rest upon concepts which resemble those used in the natural or physical sciences and do indeed illuminate novel aspects of the real world.

---

[1] R. J. Chorley, 'Geography and Analogue Theory', *Annals of the Association of American Geographers* (1964), Vol 54, p. 137.

Epilogue

This study has attempted to give an outline of selected aspects of quantitative and theoretical geography and to afford glimpses of common elements that have helped shape nations and individual states. Roman law and order, the civilizing power of Christianity, and the economic drive of the Germanic peoples, has been felt both on the mainland of Europe and on the off-shore islands.

Into the melting-pots of European nations went Celtic, Latin and Germanic raw materials, but in the fused units are identifiable national characteristics which can still be detected. Anglo-Saxon, Welsh, Irish and Scottish temperaments are united but still recognizable within the British people. With the decline of Latin as a universal European tongue, so national languages became entrenched, and barriers to exchange of ideas were erected. Our brief studies of place-names and of the Swiss peoples suggest that language need not be an insurmountable barrier to unity. Studying national characteristics through national literature, even if translated, leads to an appreciation of the contribution that individual states have made to the cultural and economic development of Europe.

Insularity must now be an anachronism on 'spaceship earth' for we now see the need to manage and conserve resources. Geographers, as students of regional policy, will become graduates of policy-making, and hob-nob with the politicians who are concerned with the management of man and the environment, whether it be urban or rural.

Population studies have formed a substantial part of this book, for we Europeans have a duty not only *not* to misuse the earth's resources, but also *not* to reproduce ourselves in such numbers that our environment cannot sustain us. Government control of economic growth will therefore become a key used for unlocking the door of European understanding. Once we Europeans really understand each other then we may attempt to better understand non-Europeans.

In 1973 Britain joined the European Economic Community (Common Market) and this organization hopes to achieve an economic and monetary union. The planned co-ordination of industrial policies within this Community should not only improve working conditions for all, but should also remove trade barriers. Poorer regions will be helped through a common fund. The last chapter of this textbook briefly reviews some of the problems connected with the revitalization of old industrial areas and correcting imbalance within regions and within nations.

Geographers know that seas and rivers may unite as well as divide and that mountain ranges may challenge man or help create nationalism.

The year 1973 should be a landmark in the story of the geography of the British peoples, for the lively present is but the start of the future.

Reference Appendix

USEFUL TYPES OF GRAPH PAPERS

When the relationship of two variables is to be plotted, three basic types of graph paper are available for this purpose: linear, semi-log (log-linear) or log-log. The one selected for any relationship depends upon the way the two variables (for easy reference we will call them x and y) either increase or decrease.

Where either or both x and y increase (decrease) as arithmetic series, then a graph paper with either one or both scales in linear form should be selected. An arithmetic series is of the form $y = ax + b$ where a and b are constants. For example:

$$\text{if } y = 2x + 1$$
when $x = 0$ 1   2   3   4 – – – –
then $y = 1$ 3   5   7   9 – – – –

$$\text{and if } y = \tfrac{1}{2}x + 1$$
when $x = 0$ 1   2   3   4 – – – –
then $y = 1$ $1\frac{1}{2}$ 2 $2\frac{1}{2}$ 3 – – – –

Here the series increase or decrease by a constant amount.

However, where either or both x and y increase or decrease as a power index, then a log-scale graph paper can be useful. A power series (geometric progression) is one such as a^x, where a is a constant and in numerical evaluation would be:

$$\text{for } y = 2^x$$
if $x = 0$ 1   2   3   4   5 – – – –
then $y = 1$ 2   4   8   16   32 – – –

$$\text{and for } y = 3^x$$
if $x = 0$ 1   2   3   4   5 – – – –
then $y = 1$ 3   9   27   81   243 – – –

Another type of power series is that of the polynomial, whose form is $y = x^n$ where n is a constant. In this case the evaluation is:

$$\text{for } y = x^2$$
if $x = 1$ 2   3   4 – – – –
then $y = 1$ 4   9   16 – – –

$$\text{and for } y = x^3$$
if $x = 1$ 2   3   4 – – – –
then $y = 1$ 8   27   64 – – –

In this latter type of series if log y is plotted against log x then a straight-line graph results, the gradient of which is the index of the series. In these types of series the numbers increase more rapidly than in an arithmetic series.

Thus where *both x and y vary as arithmetic progressions, linear* graph paper should be used. Where x increases (decreases) in *arithmetic progression*, but y varies as a *geometric* progression or as a *polynomial* series, then *semi-log* paper should be used. If, however, *both* vary as *geometric* or *polynomial* series then log-log graph paper should be selected.

In plotting geometric or polynomial series on linear graph paper, the resultant graph will be of a curved form, and where rates of change are required, as indicated by the slope of the graph, then this is not possible to see at a glance nor is it easy to calculate. But the use of the logs of either or both the x and y variables will transform the graph into one of linear form. When the rate of increase (decrease) is constant, then the graph is a straight line. The steeper the angle of the straight line and the faster the rate of change.

Another advantage of a log-scale is that very widely differing values in the same data can be plotted on the same graph, for the log-scale has the effect of compressing the range of values into a smaller space.

Logs of numbers can be looked up in log tables and plotted on linear graph paper, but this is a tedious method. Hence specially printed log-graph paper is obtainable. On to this the actual numerical values can be plotted directly on the log scale. But it must be remembered that there is no log of zero and thus all log scales begin at the number one.

Each series of 10 lines on log-scale graph paper become more compressed together. These are termed one cycle and semi-log and log-log papers are available in single or multiple cycles.

Every cycle represents a power index of 10. Thus the first cycle may represent the values of y from 1 to 10, i.e. 10^0 to 10^1. The second cycle will represent the values between 10^1 and 10^2 and the individual lines will represent values 10, 20, 30 – – – 90. The third cycle will represent the values between 10^2 and 10^3 and the individual lines will have the values 100, 200, 300 – – – 1000. Each cycle represents one power higher of 10. However, the starting-point of the graph does not have to be at 10^0. If the range of values of x or y is, for example, between 1000 and 1 000 000 then the first cycle could be the 10^3 to 10^4 values, i.e. 1000, 2000, 3000 – – – – 9000 and the third cycle would represent the values 10^5 to 10^6, i.e. 100 000, 200 000, 300 000 – – – – 900 000 and 1 000 000.

PLACE-NAME ELEMENTS IN FRANCE
(Based on E. Nègre. *Les noms de lieux en France*.)

Pre-Celtic

-ara; -ar; -aran	valley settlement (Basque names)
-basa	village (Basque)
-cade	settlement by juniper trees
-car	stony site
-chaume; -calm	settlement on high, bare plateau
-chier; -crep	rocky site
-dur; -edouris	waterfall site
-gabe	torrent
-mal	scarp
-mendi	mountain settlement (Basque)
-narso	water meadow
-roc; -roche	rock; settlement on fortified height
-rone; -roné; -rot; -rod; -ro	settlement with abundant water
-sor; -sorga	source or spring

Celtic (pre-First century A.D.)

-arduenna	high, forested place
-bar; -briga	hill-top settlement
-briva	bridge-point settlement
-cambo	settlement on alluvial plain within a meander bend of the river
-condate; -comboro	confluence settlement
-dubron -rian; -renos	settlement by water
-devos; -deva	a divine place
-duro	fortified place
-lanno	on a plain
-magos	market settlement
-nanto	settlement in river valley
-nem	a sacred place
-randa	limit (frontier) of settlement
-rate	fortress
-rito	ford
-trebo	village (cf. Cornish -tre)
-uxellos	settlement on a mound
-vertra	a small fort

Latin or Roman (First to Fifth Century A.D.)

-armentaria	stable for cattle
-castra; -castras	camp
-castellum	fortified village
-etum	settlement with mineral springs
-ey; -oy; -ay	place associated with farming
-iacum	settlement
-lucus	sacred wood
-vallicula	small settlement in valley
-vicus; -vicinia	hamlet, village
-vicinium	hamlet, village
-villa	farm or country house

Germanic (Fifth to Twelfth Century A.D.)

-bach; -beke	stream
-berg; -berch	mountain
-burg	fortified outpost
-buron	mountain hut
-brunnen; -born	settlement at a spring
-dorf	village
-heim; -heem	village
-hof; -hove	farm
-ing; -ingen; -inga	homestead

Breton names (Fifth to Ninth Century A.D.)

-bren	hill (cf. Cornish -ben)
-kemper	confluence site
-ker	fortified house or hamlet
-penn	settlement on a summit (cf. Cornish -pen)
-tref	hamlet without a church

Saxon (Sixth to Tenth Century A.D.)

-bec	brookside settlement
-bu	farm
-fleur (flod)	tidal settlement
-ham	meadow
-ho	settlement on a spur
-heim	house or homestead
-ig	island settlement
-mere	sea coast settlement
-tun	farmstead

Scandinavian (Normans speaking Danish Ninth to Twelfth Century A.D.)

-haugr	homestead on a mound
-holmr	settlement on isolated hill
-lundr	small wood
-skali	hut or hamlet
-topt	homestead
-ville	town

TRANSLATION OF KEY SYMBOLS ON THE TOPOGRAPHICAL MAP OF GERMANY

GERMAN	ENGLISH
Boundaries	
Staatsgrenze	State boundary
Landesgrenze	'Länder' (County) boundary
Regierungsbezirksgrenze	Government district boundary
Stradt-und LandKreisgrenze	Town and Urban district boundary
Truppenübungsplatzgrenze	Military boundary
Naturschutzgebietsgrenze	National Park boundary
Communications	
Vollspurige Bahn mit Bahnhof, mehrgleisig	Multiple track railway with station
Vollspurige Bahn mit Haltepunkt, eingleisig	Single line railway with halt
Anschlussgleis	Branch line
Schmalspurige Bahn	Narrow-gauge railway
Zahnradbahn	Rack and pinnion railway
Strassen-und Wirtschaftsbahn	Tramway or mineral line
Seil-und Schwebebahn	Cable railway
Autobahn	Motorway
Bundesstrasse	Main roads
Strasse 1A mit Bäumreihen	A road with rows of trees
Strasse 1B mit Kilometerstein	B road with kilometre stone
Unterhalteren Fahrweg 11A	Secondary road
Feld-und Waldweg	Unpaved road or track
Fussweg	Footpath
Waldschneise	Forest track
Topographical features	
Kirche mit 2 Turmen	Church with 2 towers
Kirche mit 1 Turm	Church with 1 tower
Kapelle	Chapel
Feldkreuz, Bildstock	Cross, shrine
Friedhof	Cemetery
Denkmal	Monument
Rundfunk	Radiomast
Ruine	Ruin
Forstamt; Försterei	Forest box or Forester's house
Hervorragende Bäume	Important isolated trees
Windmühle	Windmill
Wassermühle	Water mill
Windrad	Wind pump
Schiffsmühle	Floating mill
Hohle	Cave
Erdfall, Doline	Landslip, doline
Bergwerk in Betrieb	Working mine
Bergwerk ausser Betrieb	Old mine
Schornstein frei u.i. Gebäude	Chimney free-standing or in a building
Steinbruch, Grube	Stone quarry, earthwork or pit
Trigonometrischer Punkt	Trigonometrical point
Höhenpunkt	Spot height
Eisen-und Betonbrucke	Iron and concrete bridge
Holzbrucke	Wooden bridge
Steg	Footbridge
Wagon-und Personenfahre (W.F.)	Ferry for cars and foot passengers (car ferry)
Damm, befahrbar	Dam with road across
Damm, nicht befahrbar	Dam without trackway
Steilrand, naturlich	Natural scarp or steep edge
Steilrand, Kunsklich	Artificial scarp or steep edge
Ringwall	Enclosing mounds
Hunengrab	Ancient burial-mound (barrow)
Zaun	Fence
Mauer	Wall
Hecke	Hedge
Knick (Kleiner Wall mit Hecke)	Small wall or bank with hedge
Hochspannungsleitung	Electric transmission lines
Zeltplatz	Camping site
Sportsplatz	Sports stadium
Sprungschanze	Ski jump

GERMAN	ENGLISH
Vegetation	
Laubwald	Deciduous forest
Nadelwald	Coniferous forest
Mischwald	Mixed forest
Einzelne Bäume und Gebüsch	Mixed single trees and bushes
Regelmässige	Regularly spaced trees
Baumanpflanzung	Plantations or orchards
Baumschule	Nurseries
Park	Park
Wiese und Weide mit nassen Stallen	Meadow and water-meadows
Garten	Gardens
Weingarten	Vineyards
Hopfenanpflanzung	Hops
Heide	Heath
Moor, Bruch, Sumpf	Moor, fen, marsh
Landforms	
Insel	Island
Kessel	Hollow
Kuppe	Hill-top
Felsen	Rocks
Hochflache	Plateau
Tal	Valley
Quelle, Brunnen	Spring, well
Unterirdischer Wasserlauf	Subterranean stream
Buhnen	Groyne
Uferbekleidung	Embankment
Schilf	Reeds
Trockenes Flussbett	Dry river bed
Schiffbarkeitszeichen	Limit of navigation
Wasser-graben	Drainage ditches
Siel	Sluice
Fluss	River
Bach	Stream
See	Lake
Altwasser	Cut-off meander (ox-bow lake)
Torfstich	Peat digging
Rucken	Ridge

TRANSLATION OF KEY SYMBOLS ON THE TOPOGRAPHICAL MAP OF FRANCE

FRENCH	ENGLISH
Autoroute et route à deux chaussées separées	Motorways and dual-carriageway main roads
Autoroute, route d'excellente viabilité	Highway, main road, excellent trafficability
Route de très bonne viabilité	Major road, very good trafficability
Chemin de moyenne viabilité	Minor road, fair trafficability
Chemin étroit de moyenne viabilité	Narrow minor road, fair trafficability
Chemin de viabilité médiocre ou irrégulièrement entretenu	Minor road, poor trafficability or irregularly maintained
Chemin d'exploitation, laie forestière. Sentier muletier. Sentier, layon	Cart track, forest path. Mule path. Footpath
Vestiges d'ancienne voie carrossable. Route en construction	Remains of old trafficable road. Road under construction
Routes et chemins bordés d'arbres	Main roads and minor roads bordered with trees
Chemin de fer à 4 voies	Railway—4 tracks
Chemin de fer à 2 voies	Railway—2 tracks
Chemin de fer à 1 voie	Railway—1 track
Chemins de fer à voie étroite: de 1 m—de moins de 1 m	Railway narrow gauge: 1 m—under 1 m
Voies de garage ou de service	Sidings
Gare, station. Halte, arrêt	Station. Stop
Tunnels: moins de 500 m, plus de 500 m	Tunnels: under 500 m, more than 500 m
Passage: à niveau, supérieur, inférieur, Viaduc	Crossing: level crossing, overpass, underpass, Viaduct

FRENCH	ENGLISH	FRENCH	ENGLISH
Voies en déblai et en remblai	Railways, cuttings and embankments	Limites: d'arrondissement, de canton	Boundaries: arrondissement, canton
Voies hors service	Unused railway	Limite de commune. Limite de camp	Commune boundary. Camp boundary
Pont. Passerelle, Gué, Bac, Barrage	Bridge, Footbridge, Ford, Vehicle ferry. Dam	Points géodésiques. Population en milliers d'habitants	Trig. points. Thousands of inhabitants
Lac, étang permanent. Etang à niveau variable. Etang périodique. Marais	Lake, permanent pond. Intermittent pond. Periodic pond. Swamp	Eglise. Chapelle. Calvaire. Cimetière	Church. Chapel. Calvary. Cemetery
Source. Puits, citerne. Château d'eau. Réservoirs	Spring. Well, cistern. Water tower. Reservoirs	Moulin à eau. Moulin à vent, éolienne. Gazomètre. Réservoir d'hydrocarbure	Water mill. Wind mill, wind pump. Gas tank. Petrol tank
Canal navigable: écluse, traction mécanique. Canal d'alimentation	Navigable canal: lock, mechanical traction. Feed water	Carrière à ciel ouvert. Carrière souterraine, grotte. Puits de mine. Terril	Open mine or quarry. Mine, grotto. Mine. Spoil dump
Aqueducs: sur le sol, élevé, souterrain	Aqueducts: surface, above ground, underground	Habitations troglodytiques, Monuments mégalithiques. Ruines	Troglodyte caves. Megalithic monuments. Ruins
Sables et dunes. Laisse des plus hautes mers	Sands and dunes. Contour of highest water mark		
Estran: sables, vases, rochers	Foreshore: sands, muds, rocks	Ligne d'énergie électrique. Câble transporteur	Power line. Conveying cable
Courbes isobathes (tirées des cartes du Service Central Hydrographique)	Submarine contours (compiled from the charts of the Service Central Hydrographique)	Arbres. Haies. Murs. Murs en ruines	Trees. Hedges. Walls. Ruin walls
Phare. Feu. Bateau-feu	Lighthouses. Light. Lightship	Bois	Woods
Sémaphore. Balise. Bouée. Bouée-lumineuse	Signal station. Beacon. Buoy. Light buoy	Broussailles	Brushwoods
Limites: d'état avec bornes, de département	Boundaries: international with land marks, department	Vergers, Plantations	Orchards, plantations
		Vignes	Vines

CONVERSION TABLES

LINEAR MEASURES CONVERSION TABLE

Miles	Kilometres	Kilometres	Miles
1	1·6	1	0·6
2	3·2	2	1·2
3	4·8	3	1·9
4	6·4	4	2·5
5	8·0	5	3·0
6	9·6	6	3·7
7	11·3	7	4·3
8	12·9	8	5·0
9	14·5	9	5·6
10	16·1	10	6·2
11	17·7	11	6·8
12	19·3	12	7·5
13	20·9	13	8·1
14	22·5	14	8·7
15	24·1	15	9·3

Yards	Metres	Metres	Yards
1	0·9144	1	1·093
10	9·1	10	10·9
50	45·7	50	54·7
100	91·4	100	109·4
500	457·2	500	547·0

SQUARE MEASURES CONVERSION TABLE

Acres	Hectares (Ha)	Hectares	Acres
1 (4840 yards)	0·4 (4046·8 m²)	1	2·5
2	0·8	2	5·0
3	1·2	3	7·4
4	1·6	4	9·9
5	2·0	5	12·4

METRIC SQUARE MEASURE

1 are = 100 square metres (c. 119 square yards)
1 hectare = 100 ares (c. 11 960 square yards)

MEASURE OF CAPACITY

1 litre = 0·2201 Imperial gallon
1 Imperial gallon = 4·5459 litre (British)
1 American gallon = 3·7853 litre

MEASURE OF WEIGHT

1 metric tonne = 0·984 Imperial ton
　　　　　　　 = 1·1023 USA ton (the long ton)
1 Imperial ton = 1016·05 kilogram
1 USA ton = 907·185 kilogram

ORDNANCE SURVEY ARCHAEOLOGICAL AND HISTORICAL MAPS
(with accompanying texts)

1. *Map of Southern Britain in the Iron Age* (1962).
   The approximate period covered is from the fifth century B.C. to mid-first century A.D.
2. *Map of Roman Britain* (3rd edn, 1956).
3. *Map of Britain in the Dark Ages* (2nd edn, 1966).
   This map covers the period between the end of Roman Rule and the reign of King Alfred. This was a formative period of the Anglo-Saxon Settlement.
4. *Map of Ancient Britain* (North and South Sheets) (2nd edn, 1964).
   This map marks the major visible antiquities of Great Britain older than A.D. 1066.

United Kingdom New Towns 1972

New Town	Year of designation	Population (estimated) 31 December 1972	Proposed maximum population size	Designated area in hectares (1972)
Antrim	1966	40 000	74 000	48 653
Aycliffe	1947	25 000	45 000	1 003
Ballymena	1966	50 000	96 000	65 652
Basildon	1949	82 000	134 000	3 165
Bracknell	1949	38 400	60 000	1 336
Corby	1950	50 000	83 000	1 790
Craigavon	1965	73 000	180 000	26 880
Crawley	1947	68 700	85 000	2 396
Cumbernauld	1955	35 000	100 000	1 679
Cwmbran	1949	42 000	55 000	1 275
East Kilbride	1947	66 800	100 000	4 148
Glenrothes	1948	32 000	75 000	2 333
Harlow	1947	80 000	undecided	2 588
Hatfield	1948	26 000	29 500	947
Hemel Hempstead	1947	73 000	80 000	2 392
Irvine	1966	44 000	120 000	5 022
Livingston	1962	17 500	100 000	2 708
Londonderry	1969	84 000	100 000	34 610
Milton Keynes	1967	50 000	250 000	8 900
Newtown	1967	6 300	13 000	606
Northampton	1968	138 000	260 000	8 080
Peterborough	1967	91 000	187 000	6 455
Peterlee	1948	25 750	30 000	1 133
Redditch	1964	43 600	90 000	2 906
Runcorn	1964	44 300	100 000	2 927
Skelmersdale	1961	34 000	80 000	1 668
Stevenage	1946	72 500	105 000	2 532
Telford	1968	87 000	250 000	7 790
Warrington	1968	131 000	225 000	7 535
Washington	1964	32 000	80 000	2 368
Welwyn Garden City	1948	41 600	50 000	1 747
TOTAL				263 224

N.B. No substantial development has as yet (April 1973) taken place in Central Lancashire (designated 1970) or at Stonehouse (designated 1972). Telford was originally Dawley which was designated in 1963.

Bibliography

CHAPTER 1

Allerston, P. 1970. 'English Village Development', *Transactions of the Institute of British Geographers*, vol. 51, pp. 95–109.

Baker, A. R. H., and Butlin, R. A. 1972. *Studies of Field Systems in the British Isles*.

Beresford, M. 1954. *The Lost Villages of England*.

Cameron, K. 1963. *English Place Names*.

Campbell, Eila. 1962. *The Domesday Geography of S.E. England*, ed. H. C. Darby and E. M. J. Campbell.

Chisholm, M. 1968. *Rural Settlement and Land Use*, p. 129.

Clarke, W. G. 1937. *Breckland Wilds*.

Coleman, Alice M., and Lukehurst, Clare T. 1967. *East Kent*. Geographical Association British Landscape Through Maps no. 10.

Darby, H. C. ed. 1936. *An Historical Geography of England Before A.D. 1800*.

Ekwall, E. 1936. *The Concise Oxford Dictionary of English Place Names.*

Fleure, H. J. 1950. *The Natural History of Man in Britain*.

Hoskins, W. G. 1955. *The Making of the English Landscape*.

Jones, E. 1966. *Towns and Cities*.

Lee, D. R., and Sallee, G. T. 1970. 'A Method of Measuring Shape', *Geographical Review*, vol. 60, October.

Loyn, H. R. 1962. *Anglo-Saxon England and the Norman Conquest*.

McClure, E. 1910, reprinted 1971. *British Place Names in their Historical Setting*.

McRae, S. G., and Burnham, C. P. 1973. *The Rural Landscape of Kent* (Wye College Publication).

Mitchell, J. B. 1954. *Historical Geography*.

Roden, D., and Baker, A. R. H. 1966. 'Field Systems of the Chiltern Hills and of Parts of Kent from the Late Thirteenth to the Early Seventeenth Century'. *Transactions of the Institute of British Geographers*, vol. 38, p. 79.

Yates, E. M. 1965. 'Dark Age and Medieval Settlements on the Edge of Wastes and Forests'. *Field Studies*, vol. 2, no. 2, pp. 133–53.

CHAPTER 2

Abler, R., Adams, J. S., and Gould, P. 1971. *Spatial Organisation*. See chapter 8, Movement and Transport Systems.

Bach, A. 1953–54. *Deutsche Namenkunde. Die deutschen Ortsnamen.* (Two Volumes.)

Briggs, K. 1972. *Introducing Transportation Networks*.

Bunge, W. 1966. *Theoretical Geography*. See chapter 7, Distance, Nearness and Geometry.

Christaller, W., trans. C. W. Baskin, 1966. *Central Places in Southern Germany*.

Dickinson, R. E. 1951. *The West European City*.

Elkins, T. H. 1968. *Germany*.

Everson, J. A. and FitzGerald, B. P. *Concepts in Geography*: vol. 1, 1969. *Settlement Patterns*. 2nd ed.; vol. 3, 1972. *Inside the City*.

Haggett, P., and Chorley, R. J. 1969. *Network Analysis in Geography*.

Holt, M., and Marjoram, D. T. E. 1973. *Mathematics in a Changing World*.

Houston, J. M. 1953. *A Social Geography of Europe*.

Johnson, J. H. 1967. *Urban Geography—an Introductory Analysis*.

Kaufman, A. 1972. *Points and Arrows: the Theory of Graphs*. Transworld Student Library.

Knowles, R., and Stowe, P. W. E. 1971. *Europe in Maps*, Book 2.

Mansfield, A. J., and Powrie, P. J. 1972. *France and Benelux*.

Mayhew, A. 1973. *Rural Settlement and Farming in Germany*.

Sinnhuber, K. A. 1970. *Germany: its Geography and Growth*.

Smith, C. T. 1967. *An Historical Geography of Western Europe before 1800*.

Tideswell, W. V. 1971. *An Introduction to the Analysis of Road Networks*. Geographical Association Pamphlet No. 15.

Tideswell, W. V., and Barker, S. M. 1971. *Quantitative Methods*.

Toyne, P., and Newby, P. T. 1971. *Techniques in Human Geography*.

Wrightman, M. 1971. *The Faces of Germany*.

CHAPTER 3

Clarke, J. I. 1965. *Population Geography*.

Commission Nationale Suisse de l'U.N.E.S.C.O. 1968. *Exode rural et dépeuplement de la montagne en Suisse*.

Demko, G. J., Rose, H. M., and Schnell, G. A. eds. 1970. *Population Geography: a Reader*.

Embleton, C., and King, C. A. M. 1968. *Glacial and Periglacial Geomorphology*.

Kosiński, L. English translation, 1970. *The Population of Europe*.

Ladurie, E. Le Roy. 1973. *Times of Feast, Times of Famine*.

Lunn, A. not dated. *Zermatt and the Valais*.

Mackinder, H. 1919. *Democratic Ideals and Reality*.

Mayer, K. B. 1952. *The Population of Switzerland*.

Mutton, A. F. A. 1968. *Central Europe*. See chapters 4, 5 and 6.

Parker, G. 1968. *The Logic of Unity*.

Peattie, R. 1936. *Mountain Geography*.

Small, R. J. 1970. *The Study of Landforms*.

Zelinsky, W. 1970. *A Prologue to Population Geography*.

CHAPTER 4

Bielckas, C. L., Rogers, A. W., and Wibberley, G. P. 1973. *The Distribution and Use of Second Homes in England and Wales*. (Wye College Publication.)

Capstick, M. 1972. *Some Aspects of the Economic Effects of Tourism in the Westmorland Lake District*. University of Lancaster, Department of Economics.

Clout, H. D. 1969. 'Auvergne—a challenge for country planners'. *The Geographical Magazine*, vol. 41, no. 12, pp. 918–26.

——. 1971. 'Second Homes in the Auvergne'. *The Geographical Review*, vol. LXI, pp. 530–53.

——. 1972. *The Geography of Post-War France*.

——. 1973. *Historical Geography of France*.

Downing, P., and Dower, M. 1973. *Second Homes in England and Wales*. (Countryside Commission.)

Estienne, Pierre. 1970. 'La Banlieu de Clermont-Ferrand'. *Revue D'Auvergne*, Tome 84, pp. 257–334.

Freeman, T. W. 1959. *The Conurbations of Great Britain*.

Johnson, J. H. 1967. *Urban Geography*.

Les Parcs Nationaux Français, Numéro spécial de la Revue Forestière Française 1971. Ministère de l'Agriculture.

Mansfield, A. J., and Powrie, P. J. 1972. *France and Benelux*. pp. 410–15.

Nègre, E. 1963. *Les Noms de Lieux en France*.

Peterlongo, J. M. 1972. *Guides Géologiques Régionaux. Massif Central*.

Pinchemell, P. 1969. *France—a Geographical Survey*.

Rutter, M. G. 1969. *The Geology of Western Europe*.

Scarth, A. 1966. 'The Physiography of the Fault-Scarp between the Grande Limagne and the Plateaux des Domes, Massif Central'. *Transactions of the Institute of British Geographers*, no. 38, pp. 25–40.

Theakstone, W. H., and Harrison, C. 1970. *The Analysis of Geographical Data*.

Thompson, L. B. 1970. *Modern France—a Social Economic Geography*.

CHAPTER 5

Arvill, R. 1969. *Man and Environment*. See chapters 16 and 17.

Best, R. H. 1964. *Land for New Towns*.

Best, R. H. 1972. 'March of the Concrete Jungle'. *The Geographical Magazine*, Vol. XLV, no. 1, pp. 47–51.

Blacksell, A. M. Y. 1974. *Re-building of Europe: a Geographical Analysis*.

Brown, A. J. 1972. *The Framework of Regional Economics in the United Kingdom*.

Carter, H. 1972. *The Study of Urban Geography*.

Curl, J. S. 1970. *European Cities and Society*.

Fairbrother, N. 1970. *New Lives, New Landscapes*. Penguin Books Edition, 1972.

Charre, J. G., Coyard, L. M., and Jonas, S. 1969. *Les Villes Françaises*.

Clout, H. D. 1970. 'Industrial Relocation in France'. *Geography*, vol. 55, pp. 48–63.

——. 1972. *Rural Geography: An Introductory Survey*.

Haggett, P. 1973. *Geography: A Modern Synthesis*.

Hall, P. 1966. *The World Cities*.

Howard, E. 1965. *Garden Cities of Tomorrow*. First published in 1898 as *Tomorrow: a Peaceful Path to Real Reform*.

Intermediate Areas. Report of the Hunt Committee. April 1969. (H.M.S.O.) Cmnd. 3998.

Lloyd, P. E., and Dicken, P. 1972. *Location in Space: a Theoretical Approach to Economic Geography*.

Jones, H. R., and Pocock, D. C. D. 1966. 'Some Economic and Social Implications of the Tay Road Bridge'. *Scottish Geographical Magazine*, vol. 82, no. 2, pp. 93–103.

Jones, S. J., ed. 1968. *Dundee and District*. Survey for the British Association for the Advancement of Science.

Manners, G., Keeble, D., Rodgers, B., and Warren, K. 1972. *Regional Development in Britain*.

Osborn, F. J., and Whittick, A. 1969. *The New Towns: the Answer to Megalopolis* 2nd ed. 1972.

Riboud, J. 1965. *Développement Urbain*.

Tayside: Potential for Development. 1970. HMSO Regional Report.

Tuppen, J. 1972. 'Le Vaudreuil: an Advance in the French New Town Concept'. *Town and Country Planning*, vol. 40, no. 6.

Walford, R. 1969. *Games in Geography*.

NOTE

1. See also the Central Office of Information Reference pamphlet 44, *The New Towns of Britain* (HMSO, 1972), and the January 1973 New Towns Special Issue of *Town and Country Planning*, the journal of the Town and Country Planning Association (vol. 41, no. 1).

2. A useful teaching techniques journal is *Classroom Geographer*, available from N. E. Sealey, 3 Wensleydale, Luton, Bedfordshire.

CHAPTER 6

Chisholm, M. 1968. *Rural Settlement and Land Use*.

Chorley, R. J., and Haggett, P. 1967. *Models in Geography*.

Cox, K. 1972. *Man, Location and Behaviour*.

Davies, W. K. D. (ed.) 1972. *The Conceptual Revolution in Geography*.

Haggett, P. 1965. *Locational Analysis in Human Geography*.

Hall, P. 1966. *Von Thünen's Isolated State*.

Lloyd, P. E., and Dickens, P. 1972. *Location in Space: A Theoretical Approach to Economic Geography*.

Money, D. C. 1972. *Patterns of Settlement* (Chapters 7 and 8).

Riley, R. C. 1973. *Industrial Geography*.

Smith, D. M. 1971. *Industrial Location: An Economic Geographical Analysis*.

Weber, A. Translation by C. J. Friedrich, 1957. *Theory of the Location of Industries*.

GENERAL REFERENCE TEXTS

Queencez, G., ed. 1967. *Vocabularium Geographicum*. A dictionary of geographical terms in French, German, Italian, Dutch, English and Spanish for use in schools. (Obtainable from Presses Academiques Européennes, Bruxelles 6, Belgium.)

Schieferdecker, A. A. G., ed. 1959. *Geological Nomenclature*. A dictionary of physical terms in English, Dutch, French and German. (Obtainable from Royal Geological and Mining Society of the Netherlands.)

MAP WORK AND CARTOGRAPHY

Crone, G. R. 1966. *Maps and Their Makers*.

Dickinson, G. C. 1969. *Maps and Air Photographs*.

——. 1963. *Statistical Mapping and the Presentation of Statistics*.

Dury, G. H. 1967. *Map Interpretation*. 3rd ed.

Guest, A. 1974. *Advanced Practical Geography*. 4th ed.

Knowles, R., and Stowe, P. W. E. *Europe in Maps: Topographical Map Studies of Western Europe*. Two vols: Vol. I, 1969; Vol. II, 1971.

Raisz, H. 1962. *Principles of Cartography*.

Robinson, A. H. 1965. *Elements of Cartography*. International Edition—2nd ed.

Tooley, R. V., and Bricker, C. 1969. *A History of Cartography*.

Wood, Margaret. 1968. *Foreign Maps and Landscapes*.

Index to Exercises

General Index

Auszug aus der Zeichenerklärung

Grenzen

————————	Staatsgrenze
—∗—∗—∗—∗—∗—	Landesgrenze
—·—·—·—·—	Regierungsbezirksgrenze
— — — — —	Kreisgrenze
–· –· –· –·	Truppenübungsplatzgrenze
··············	Naturschutzgebietsgrenze

Verkehrsnetz

Bahnhof	Vollspurige Bahn, mehrgleisig
Haltepunkt	Vollspurige Bahn, eingleisig
	Schmalspurige Bahn
	Straßen- und Wirtschaftsbahn
—o—o—o—o—	Seil- und Schwebebahn
im Bau	Autobahn oder Autostraße mit Mittelstreifen
	Autostraße ohne Mittelstreifen
	Hochstraße
E5 10	Europa- und Bundesstraßennummer
	Hauptstraße (IA) mit Baumreihen
	Nebenstraße (IB) mit Kilometerstein
	Befestigter Fahrweg (II) (Verbindungs- und Hauptwirtschaftsweg)
	Wirtschaftsweg. Feld- und Waldweg (III)
------+-----	Fußweg mit Steg

Topographische Einzelzeichen

⌁	Kirche, mehrtürmig	·149	Höhenpunkt
♂	Kirche, eintürmig oder ohne Turm	△307	Trigonometrischer Bodenpunkt
+	Kapelle	♂ ♂	Trigonometrische Hochpunkte: Kirche, Turm, Schornstein
†	Feldkreuz, Bildstock	⇌ ⇌	Eiserne Brücke. Betonbrücke
[⋮]	Friedhof	⌣	Holzbrücke
⯗	Ehrenfriedhof	⊟⊟⊟	Hebe- oder Drehbrücke
⚑	Denkmal. Denkstein	●-□-□	Eisenbahn-, Wagen- und Personenfähre
♂	Turm	⊥⊥⊥⊥	Steilrand
∘	Schornstein	⊤⊤⊤⊤	Rain
▣	Turm oder Schornstein; auf Gebäude stehend	⫿⫿⫿	Damm, befahrbar
⚲	Funkturm	⩔⩔⩔	Damm, nicht befahrbar
⊤	Tankstelle	🝔 🝕	Steinbruch, Grube
⚱	Windrad	▭	Ringwall
✿	Wassermühle	⊙ ∘	Hünengrab (Grabhügel)
♈	Forstamt, Försterei	⏂ ⏂	Mauerreste, Ruine
⌘ ⚘ ⚘	Hervorragende Bäume	+++++	Mauer, Zaun
⚒	Bergwerk in Betrieb	·········	Hecke
⚒	Bergwerk außer Betrieb	⌐⌐⌐⌐	Knick, kleiner Wall mit Hecke
∩	Höhle	→—	Starkstromleitung
⬭	Sportplatz	‖‖‖‖	Bruchfeld
⛺	Zeltplatz		

Bodenbewachsung

Schneise	Laubwald
	Nadelwald
	Baumschule
	Mischwald
	Bäume und Gebüsch
	Regelmäßige Baumpflanzung. Obstbaumgut mit und ohne Wiese
	Heide mit einzelnen Bäumen und Büschen
	Wiese u. Weide mit nassen Stellen, Bäumen und Büschen
	Weingarten
	Hopfenanpflanzung
	Garten
	Park

Abkürzungen

AT	Aussichtsturm	...kp, Kp	Kapelle
B	Bach	Krhs	Krankenhaus
B	Berg	M	Mühle
...bf, Bf	Bahnhof	ND	Naturdenkmal
...br, Br	Brunnen	NSG	Naturschutzgebiet
ehem	ehemalig	PW	Pumpwerk
EW	Elektrizitätswerk	qu, Qu	Quelle
Gr	Groß	R	Ruine
H	Hütte	Rhs	Rasthaus
...hs, Hs	Haus	Sch	Scheune, Schuppen, Stall
Hbf	Hauptbahnhof	Schl	Schloß
Hp	Haltepunkt	UW	Umspannwerk
Hst	Haltestelle	Wbh	Wasserbehälter
JH	Jugendherberge	...whr, Whr	Weiher
KD	Kulturgesch. Denkmal	Whs	Wirtshaus
Kl	klein	WT	Wasserturm
Kläranl	Kläranlage	WW	Wasserwerk

WANDSWORTH PUBLIC LIBRARIES

WANDSWORTH PUBLIC LIBRARIES M.S.C.

Gewässer, Bodenformen

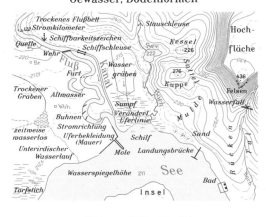

	100 m-Linie
	10 m-Linie
	5 m-Linie
	2,5 m-Linie

Die Höhen sind in Metern über Normal-Null angegeben.

Key 1

To accompany extract from Topographischekarte, Map 2

MAN AND LANDSCAPE by Arthur Guest
Heinemann Educational Books, 1974
Reproduced with the permission of the
Landesvermessungsamt Rheinland-Pfalz

Key 1

To accompany extract from Topographischekarte, Map 2

MAN AND LANDSCAPE by Arthur Guest
Heinemann Educational Books, 1974
Reproduced with the permission of the
Landesvermessungsamt Rheinland-Pfalz

Signes conventionnels

	1:25 000	1:50 000	1:100 000
Gare importante.			
Gare, station.	1:25 000		
	1:50 000		
Chemin de fer à voie normale double. Halte.			
Chemin de fer à voie normale unique. Halte.			
Chemin de fer à voie étroite, à crémaillère, funiculaire. Halte.			
Chemin de fer à voie étroite sur route. Halte.			
Voie industrielle.			
Téléférique pour transport de personnes, télésiège.			
Téléférique pour transport de matériel.			
Monte-pente.			
Ponts de chemin de fer, viaducs.			
Tunnel, galerie.			
Autoroute de 1ère classe, 2 chaussées séparées à sens unique.			
Autoroute de 2ème classe, plusieurs voies non séparées.			
Route principale à trafic mixte.			
Route de 1ère classe, largeur utile : 5 m au minimum.			
Route de 2ème classe, largeur utile : 3 ~ 5 m.			
Route de 3ème classe, largeur utile : 2.2 ~ 3.0 m.			
Chemin carrossable entretenu.			
Chemin de dévestiture, chemin muletier en montagne.			
Sentier. Traces de sentier, passage en montagne.			
Passage habituel sur glaciers et névés.			
Vestiges d'anciennes routes et d'anciens chemins.			
Piste de bobsleigh. Dévaloir.			

	1:25 000	1:50 000	1:100 000
Pont. Pont couvert.			
Ponts carrossables. Passerelle. Aqueduc.	1:25 000 / 1:50 000		
Galerie. Tunnels routiers.			
Passages à niveau.			
Passages sur voie.	1:25 000 / 1:50 000		
Passages sous voie.			
Limite d'état, bornes avec leurs numeros.			
Limite de canton, bornes.			
Limite de district, bornes.			
Limite de commune, bornes.			
Point de triangulation de 1er - 3ème ordre. (au 1:100 000, seulement avec pyramide)		△ 2042.6	△ 2042
Points de triangulation de 4ème ordre.	× 1966.6	· 1165.0	
Points topographiques cotés.	× 1482	· 2364	× 1482 · 2364
Maison. Maison avec pont de grange important. Auberge isolée.	1:25 000 / 1:50 000		
Eglise. Chapelle.			
Gazomètre. Tour isolée, cheminée d'usine. Tour d'observation.			
Ruine. Palafittes (station lacustre).			
Murs. Mur sec.			
Monument. Croix, oratoire.			
Caverne, grotte. Bloc erratique.			
Cimetière. Stand important.			
Station radio. Station de transformateurs à ciel ouvert.			
Ligne électrique à haute tension et à longue portée.			

	1:25 000	1:50 000	1:100 000
Courbes de niveau directrices, équidistance 200 m.	1:50 000		
Courbes de niveau directrices, équidistance 100 m.	1:25 000		
Courbes de niveau de 50 m.			
Courbes de niveau de 20 m.	1:50 000 / 1:25 000 dans les Alpes		
Courbes de niveau de 10 m.	1:25 000 Plateau, Jura		
Courbes intermédiaires de 25 m.			
Courbes intermédiaires de 10 m.	1:25 000 dans les Alpes / 1:50 000		
Courbes intermédiaires de 5 m.	1:25 000 Plateau, Jura		
Talus. Talus de pierre.			
Dépression. Culmination.			
Carrière. Gravière. Glaisière.			
Glissement. Ravinement rocheux.			
Remblai. Déblai.			
Rocher et pierrier. (Au 1:25 000 courbes de 100 m dans le rocher)	1:25 000 / 1:50 000		
Marais. Tourbière.			
1 Forêt. 2 Forêt clairsemée. 3 Buissons	1:25 000 / 1:50 000		
Forêt, limite supérieure en montagne.			
Parc. Allée. Arbre isolé, bosquet.	1:25 000 / 1:50 000		
Haie. Châtaigniers.	1:25 000 / 1:50 000		
Vergers. Pépinière.	1:25 000		
Vignes.			

	1:25 000	1:50 000	1:100 000
Lac. Cote du fond. Cote du niveau moyen. 1 Débarcadère. 2 Port. 3 Bains. 4 Rive marécageuse.			
Lac d'accumulation. Barrage ou digue. Cote du niveau maximum.			
Lac à niveau très variable. Etang, piscine.			
Réservoir. Fontaine. Citerne.	1:25 000 / 1:50 000		
Fleuve ou rivière. Ancien lit. Endiguement.			
Fleuve ou rivière. Barrage avec passage. Barrage sans passage.			
Fleuve ou rivière. Bac passant les véhicules. Bac passant les personnes.			
Ruisseaux. 1 Endiguement. 2 Cascade. 3 Source. 4 Débit intermittent. 5 Ravine. 6 Dépotoir. 7 Entonnoir.			
Ruisseau, rivière ou fleuve.			
Glacier. Moraines.			
Canaux à ciel ouvert.			
Canaux recouverts ou souterrains.			
Conduite forcée. Conduite forcée souterraine. 1:25 000 conduite multiple			

WANDSWORTH PUBLIC LIBRARIES M.S.C.

Key 2

To accompany extract from the Landeskarte der Schweiz, Map 3

MAN AND LANDSCAPE by Arthur Guest
Heinemann Educational Books, 1974
Reproduced with the permission of the
Eidgenössische Landestopographie

WANDSWORTH PUBLIC LIBRARIES ★ M.S.C.

Pont. Passerelle. Gué. Bac. Barrage.

Lac, étang permanent. Etang à niveau variable. Etang périodique. Marais.

Source. Puits, citerne. Château d'eau. Réservoirs.

Canal navigable : écluse, traction mécanique. Canal d'alimentation.

Aqueducs : sur le sol, élevé, souterrain.

Sables et dunes. Laisse des plus hautes mers.

Estran : sables, vases, rochers.

Courbes isobathes.

Phare. Feu. Bateau-feu.

Sémaphore. Balise. Bouée. Bouée lumineuse.

Surfaces bâties { 1 - Forte densité.
{ 2 - Densité moyenne.

Constructions non agglomérées.

Eglise. Chapelle. Calvaire. Cimetière.

Moulin à eau. Moulin à vent, éolienne. Gazomètre. Réservoir d'hydrocarbure.

Points géodésiques. Population en milliers d'habitants.

Carrière à ciel ouvert. Carrière souterraine, grotte. Puits de mine. Terril.

Habitations troglodytiques. Monuments mégalithiques. Ruines.

Ligne d'énergie électrique. Câble transporteur.

Arbres. Haies. Murs. Murs en ruines.

Autoroute et route à deux chaussées séparées.

Autoroute, route d'excellente viabilité.

Route de très bonne viabilité.

Route ou chemin de bonne viabilité.

Chemin de moyenne viabilité.

Chemin étroit de moyenne viabilité.

Chemin de viabilité médiocre ou irrégulièrement entretenu.

Chemin d'exploitation, laie forestière. Sentier muletier. Sentier, layon.

Vestiges d'ancienne voie carrossable. Route en construction.

Routes et chemins bordés d'arbres.

Chemin de fer à 4 voies.

Chemin de fer à 2 voies.

Chemin de fer à 1 voie.

Chemins de fer à voie étroite : de 1 m — de moins de 1 m

Voies de garage ou de service.

Gare, station. Halte, arrêt.

Tunnels : moins de 500 m, plus de 500 m

Limites : d'état avec bornes, de département.

Limites : d'arrondissement, de canton.

Limite de commune. Limite de camp.

Echelle 1 : 50 000

mètres 1 000   500   0   1   2   3   4   5 kilomètres

Figuré du terrain

Rochers et glaciers.

Courbes, talus et point coté.

Dans les cuvettes, la flèche est dirigée vers le fond.

Bois

Broussailles

Vergers . Plantations

Vignes

Key 3

To accompany extract from the Carte Nationale, Map 4

MAN AND LANDSCAPE by Arthur Guest
Heinemann Educational Books, 1974
Reproduced with the permission of the
Institut Geographique National

Key 3

To accompany extract from the Carte Nationale, Map 4

MAN AND LANDSCAPE by Arthur Guest
Heinemann Educational Books, 1974
Reproduced with the permission of the
Institut Geographique National

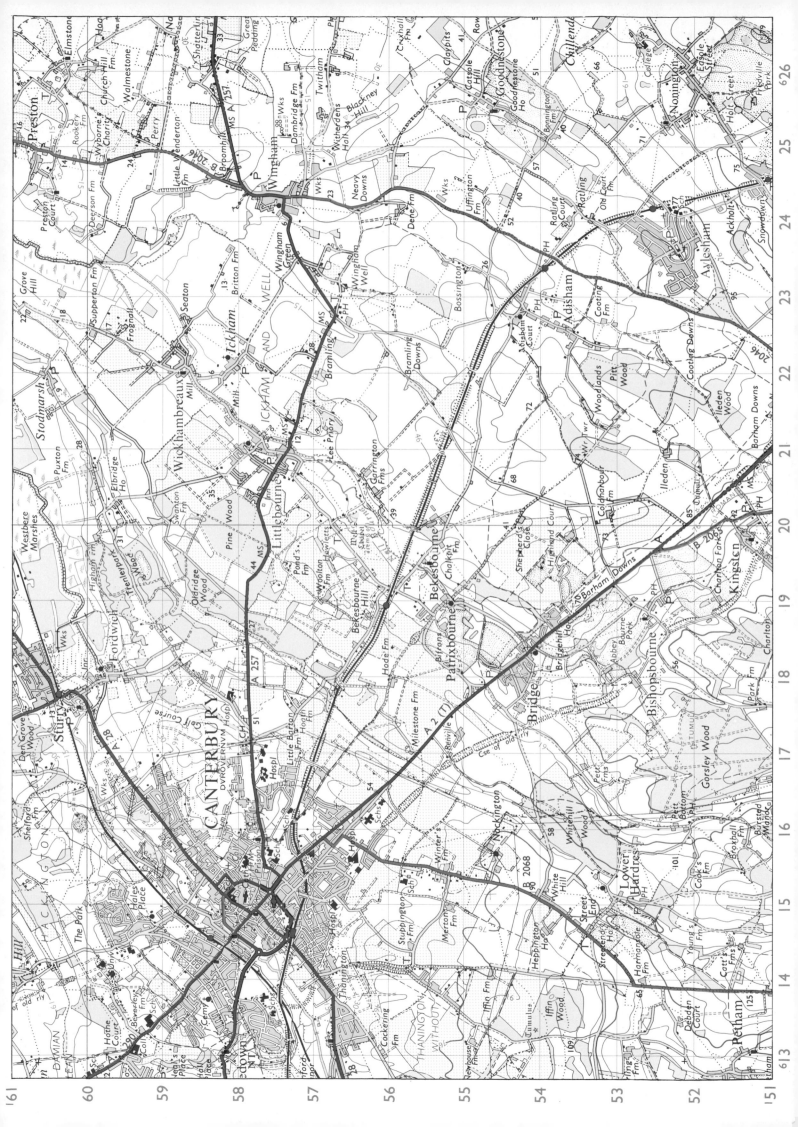

Map 1: Canterbury

Extract from Ordnance Survey Sheet 179

Scale 1 : 50 000

MAN AND LANDSCAPE by Arthur Guest
Heinemann Educational Books, 1974
*Reproduced from the Ordnance Survey Map with
the sanction of the Controller of H.M. Stationery Office*

WANDSWORTH PUBLIC LIBRARIES M.S.C.

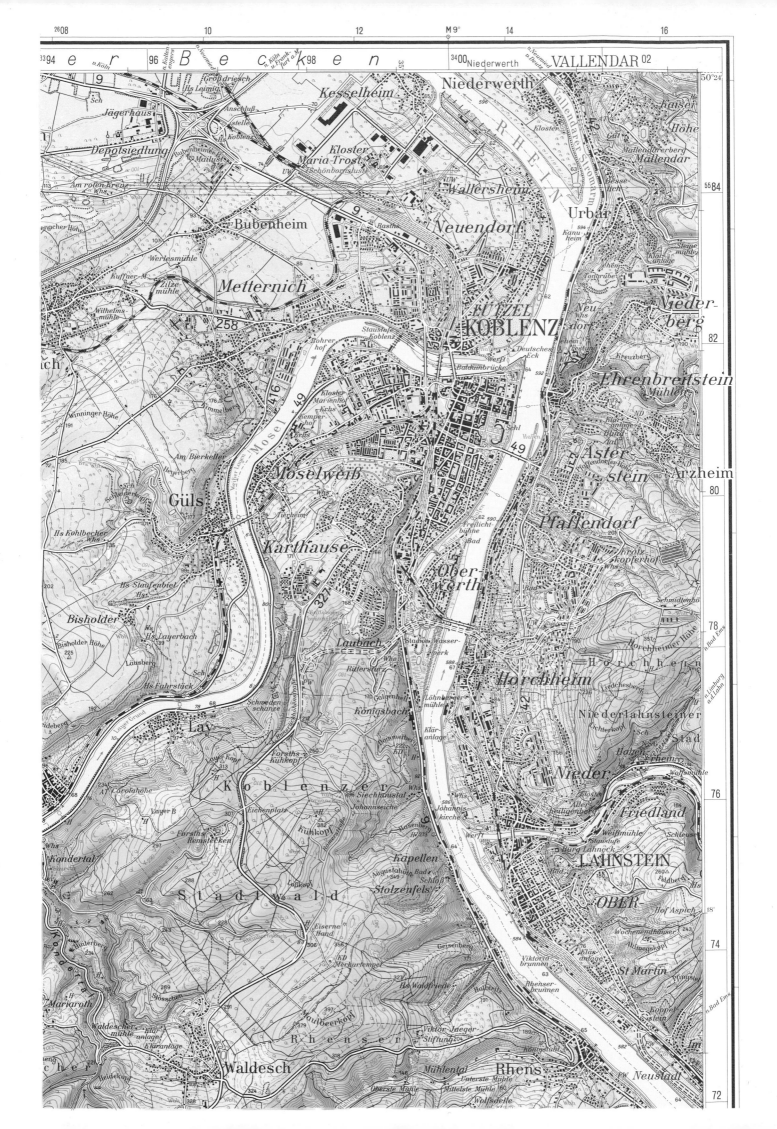

Map 2: Koblenz

Extract from Topographischekarte L5710
Scale 1: 50 000

MAN AND LANDSCAPE by Arthur Guest
Heinemann Educational Books, 1974
Reproduced with the permission of the
Landesvermessungsamt Rheinland-Pfalz

WANDSWORTH PUBLIC LIBRARIES M.S.C.

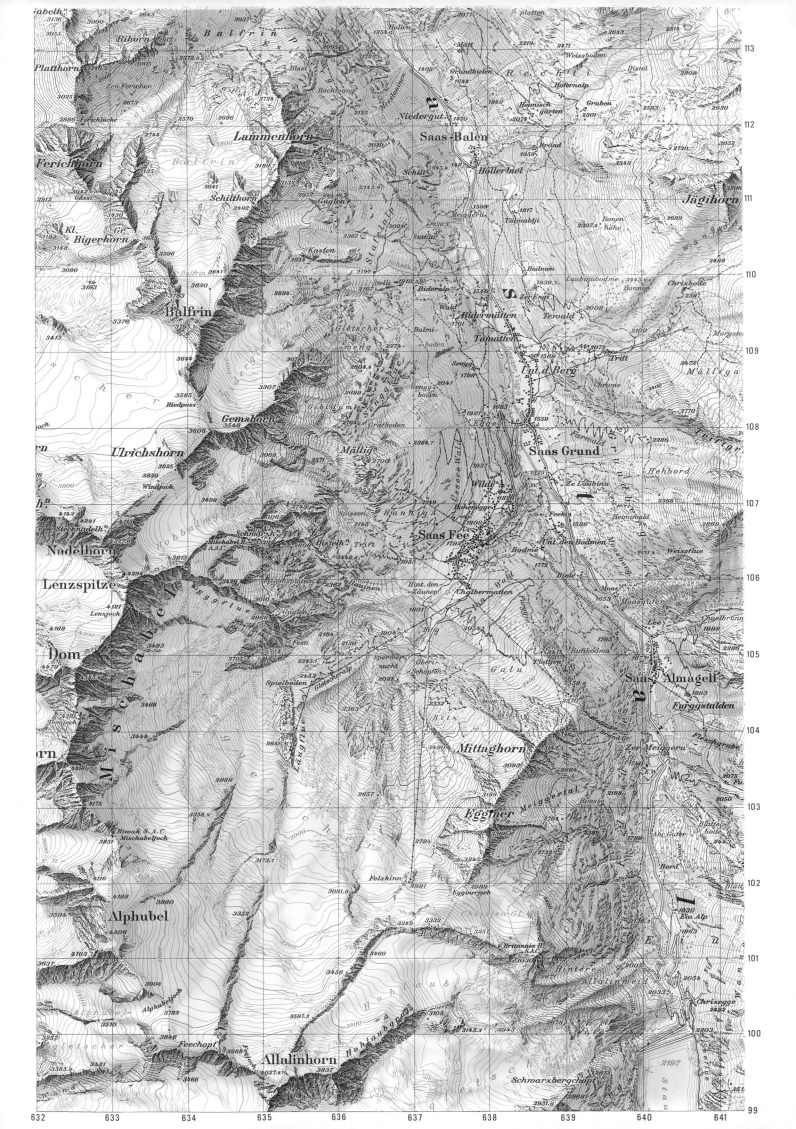

Map 3: Upper Saas Valley

Extract from Landeskarte der Schweiz, sheets 274 and 284

Scale 1: 50 000

MAN AND LANDSCAPE by Arthur Guest
Heinemann Educational Books, 1974
Reproduced with the permission of the
Eidgenössische Landestopographie

2092 2091 2090 2089 2088 2087 2086 2085 2084

CLERMONT
Montferrand
St-Jean
Aubière
Beaumont
Blanzat
Sayat
Chanat-la-Mouteyre
Nohanent
Durtol
Chamalières
Royat
Orcines
Ternant
Sarcenat
le Gressigny
Fontanas
Montrodeix
Solagnat
la Baraque
le Cheix
Villeneuve

Puy de Chanturgue · 553
Côtes Trémonteix
Puy de Var
Bancillon
le Maupas
Monjuzet

Puy Chaumont 1111
Puy de Chaumont
des Goules 969
Petit Sarcoui 1038
Grand Sarcoui 1147
Puy des Goules 997
Col des Goules
Puy Pariou 1209
Puy de Fraisse
Puy de Dôme 1464
Tour de Téléc.
Temple de Mercure
Petit Puy de Dôme 1079
Puy de la Vache
Puy de Charmes
Puy de Grave Noire 822
Puy de Charade 904
Charade
Bois de la Pauze
Mont Miel
Golf
Solagnat 782
Sagne Vida
Petit Puy de Manson 997
St-Aubin 999
Marmoison
Roche Merle 924
Cr Ste-Anne

N. 141
D. 941
D. 52e
D. 90
D. 68
D. 21
150 kV

Puy Chopine 1181
Croix Mor? 1011
Puy de Pérady
Puy du Suchet
le Petit Suchet 1197
la Cime de la Plaine
Montchal 1023
Montchatif 973
Camp Militaire
la Fontaine du Berger
Montchâtre 927
Puy Plantias
Calv. 884
Enval
la Font de l'Arbre
Chât. de Montrodeix 916
Poste Électr.
Puy de Couleyras 921
Chemin de la Roche Pertuisade 864
les Perrières
Pont de la Chèvre
les Moines
Chemin des Gouts 920

Bois de Fontmagne
Berger du
Suquet Bonnet

l'Étang
Bois de Chanal
Bois de Clerzat
la Mouteyre
Côte Verse
Fontaneyre
Suquet Morand 857
Bois de Ribage
Puy Mergue
Bonnabry
Bellevue
la Bosse
Puy de Pégoul
Côte de Pégoul
Puy Charmont 678
Turn de la Côte Noire 708
Bois de la Razerie
Tuf de Cheval
le Fer de Varoux 599
Turn de Varoux
la Garde 692
Bois de la Classagne 636
Pont de la Classagne
Puy des Paradis 631
Route de l'Adou

les Vergnes
la Plaine
les Fourches
la Croix de Neyra-Flamina 334
Champ Cros
Poste Électr.
Cr Bertrand
Chambert
Massaud
Bédat
le Caire Maronne 445
le Chevalard
la Tannerie
les Sagnes R.
St-Vincent 438
la Verrède 490

Villars
Puy de Monfaudoux
Ormeaux
Puy de Gravenoire
Raye Dieu
Massage
Montpoly
Boissejour
Loradoux
la Gauthière
la Pradelle
Herbet
St-Jacques 394
Pourliat
Puy d'Aubière 464
les Gravières

Map 4: Clermont-Ferrand

Extract from Carte Nationale, Sheet XXV–31

Scale 1: 50 000

MAN AND LANDSCAPE by Arthur Guest
Heinemann Educational Books, 1974
Reproduced with the permission of the
Institut Geographique National

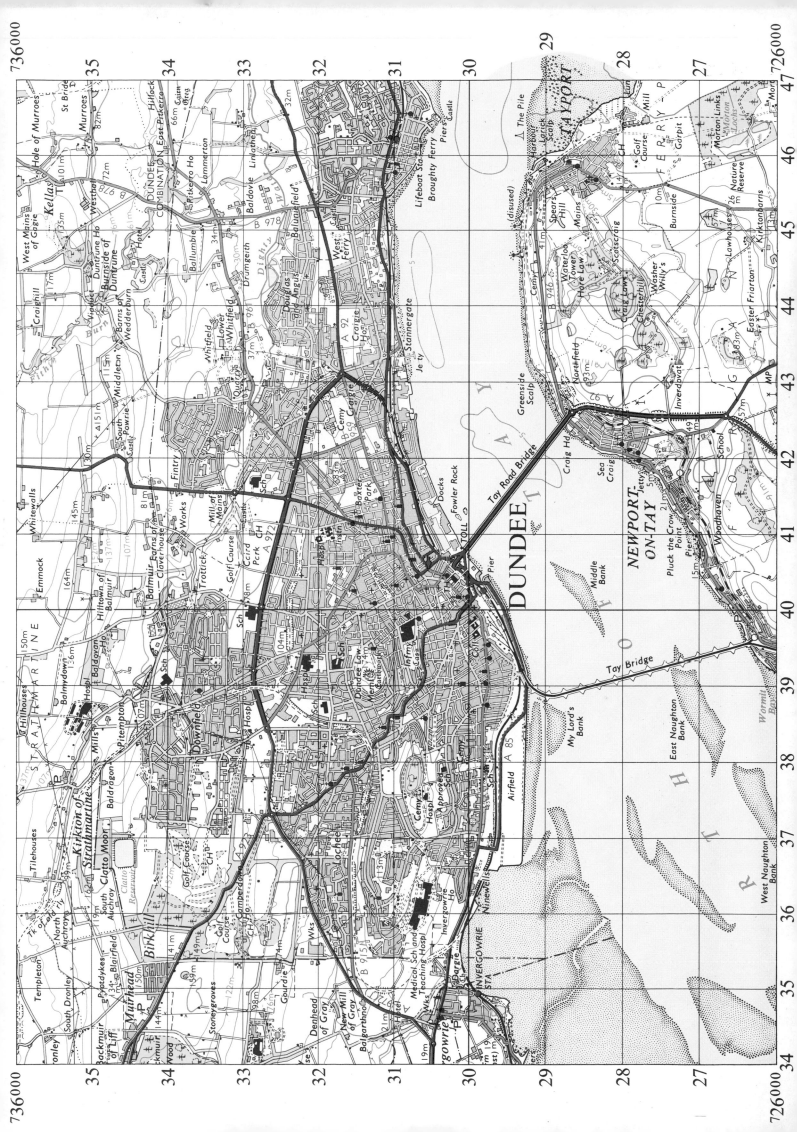

Map 5: Dundee

Extract from Ordnance Survey, Sheet 50 (M)

Scale 1: 50 000

MAN AND LANDSCAPE by Arthur Guest
Heinemann Educational Books, 1974
*Reproduced from the Ordnance Survey Map with the
sanction of the Controller of H.M. Stationery Office*

WANDSWORTH PUBLIC LIBRARIES M.S.C.